D0231464

The
Economist

Pocket
World in
Figures

2016 Edition

THE ECONOMIST IN ASSOCIATION WITH
PROFILE BOOKS LTD

Published by
Profile Books Ltd
3 Holford Yard
Bevin Way
London WC1X 9HD

This edition published by Profile Books in association with
The Economist, 2015

Copyright © The Economist Newspaper Ltd, 1991, 1992,
1993, 1994, 1995, 1996, 1997, 1998, 1999, 2000, 2001, 2002, 2003,
2004, 2005, 2006, 2007, 2008, 2009, 2010, 2011, 2012, 2013, 2014, 2015

Material researched and compiled by
Andrea Burgess, Mark Doyle, Lisa Davies, Ian Emery,
Andrew Gilbert, Conrad Heine, Carol Howard, David McKelvey,
Roxana Willis, Philip Wroe

All rights reserved. Without limiting the rights under copyright
reserved above, no part of this publication may be reproduced,
stored in or introduced into a retrieval system, or transmitted, in any
form or by any means (electronic, mechanical, photocopying,
recording or otherwise), without the prior written permission of
both the copyright owner and the above publisher of this book.

The greatest care has been taken in compiling this book. However,
no responsibility can be accepted by the publishers or compilers
for the accuracy of the information presented.

Typeset in Officina by MacGuru Ltd
info@macguru.org.uk

Printed and bound in Italy by L.E.G.O. Spa

A CIP catalogue record for this book is available
from the British Library

ISBN 978 1 78125 447 9

Contents

CONTENTS

CONTENTS

Welcome

I am delighted to introduce the 25th annual edition of *The Economist Pocket World in Figures*.

Since 1991 when the first edition was published the world has undergone major demographic, economic and technological changes. No longer do we print out individual sheets of paper with lists of complex data and send them off in the post to be published. Now we upload our spreadsheets to the cloud so that we can share the information with our contributors and colleagues all around the world.

In the past quarter of a century this book has evolved with the times. We now embrace the internet, mobile phones and renewable energy. This book has tracked the good – for example, reductions in infant mortality – and the bad, such as the rise of obesity and diabetes. In the process, the rankings have swelled to cover 183 countries and the country profiles have risen from 60 to 67, with added profiles of the euro area and the world. The *Pocket World in Figures* provides an increasingly detailed, ever-changing portrait of the world we live in and is an essential resource for our globally curious readers.

Zanny Minton Beddoes
Editor-in-Chief, *The Economist*

Pocket World in Figures presents and analyses data about the world in two sections:

The **world rankings** consider and rank the performance of 183 countries against a range of indicators. These are countries which had (in 2013) or have recently had a population of at least 1m or a GDP of at least $3bn; they are listed on pages 250–53. New rankings this year include topics as diverse as NEET (not in education, employment or training) rates, employment costs, ports, gambling and football World Cup winners.

The **country profiles** look in detail at 67 major countries, listed on page 109, plus profiles of the euro area and the world.

To celebrate our 25th anniversary, this 2016 edition of *The Economist Pocket World in Figures* includes a special "Twenty-five years on" feature which looks at how the world has changed since our first edition was published back in 1991. This reflects not only on changes to the data, but how the indicators themselves have shifted (see pages 10–12).

Notes

The extent and quality of the statistics available varies from country to country. Every care has been taken to specify the broad definitions on which the data are based and to indicate cases where data quality or technical difficulties are such that interpretation of the figures is likely to be seriously affected. Nevertheless, figures from individual countries may differ from standard international statistical definitions. The term "country" can also refer to territories or economic entities.

Definitions of the statistics shown are given on the relevant page or in the glossary on pages 248–9. Figures may not add exactly to totals, or percentages to 100, because of rounding or, in the case of GDP, statistical adjustment. Sums of money have generally been converted to US dollars at the official exchange rate ruling at the time to which the figures refer.

Some country definitions

Macedonia is officially known as the Former Yugoslav Republic of Macedonia. Data for Cyprus normally refer to Greek Cyprus only. Data for China does not include Hong Kong or Macau. Data for Sudan are largely for the country before it became two countries, Sudan and South Sudan, in July 2011. For countries such as Morocco they exclude disputed areas. Congo-Kinshasa refers to the Democratic Republic of Congo, formerly known as Zaire. Congo-Brazzaville refers to the other Congo. The Netherlands Antilles was dissolved in 2011 but continues to appear in some data; Curaçao qualifies for inclusion but there are few data as yet. Data for the EU refer to the 28 members as at January 1 2008, unless otherwise noted. Euro area data normally refer to the 18 members that had adopted the euro as at December 31 2014: Austria, Belgium, Cyprus, Estonia, France, Finland, Germany, Greece, Ireland, Italy, Latvia, Luxembourg, Malta, Netherlands, Portugal, Slovakia, Slovenia and Spain. (Lithuania joined the euro area on January 1 2015.) At the time of going to press, uncertainty remained over Greece's future as part of the euro zone. For more information about the EU and the euro area see the glossary on pages 248–9.

Statistical basis

The all-important factor in a book of this kind is to be able to make reliable comparisons between countries. Although this is never quite possible for the reasons stated above, the best route, which this book takes, is to compare data for the same year or period and to use actual, not estimated, figures wherever possible. In some cases, only OECD members are considered. Where a country's data is excessively out of date, it is excluded. The research for this edition was carried out in 2015 using the latest available sources that present data on an internationally comparable basis.

Data in the country profiles, unless otherwise indicated, refer to the year ending December 31 2013. Life expectancy and death rates are based on 2015–20 estimated averages; fertility rates for 2013, crude birth rates for 2014, energy data for 2011–12 and religion for 2010; marriage and divorce, employment, health and education, consumer goods and services data refer to the latest year for which figures are available.

Other definitions

Data shown in country profiles may not always be consistent with those shown in the world rankings because the definitions or years covered can differ.

Statistics for principal exports and principal imports are normally based on customs statistics. These are generally compiled on different definitions to the visible exports and imports figures shown in the balance of payments section.

Energy consumption data are not always reliable, particularly for the major oil producing countries; consumption per person data may therefore be higher than in reality. Energy exports can exceed production and imports can exceed consumption if transit operations distort trade data or oil is imported for refining and re-exported.

Abbreviations and conventions
(see also glossary on pages 248–9)

bn	billion (one thousand million)	km	kilometre
EU	European Union	m	million
GDP	gross domestic product	PPP	purchasing power parity
GNI	gross national income	TOE	tonnes of oil equivalent
ha	hectare	trn	trillion (one thousand billion)
kg	kilogram	...	not available

Twenty-five years on

In the past 25 years the planet's population has surged and its distribution has been far from equal. Developing countries have experienced booms while developed economies have stagnated. India added 418m people to its population between 1988 (the base year for data in the first edition of the *Pocket World in Figures*, published in 1991) and 2013 (the base year for this edition). Germany and Japan, meanwhile, mustered fewer than 9m between them.

Alongside this, the world has seen dramatic urbanisation, most pronounced in China and India. In 1988, Seoul, South Korea's capital, was one of the world's biggest cities with a population of 10m. Today, it does not even make the top 30. The world's biggest city is still Tokyo, with a population now almost four times that of Seoul. In 2015, six cities in China and five in India were larger than Seoul. (For full rankings, see page 21.)

World's biggest cities
Population in urban agglomeration, m

1988			2015		
1	Tokyo, Japan	31.6	1	Tokyo, Japan	38.0
2	Osaka, Japan	18.1	2	Delhi, India	25.7
3	New York, US	16.0	3	Shanghai, China	23.7
4	Mexico City, Mexico	15.1	4	São Paulo, Brazil	21.1
5	São Paulo, Brazil	14.2	5	Mumbai, India	21.0
6	Mumbai, India	11.6		Mexico City, Mexico	21.0
7	Los Angeles, US	10.6	7	Beijing, China	20.4
8	Kolkata, India	10.5	8	Osaka, Japan	20.2
9	Buenos Aires, Argentina	10.3	9	Cairo, Egypt	18.8
10	Seoul, South Korea	10.0	10	New York, US	18.6

As poorer countries have developed, birth rates and fertility rates have fallen steadily. In Kenya, for example, the average number of children born to each woman has dropped from 8.1 in the late 1980s to 4.3 in 2013 (see page 19). In many rich world countries, however, they are beginning to rise.

As health care, diet and nutrition have improved, so has life expectancy. In 1988 Japan topped the table with an average of 78 years. In the 25 years since, Mexico, Lebanon, Cuba, the Czech Republic and dozens more have improved on this. Monaco now ranks highest with a remarkable 89 years (see page 80). At the other end of the spectrum, Sierra Leoneans are now expected to live to 47, six years more than in 1988. As a result of such gains, the percentage of people aged over 65 has surged. In the 1980s, not a single country had to cope with 20% of its population being over 65. Now Japan, Germany and Italy all face this. African countries, however, continue to have the world's youngest populations. In the late 1980s, 40–50% of people were under 15 years old across much of the continent. In 2013, this remained the case (see page 20).

Despite the health improvements, an AIDS pandemic has gripped Africa throughout this period. Twenty-five years ago Congo-Brazzaville reported 66 cases per 100,000 people, by far the highest rate on the continent. Now 22 African countries report more than 100 deaths per 100,000 (see page 85). Even this rate is substantially down from the mid-2000s.

The causes of death have changed as people's lifestyles have become increasingly comfortable. In many developed countries, the average person has some 3,000 calories per day available for consumption (see page 87). As a result, diabetes and obesity, not recorded in the *Pocket World in Figures* until 2005 and 2006 respectively, are now endemic (see page 84). On a more positive note, smoking has fallen steeply in the rich world. The Greeks, previously serial puffers, have halved their cigarette intake to an average of four-and-a-half a day per person (see page 100).

In the rich world the marriage rate has fallen, with a third fewer unions in the United States than 25 years ago. Divorce rates have also fallen, down by two-fifths in the United States (see pages 88–9). Globally, more young women than young men graduate from university every year. And this increased focus on careers has pushed back the average age of marriage. In the United Kingdom the average age of a bride is now 32, up from 24 in 1987.

Perhaps the most startling backward step in the past 25 years has taken place in the Americas. In 1986, only two countries in the world had murder rates above 20 per 100,000 people: Philippines at 38.7, and Lesotho, at 36.4. Now, 13 countries in the Americas alone exceed this (see page 101).

Murders
Homicides per 100,000 population

1986			2012 or latest		
1	Philippines	38.7	1	Honduras	91.0
2	Lesotho	36.4	2	Venezuela	53.6
3	Sri Lanka	18.9	3	Virgin Islands (US)	52.6
4	Jamaica	18.0	4	El Salvador	41.5
5	Guyana	15.6	5	Jamaica	39.1
6	Lebanon	13.2	6	Lesotho	38.0
7	Zimbabwe	12.6	7	Guatemala	34.6
8	Thailand	12.4	8	Colombia	30.7
9	Bahamas	12.2		South Africa	30.7
10	Botswana	11.0	10	Bahamas	29.7

The economic scene over the past quarter-century has been dominated by the rise of China. With an average annual growth rate of 9.7%, it is now the world's second largest economy. (Only one country has exceeded 10% annual growth across the entire period – Equatorial Guinea, with 18%.)

Biggest economies
$bn, 2013 prices

1988			2013		
1	United States	9,612	1	United States	16,768
2	Japan	5,630	2	China	9,240
3	West Germany	2,379	3	Japan	4,920
4	France	1,869	4	Germany	3,730
5	Italy	1,631	5	France	2,806
6	United Kingdom	1,627	6	United Kingdom	2,678
7	USSR	1,148	7	Brazil	2,246
8	Canada	961	8	Italy	2,149
9	Brazil	697	9	Russia	2,097
10	Spain	666	10	India	1,875

China's GDP per person has risen eightfold to $6,807. It may not compete with Monaco's $173,000 per person (see page 28), but in these years it has pulled roughly 600m of its population above the poverty line ($1.25 a day in 2005 prices). It has also become by far the largest consumer of the world's resources (see pages 52–7).

China's industrial output, which was a seventh of the United States' in 1988, overtook it in 2010. As a result, China's share of world exports has risen from 1.4% to 10.4%, behind only the United States and the euro area (see page 34).

Thanks to the rapid evolution of consumer goods, the items ranked in 1988 for the first edition have almost all been replaced. No longer does the *Pocket World in Figures* compile statistics on the share of households with video cassette recorders, microwaves and dishwashers. It now ranks mobile phone ownership, computer sales and the number of broadband subscribers (see pages 92–3).

In many ways, the world we documented in 1988 seems a simpler, more innocent time. Hans Christian Andersen and Enid Blyton were among the most translated authors in the world and there were no rankings for teenage pregnancies, gambling, prisoners, robberies and refugees (see pages 18, 100, 101 and 25, respectively). In part that is because there are more, and better, data available today. And for all that's changed, for better or worse, there is one constant truth: France still draws the most tourists in the world (see page 77).

World rankings

Countries: natural facts

Countries: the largest[a]
'000 sq km

1	Russia	17,098	31	Tanzania	947
2	Canada	9,985	32	Nigeria	924
3	United States	9,834	33	Venezuela	912
4	China	9,597	34	Namibia	824
5	Brazil	8,515	35	Mozambique	802
6	Australia	7,692	36	Pakistan	796
7	India	3,287	37	Turkey	784
8	Argentina	2,780	38	Chile	756
9	Kazakhstan	2,725	39	Zambia	753
10	Algeria	2,382	40	Myanmar	677
11	Congo-Kinshasa	2,345	41	Afghanistan	653
12	Saudi Arabia	2,207	42	South Sudan	644
13	Greenland	2,166	43	Somalia	638
14	Mexico	1,964	44	Central African Rep.	623
15	Indonesia	1,911	45	Ukraine	604
16	Sudan	1,879	46	Kenya	592
17	Libya	1,760	47	Madagascar	587
18	Iran	1,629	48	Botswana	582
19	Mongolia	1,564	49	France	552
20	Peru	1,285	50	Yemen	528
21	Chad	1,284	51	Thailand	513
22	Niger	1,267	52	Spain	506
23	Angola	1,247	53	Turkmenistan	488
24	Mali	1,240	54	Cameroon	476
25	South Africa	1,221	55	Papua New Guinea	463
26	Colombia	1,142	56	Sweden	450
27	Ethiopia	1,104	57	Morocco	447
28	Bolivia	1,099		Uzbekistan	447
29	Mauritania	1,031	59	Iraq	435
30	Egypt	1,002	60	Paraguay	407

Mountains: the highest[b]

	Name	Location	Height (m)
1	Everest	China-Nepal	8,848
2	K2 (Godwin Austen)	China-Jammu and Kashmir	8,611
3	Kangchenjunga	India-Nepal	8,586
4	Lhotse	China-Nepal	8,516
5	Makalu	China-Nepal	8,463
6	Cho Oyu	China-Nepal	8,201
7	Dhaulagiri	Nepal	8,167
8	Manaslu	Nepal	8,163
9	Nanga Parbat	China-Jammu and Kashmir	8,126
10	Annapurna I	Nepal	8,091
11	Gasherbrum I	China-Jammu and Kashmir	8,068
12	Broad Peak	China-Jammu and Kashmir	8,047
13	Gasherbrum II	China-Jammu and Kashmir	8,035
14	Xixabangma Feng	China	8,012

a Includes freshwater.
b Includes separate peaks which are part of the same massif.

Rivers: *the longest*

Name	Location	Length (km)
1 Nile	Africa	6,695
2 Amazon	South America	6,516
3 Yangtze	Asia	6,380
4 Mississippi-Missouri system	North America	5,959
5 Ob'-Irtysh	Asia	5,568
6 Yenisey-Angara-Selanga	Asia	5,550
7 Huang He (Yellow)	Asia	5,464
8 Congo	Africa	4,667
9 Río de la Plata-Paraná	South America	4,500
10 Irtysh	Asia	4,440

Deserts: *the largest non-polar*

Name	Location	Area ('000 sq km)
1 Sahara	Northern Africa	8,600
2 Arabian	South-western Asia	2,300
3 Gobi	Mongolia/China	1,300
4 Patagonian	Argentina	673
5 Syrian	Middle East	520
6 Great Basin	South-western United States	492
7 Great Victoria	Western and Southern Australia	422
8 Great Sandy	Western Australia	395

Lakes: *the largest*

Name	Location	Area ('000 sq km)
1 Caspian Sea	Central Asia	371
2 Superior	Canada/United States	82
3 Victoria	East Africa	69
4 Huron	Canada/United States	60
5 Michigan	United States	58
6 Tanganyika	East Africa	33
7 Baikal	Russia	31
Great Bear	Canada	31

Islands: *the largest*

Name	Location	Area ('000 sq km)
1 Greenland	North Atlantic Ocean	2,176
2 New Guinea	South-west Pacific Ocean	809
3 Borneo	Western Pacific Ocean	746
4 Madagascar	Indian Ocean	587
5 Baffin	North Atlantic Ocean	507
6 Sumatra	North-east Indian Ocean	474
7 Honshu	Sea of Japan-Pacific Ocean	227
8 Great Britain	Off coast of north-west Europe	218

Notes: Estimates of the lengths of rivers vary widely depending on eg, the path to take through a delta. The definition of a desert is normally a mean annual precipitation value equal to 250ml or less. Australia is defined as a continent rather than an island.

Population: size and growth

Largest populations
Million, 2013

1	China	1,385.6	37	Canada	35.2
2	India	1,252.1	38	Iraq	33.8
3	United States	320.1	39	Morocco	33.0
4	Indonesia	249.9	40	Afghanistan	30.6
5	Brazil	200.4	41	Peru	30.4
6	Pakistan	182.1		Venezuela	30.4
7	Nigeria	173.6	43	Malaysia	29.7
8	Bangladesh	156.6	44	Uzbekistan	28.9
9	Russia	142.8	45	Saudi Arabia	28.8
10	Japan	127.1	46	Nepal	27.8
11	Mexico	122.3	47	Ghana	25.9
12	Philippines	98.4	48	Mozambique	25.8
13	Ethiopia	94.1	49	North Korea	24.9
14	Vietnam	91.7	50	Yemen	24.4
15	Germany	82.7	51	Australia	23.3
16	Egypt	82.1		Taiwan	23.3
17	Iran	77.4	53	Madagascar	22.9
18	Turkey	74.9	54	Cameroon	22.3
19	Congo-Kinshasa	67.5	55	Syria	21.9
20	Thailand	67.0	56	Romania	21.7
21	France	64.3	57	Angola	21.5
22	United Kingdom	63.1	58	Sri Lanka	21.3
23	Italy	61.0	59	Ivory Coast	20.3
24	Myanmar	53.3	60	Niger	17.8
25	South Africa	52.8	61	Chile	17.6
26	South Korea	49.3	62	Burkina Faso	16.9
	Tanzania	49.3	63	Netherlands	16.8
28	Colombia	48.3	64	Kazakhstan	16.4
29	Spain	46.9		Malawi	16.4
30	Ukraine	45.2	66	Ecuador	15.7
31	Kenya	44.4	67	Guatemala	15.5
32	Argentina	41.4	68	Mali	15.3
33	Algeria	39.2	69	Cambodia	15.1
34	Poland	38.2	70	Zambia	14.5
35	Sudan	38.0	71	Senegal	14.1
36	Uganda	37.6			

Largest populations
Million, 2050

1	India	1,620	11	Mexico	156
2	China	1,385	12	Congo-Kinshasa	155
3	Nigeria	440	13	Tanzania	129
4	United States	401	14	Egypt	122
5	Indonesia	321	15	Russia	121
6	Pakistan	271	16	Japan	108
7	Brazil	231	17	Uganda	104
8	Bangladesh	202		Vietnam	104
9	Ethiopia	188	19	Iran	101
10	Philippines	157	20	Kenya	97

Note: Populations include migrant workers.

Fastest growing populations
Average annual % change, 2015–20

1	Niger	3.9		South Sudan	2.6
2	Mali	3.2		Zimbabwe	2.6
	Uganda	3.2	24	Benin	2.5
	Zambia	3.2	25	Cameroon	2.4
5	Gambia, The	3.1		Congo-Brazzaville	2.4
6	Angola	3.0		Ethiopia	2.4
	Burundi	3.0		Guinea	2.4
8	Chad	2.9		Liberia	2.4
	Syria	2.9		Mozambique	2.4
	Tanzania	2.9		Togo	2.4
11	Malawi	2.8		West Bank & Gaza	2.4
	Somalia	2.8	33	Guinea-Bissau	2.3
13	Burkina Faso	2.7		Kuwait	2.3
	Eritrea	2.7		Mauritania	2.3
	Kenya	2.7		Sudan	2.3
	Nigeria	2.7	37	Afghanistan	2.2
	Senegal	2.7		Gabon	2.2
18	Congo-Kinshasa	2.6		Ivory Coast	2.2
	Equatorial Guinea	2.6		Tajikistan	2.2
	Iraq	2.6	41	Yemen	2.1
	Rwanda	2.6	42	United Arab Emirates	2.0

Slowest growing populations
Average annual % change, 2015–20

1	Bulgaria	-0.8		Trinidad & Tobago	0.0
2	Lebanon	-0.7		Virgin Islands (US)	0.0
	Moldova	-0.7	29	Italy	0.1
	Ukraine	-0.7		Slovenia	0.1
5	Latvia	-0.6		Thailand	0.1
	Serbia	-0.6	32	Bermuda	0.2
7	Belarus	-0.5		Malta	0.2
	Georgia	-0.5		Martinique	0.2
9	Croatia	-0.4		Netherlands	0.2
	Lithuania	-0.4	36	Albania	0.3
11	Estonia	-0.3		Belgium	0.3
	Romania	-0.3		Czech Republic	0.3
	Russia	-0.3		Finland	0.3
14	Bosnia & Herz.	-0.2		Mauritius	0.3
	Cuba	-0.2		Spain	0.3
	Germany	-0.2		Uruguay	0.3
	Hungary	-0.2	43	Austria	0.4
	Japan	-0.2		China	0.4
19	Greece	-0.1		Denmark	0.4
	Montenegro	-0.1		Guadeloupe	0.4
	Portugal	-0.1		South Korea	0.4
22	Armenia	0.0	48	Barbados	0.5
	Macedonia	0.0		Channel Islands	0.5
	Poland	0.0		France	0.5
	Puerto Rico	0.0		Jamaica	0.5
	Slovakia	0.0		North Korea	0.5

Population: matters of breeding and sex

Crude birth rates
Births per 1,000 population, 2014

Highest			Lowest		
1	Niger	50	1	Monaco	6
2	Chad	48	2	Andorra	8
3	Central African Rep.	47		Bosnia & Herz.	8
4	Angola	46		Germany	8
	Congo-Kinshasa	46		Hong Kong	8
6	Burundi	45		Japan	8
	Zambia	45		Portugal	8
8	Somalia	44		Taiwan	8
9	Burkina Faso	43	9	Austria	9
	Mozambique	43		Bulgaria	9
	Uganda	43		Greece	9
12	Mali	42		Hungary	9
13	Gambia, The	41		Italy	9
14	Malawi	40		South Korea	9
	Senegal	40		Serbia	9
	Tanzania	40		Singapore	9
17	Cameroon	39		Spain	9
	Nigeria	39			
19	Congo-Brazzaville	38			
	Guinea	38			
	Guinea-Bissau	38			
	Sierra Leone	38			

Most births
By mother's age group, '000, 2005–10

Aged 15–19			Aged 45–49		
1	India	13,940	1	Nigeria	651
2	Nigeria	4,707	2	India	557
3	Bangladesh	3,413	3	Pakistan	256
4	Brazil	3,155	4	China	197
5	Indonesia	2,676	5	Congo-Kinshasa	186
6	China	2,418	6	Indonesia	172
7	United States	2,109	7	Ethiopia	167
8	Congo-Kinshasa	2,043	8	Kenya	119
9	Ethiopia	2,001	9	Sudan	82
10	Mexico	1,941	10	Mozambique	79
11	Tanzania	1,461	11	Morocco	68
12	Pakistan	1,422	12	Philippines	64
13	Uganda	1,292	13	Brazil	61
14	Philippines	1,246	14	Uganda	59
15	Kenya	1,064	15	Afghanistan	55
16	Mozambique	956		Niger	55
17	Sudan	935		Somalia	55
18	Egypt	926	18	Tanzania	53
19	Angola	923	19	Saudi Arabia	52
20	Afghanistan	824	20	South Africa	50
21	Colombia	782	21	Yemen	49
22	Russia	754	22	Bangladesh	48
23	Niger	753	23	South Sudan	43

Fertility rates
Average number of children per woman, 2013

Highest			Lowest		
1	Niger	7.6	1	Andorra	1.1
2	South Sudan	7.0		Hong Kong	1.1
3	Chad	6.6		Taiwan	1.1
	Congo-Kinshasa	6.6	4	Macau	1.2
	Somalia	6.6		Moldova	1.2
6	Angola	6.2		Poland	1.2
	Central African Rep.	6.2		Portugal	1.2
8	Burundi	6.1		Singapore	1.2
	Mali	6.1		South Korea	1.2
10	Zambia	6.0	10	Bosnia & Herz.	1.3
11	Burkina Faso	5.9		Greece	1.3
	Uganda	5.9		Hungary	1.3
13	Mozambique	5.7		Romania	1.3
	Timor-Leste	5.7		Slovakia	1.3
15	Gambia, The	5.6		Spain	1.3
	Nigeria	5.6	16	Austria	1.4
17	Malawi	5.5		Germany	1.4
18	Senegal	5.3		Italy	1.4
	Tanzania	5.3		Japan	1.4
20	Sudan	5.2		Malta	1.4
21	Afghanistan	5.1		Mauritius	1.4
	Cameroon	5.1		Monaco	1.4
	Guinea	5.1		Serbia	1.4

Sex ratios
Males per 100 females, 2010

Highest			Lowest		
1	Qatar	312.2	1	Latvia	84.1
2	United Arab Emirates	240.2	2	Martinique	85.6
3	Bahrain	165.7	3	Lithuania	85.7
4	Kuwait	148.5		Ukraine	85.7
5	Oman	142.1	5	Russia	85.9
6	Saudi Arabia	129.7	6	Estonia	86.4
7	Bhutan	115.8	7	Belarus	86.9
8	China	107.4	8	Hong Kong	88.1
9	India	107.2	9	Georgia	89.2
10	Armenia	105.8	10	Guadeloupe	89.3
11	Pakistan	105.6	11	Moldova	90.2
12	Equatorial Guinea	105.2	12	Hungary	90.5
13	French Polynesia	105.0	13	El Salvador	90.6
14	Jordan	104.6	14	Virgin Islands (US)	91.5
15	Ivory Coast	104.5	15	Macau	92.2
16	Cyprus	104.3	16	Puerto Rico	92.5
	Fiji	104.3	17	Kazakhstan	93.1
18	Papua New Guinea	104.1	18	Croatia	93.2
	Syria	104.1	19	Uruguay	93.3
20	Lebanon	104.0	20	Poland	93.4
21	Libya	103.8	21	France	93.6
22	Nigeria	103.4			

Population: age

Median age[a]

Highest, 2013

1	Monaco	50.5
2	Japan	45.9
3	Germany	45.5
4	Italy	44.3
5	Bulgaria	43.0
6	Greece	42.8
7	Austria	42.7
8	Bermuda	42.6
	Croatia	42.6
10	Hong Kong	42.4
	Slovenia	42.4
12	Finland	42.3
13	Portugal	42.2
14	Liechtenstein	42.1
15	Channel Islands	42.0
	Switzerland	42.0
17	Andorra	41.8
	Netherlands	41.8
19	Martinique	41.7
20	Belgium	41.6
21	Latvia	41.5
22	Spain	41.4
23	Denmark	41.1

Lowest, 2013

1	Niger	15.0
2	Chad	15.8
	Uganda	15.8
4	Angola	16.3
	Mali	16.3
	Somalia	16.3
7	Afghanistan	16.5
8	Timor-Leste	16.6
	Zambia	16.6
10	Gambia, The	17.0
11	Burkina Faso	17.1
12	Malawi	17.2
13	Mozambique	17.3
14	Congo-Kinshasa	17.4
15	Tanzania	17.5
16	Burundi	17.6
17	Nigeria	17.8
18	Senegal	18.1
19	Ethiopia	18.2
	Rwanda	18.2
21	Cameroon	18.3

Most old people

% of population aged 60 or over, 2013

1	Monaco	35.9
2	Japan	32.3
3	Italy	27.2
4	Germany	27.1
5	Bulgaria	26.4
6	Finland	26.3
7	Greece	25.7
8	Sweden	25.5
9	Croatia	25.1
10	Portugal	24.7
11	Latvia	24.3
12	Denmark	24.1
	Estonia	24.1
	France	24.1
15	Belgium	24.0
16	Hungary	23.9
17	Slovenia	23.8
18	Austria	23.7
	Czech Republic	23.7
20	Malta	23.5
21	Netherlands	23.4
	Switzerland	23.4
23	United Kingdom	23.2

Most young people

% of population aged 0–14, 2013

1	Niger	50.1
2	Chad	48.4
	Uganda	48.4
4	Angola	47.5
5	Mali	47.4
6	Somalia	47.2
7	Afghanistan	46.6
8	Gambia, The	45.9
9	Timor-Leste	45.8
10	Burkina Faso	45.5
11	Mozambique	45.4
12	Malawi	45.3
13	Congo-Kinshasa	45.0
14	Tanzania	44.9
15	Burundi	44.6
16	Nigeria	44.4
17	Senegal	43.5
18	Eritrea	43.2
19	Cameroon	43.0
20	Liberia	42.9
	Rwanda	42.9
22	Benin	42.8
23	Ethiopia	42.7

a Age at which there is an equal number of people above and below.

City living

Biggest cities[a]
Population, m, 2015

1	Tokyo, Japan	38.0		Hong Kong	7.3
2	Delhi, India	25.7	48	Foshan, China	7.0
3	Shanghai, China	23.7	49	Kuala Lumpur, Malaysia	6.8
4	São Paulo, Brazil	21.1	50	Baghdad, Iraq	6.6
5	Mexico City, Mexico	21.0	51	Santiago, Chile	6.5
	Mumbai, India	21.0	52	Hangzhou, China	6.4
7	Beijing, China	20.4		Riyadh, Saudi Arabia	6.4
8	Osaka, Japan	20.2	54	Shenyang, China	6.3
9	Cairo, Egypt	18.8	55	Madrid, Spain	6.2
10	New York, US	18.6	56	Toronto, Canada	6.0
11	Dhaka, Bangladesh	17.6		Xian, China	6.0
12	Karachi, Pakistan	16.6	58	Miami, US	5.8
13	Buenos Aires, Argentina	15.2	59	Belo Horizonte, Brazil	5.7
14	Kolkata, India	14.9		Dallas, US	5.7
15	Istanbul, Turkey	14.2		Pune, India	5.7
16	Chongqing, China	13.3		Surat, India	5.7
17	Lagos, Nigeria	13.1	63	Houston, US	5.6
18	Manila, Philippines	12.9		Philadelphia, US	5.6
	Rio de Janeiro, Brazil	12.9		Singapore	5.6
20	Guangzhou, China	12.5	66	Harbin, China	5.5
21	Los Angeles, US	12.3		Kitakyushu, Japan	5.5
22	Moscow, Russia	12.2		Luanda, Angola	5.5
23	Kinshasa, Congo-Kinshasa	11.6		Suzhou, China	5.5
24	Tianjin, China	11.2	70	Barcelona, Spain	5.3
25	Paris, France	10.8	71	Atlanta, US	5.1
26	Shenzhen, China	10.7		Dar es Salaam, Tanzania	5.1
27	Jakarta, Indonesia	10.3		Khartoum, Sudan	5.1
	London, UK	10.3	74	St Petersburg, Russia	5.0
29	Bangalore, India	10.1		Washington, DC, US	5.0
30	Chennai, India	9.9	76	Abidjan, Ivory Coast	4.9
	Lima, Peru	9.9	77	Alexandria, Egypt	4.8
32	Bogotá, Colombia	9.8		Guadalajara, Mexico	4.8
	Seoul, South Korea	9.8		Yangon, Myanmar	4.8
34	Johannesburg, South Africa	9.4	80	Ankara, Turkey	4.7
	Nagoya, Japan	9.4	81	Kabul, Afghanistan	4.6
36	Bangkok, Thailand	9.3		Qingdao, China	4.6
37	Hyderabad, India	8.9	83	Chittagong, Bangladesh	4.5
38	Chicago, US	8.7		Dalian, China	4.5
	Lahore, Pakistan	8.7		Monterrey, Mexico	4.5
40	Tehran, Iran	8.4		Sydney, Australia	4.5
41	Wuhan, China	7.9	87	Xiamen, China	4.4
42	Chengdu, China	7.6		Zhengzhou, China	4.4
43	Dongguan, China	7.4	89	Boston, US	4.2
	Nanjing, China	7.4		Brasília, Brazil	4.2
45	Ahmadabad, India	7.3		Melbourne, Australia	4.2
	Ho Chi Minh City, Vietnam	7.3	92	Jeddah, Saudi Arabia	4.1
				Phoenix, US	4.1

a Urban agglomerations. Data may change from year to year based on reassessments of agglomeration boundaries.

City growth
Biggest 100 cities, % change, 2015–20

Fastest

1	Dar es Salaam, Tanzania	5.5
2	Xiamen, China	5.4
3	Suzhou, China	4.6
4	Luanda, Angola	4.3
5	Kabul, Afghanistan	4.2
	Lagos, Nigeria	4.2
7	Kinshasa, Congo-Kinshasa	4.0
	Nairobi, Kenya	4.0
9	Guangzhou, China	3.9
10	Surat, India	3.8
11	Dhaka, Bangladesh	3.5
	Hangzhou, China	3.5
13	Abidjan, Ivory Coast	3.4
	Beijing, China	3.4

Slowest

1	Kitakyushu, Japan	-0.2
2	Seoul, South Korea	0.1
	St Petersburg, Russia	0.1
4	Los Angeles, US	0.2
	Nagoya, Japan	0.2
	New York, US	0.2
	Tokyo, Japan	0.2
8	Boston, US	0.3
	Chicago, US	0.3
	Osaka, Japan	0.3
11	Philadelphia, US	0.4
12	Moscow, Russia	0.5
13	Hong Kong	0.6
	Santiago, Chile	0.6

Single city importance
Highest % residing in a single city, 2015

1	Hong Kong	100.0
	Macau	100.0
	Singapore	100.0
4	Kuwait City, Kuwait	77.5
5	San Juan, Puerto Rico	66.9
6	Montevideo, Uruguay	49.8
7	Ulaanbaatar, Mongolia	47.1
8	Tel Aviv, Israel	45.6
9	Beirut, Lebanon	44.1
10	Panama City, Panama	41.9
11	Brazzaville, Congo-Brazzaville	40.4
	Libreville, Gabon	40.4
13	Santiago, Chile	36.3

14	Buenos Aires, Argentina	36.0
15	Yerevan, Armenia	34.9
16	Asunción, Paraguay	33.5
17	Lima, Peru	31.8
18	Riga, Latvia	30.6
	Tallinn, Estonia	30.6
20	Doha, Qatar	30.5
21	Manama, Bahrain	30.2
22	Tokyo, Japan	30.0
23	Auckland, New Zealand	29.2
24	Al-Rayyan, Qatar	28.8
25	Monrovia, Liberia	28.1
26	Santo Domingo, Dominican Rep.	27.7

Urban growth
Average annual % change, 2010–15

Highest

1	Oman	8.5
2	Rwanda	6.4
3	Qatar	6.0
4	Burkina Faso	5.9
5	Burundi	5.7
6	Tanzania	5.4
	Uganda	5.4
8	Eritrea	5.1
	Mali	5.1
	Niger	5.1
	South Sudan	5.1
12	Angola	5.0
13	Ethiopia	4.9
	Laos	4.9

Lowest

1	Trinidad & Tobago	-1.2
2	Latvia	-0.7
	Moldova	-0.7
4	Lithuania	-0.5
5	Estonia	-0.4
6	Bulgaria	-0.3
	Serbia	-0.3
	Slovakia	-0.3
	Ukraine	-0.3
10	Puerto Rico	-0.2

Urban population
%, 2015

Highest			Lowest		
1	Bermuda	100.0	1	Trinidad & Tobago	8.4
	Hong Kong	100.0	2	Burundi	12.1
	Macau	100.0	3	Papua New Guinea	13.0
	Monaco	100.0	4	Liechtenstein	14.3
	Singapore	100.0	5	Uganda	16.1
6	Qatar	99.2	6	Malawi	16.3
7	Guadeloupe	98.4	7	Sri Lanka	18.4
8	Kuwait	98.3	8	Nepal	18.6
9	Belgium	97.9	9	Niger	18.7
10	Malta	95.4	10	South Sudan	18.8
11	Uruguay	95.3	11	Ethiopia	19.5
	Virgin Islands (US)	95.3	12	Cambodia	20.7
13	Réunion	95.0	13	Swaziland	21.3

Biggest urban populations
m, 2015

1	China	779.5	15	United Kingdom	52.7
2	India	419.9	16	France	51.7
3	United States	265.4	17	Philippines	45.2
4	Brazil	174.5	18	Italy	42.2
5	Indonesia	137.4	19	South Korea	41.0
6	Japan	118.6	20	Argentina	38.7
7	Russia	105.2	21	Colombia	37.9
8	Mexico	99.2	22	Spain	37.6
9	Nigeria	87.7	23	Egypt	36.5
10	Pakistan	72.9	24	South Africa	34.7
11	Germany	62.2	25	Thailand	34.0
12	Iran	58.3	26	Vietnam	31.4
13	Turkey	56.3	27	Ukraine	31.1
14	Bangladesh	55.0	28	Congo-Kinshasa	30.3

Biggest rural populations
m, 2015

1	India	879.7	17	Myanmar	32.5
2	China	608.2	18	Uganda	32.4
3	Pakistan	118.4	19	Brazil	29.1
4	Indonesia	116.5	20	Afghanistan	27.6
5	Bangladesh	110.2	21	Nepal	26.6
6	Nigeria	86.2	22	Mexico	25.0
7	Ethiopia	75.4	23	Sudan	24.8
8	Vietnam	61.4	24	Iran	23.6
9	United States	54.0	25	Germany	20.8
10	Philippines	50.9	26	Turkey	19.2
11	Egypt	49.2	27	Italy	18.9
12	Congo-Kinshasa	47.8	28	South Africa	18.6
13	Thailand	45.6	29	Uzbekistan	18.5
14	Tanzania	37.4	30	Sri Lanka	18.4
15	Russia	36.2	31	Yemen	18.3
16	Kenya	34.5	32	Mozambique	17.7

City liveability[a]
100 = ideal, 0 = intolerable, 2014

Best

1	Melbourne, Australia	97.7
2	Vienna, Austria	97.4
3	Vancouver, Canada	97.3
4	Toronto, Canada	97.2
5	Adelaide, Australia	96.6
	Calgary, Canada	96.6
7	Sydney, Australia	96.1
8	Helsinki, Finland	96.0
9	Perth, Australia	95.9
10	Auckland, New Zealand	95.7

Worst

1	Damascus, Syria	30.5
2	Dhaka, Bangladesh	38.7
3	Lagos, Nigeria	38.9
	Port Moresby, Papua New Guinea	38.9
5	Algiers, Algeria	40.9
	Karachi, Pakistan	40.9
7	Harare, Zimbabwe	42.6
8	Douala, Cameroon	44.0
9	Tripoli, Libya	44.2
10	Abidjan, Ivory Coast	44.9

Tallest buildings[b]
Metres

1	Burj Khalifa, Dubai	828.0
2	Makkah Royal Clock Tower Hotel, Mecca	601.0
3	One World Trade Centre, New York	541.3
4	Taipei 101, Taipei	508.0
5	World Financial Centre, Shanghai	492.0
6	International Commerce Centre, Hong Kong	484.0
7	Petronas Towers, Kuala Lumpur	451.9
8	Zifeng Tower, Nanjing	450.0
9	Willis Tower, Chicago	442.1
10	KK100, Shenzhen	441.8
11	International Financial Centre, Guangzhou	438.6
12	Trump International Hotel and Tower, Chicago	423.2
13	Jin Mao Tower, Shanghai	420.5

14	Princess Tower, Dubai	413.4
15	Al Hamra Tower, Kuwait City	412.6
16	Two International Finance Centre, Hong Kong	412.0
17	23 Marina, Dubai	392.4
18	CITIC Plaza, Guangzhou	390.2
19	Shun Hing Square, Shenzhen	384.0
20	Burj Mohammed Bin Rashid Tower, Abu Dhabi	381.2
21	Empire State Building, New York	381.0
22	Elite Residence, Dubai	380.5
23	Central Plaza, Hong Kong	373.9
24	Bank of China Tower, Hong Kong	367.4

Tallest buildings in Europe[b]
Metres

1	Mercury City Tower, Moscow	338.8
2	The Shard, London	306.0
3	Capital City Tower, Moscow	301.8
4	Naberezhnaya Tower C, Moscow	268.4
5	Triumph Palace, Moscow	264.1

6	Sapphire Tower, Istanbul	261.0
7	Commerzbank Tower, Frankfurt	259.0
8	Capital City Tower, St Petersburg	257.2
9	MesseTurm, Frankfurt	256.5
10	Torre de Cristal, Madrid	249.0

a EIU liveability index, based on a range of factors including stability, health care, culture, education, infrastructure.
b Completed buildings.

Refugees and asylum seekers

Refugees[a], country of origin
'000, 2013

1	Afghanistan	2,556.6	11	Central African Rep.	252.9
2	Syria	2,468.4	12	China	195.1
3	Somalia	1,121.7	13	Mali	152.9
4	Sudan	649.3	14	Sri Lanka	123.1
5	Congo-Kinshasa	499.6	15	South Sudan	114.5
6	Myanmar	479.6	16	West Bank & Gaza	96.0
7	Iraq	401.4	17	Ivory Coast	85.7
8	Colombia	396.6	18	Rwanda	83.9
9	Vietnam	314.1	19	Ethiopia	77.1
10	Eritrea	308.0	20	Iran	75.0

Countries with largest refugee[a] populations
'000, 2013

1	Pakistan	1,616.5	11	Iraq	246.3
2	Iran	857.4	12	Yemen	241.3
3	Lebanon	856.5	13	France	232.5
4	Jordan	641.9	14	Bangladesh	231.1
5	Turkey	609.9	15	Egypt	230.1
6	Kenya	534.9	16	South Sudan	229.6
7	Chad	434.5	17	Uganda	220.6
8	Ethiopia	433.9	18	Venezuela	204.3
9	China	301.0	19	India	188.4
10	United States	263.6	20	Germany	187.6

Origin of asylum applications to industrialised countries
'000, 2013

1	Syria	56.4	11	Nigeria	14.9
2	Russia	39.8	12	Albania	11.3
3	Afghanistan	38.7	13	Sri Lanka	10.6
4	Iraq	38.2	14	Egypt	9.8
5	Serbia[b]	34.7	15	Bangladesh	9.7
6	Pakistan	26.3	16	Mexico	9.4
7	Iran	23.9	17	Georgia	9.1
8	Somalia	23.1	18	Algeria	8.8
9	Eritrea	21.8	19	Congo-Kinshasa	8.5
10	China	20.2	20	Macedonia	7.7

Asylum applications in industrialised countries
'000, 2013

1	Germany	109.6	9	Switzerland	19.4
2	United States	88.4	10	Hungary	18.6
3	France	60.1	11	Austria	17.5
4	Sweden	54.3	12	Netherlands	14.4
5	Turkey	44.8	13	Poland	14.0
6	United Kingdom	29.2	14	Belgium	12.5
7	Italy	27.8	15	Norway	11.5
8	Australia	24.3	16	Canada	10.4

a According to UNHCR. Includes people in "refugee-like situations".
b Includes Kosovo.

The world economy

Biggest economies
GDP, $bn, 2013

1	United States	16,768	23	Poland	526
2	China	9,240	24	Belgium	525
3	Japan	4,920	25	Nigeria	522
4	Germany	3,730	26	Norway	513
5	France[a]	2,806	27	Taiwan	511
6	United Kingdom	2,678	28	Venezuela	438
7	Brazil	2,246	29	Austria	428
8	Italy	2,149	30	United Arab Emirates	402
9	Russia	2,097	31	Thailand	387
10	India	1,875	32	Colombia	378
11	Canada	1,827	33	Iran	369
12	Australia	1,560	34	South Africa	366
13	Spain	1,393	35	Denmark	336
14	South Korea	1,305	36	Malaysia	313
15	Mexico	1,261	37	Singapore	298
16	Indonesia	868	38	Israel	291
17	Netherlands	854	39	Chile	277
18	Turkey	822	40	Hong Kong	274
19	Saudi Arabia	748	41	Egypt	272
20	Switzerland	685		Philippines	272
21	Argentina	610	43	Finland	267
22	Sweden	580	44	Greece	242

Biggest economies by purchasing power
GDP PPP, $bn, 2013

1	United States	16,768	24	Poland	912
2	China	16,162	25	Egypt	910
3	India	6,784	26	Pakistan	838
4	Japan	4,613	27	Netherlands	776
5	Russia	3,623	28	Malaysia	694
6	Germany	3,539	29	South Africa	684
7	Brazil	3,013	30	Philippines	643
8	France	2,475	31	Colombia	600
9	United Kingdom	2,453	32	Venezuela	553
10	Indonesia	2,389	33	United Arab Emirates[b]	551
11	Italy	2,125	34	Algeria	522
12	Mexico	2,003	35	Iraq	500
13	South Korea	1,660	36	Vietnam	475
14	Saudi Arabia	1,546	37	Belgium	465
15	Spain	1,543	38	Bangladesh	462
16	Canada	1,503	39	Switzerland	461
17	Turkey	1,407	40	Sweden	429
18	Iran	1,207	41	Singapore	425
19	Taiwan	1,021	42	Ukraine	400
20	Australia	999	43	Kazakhstan	395
21	Nigeria	973	44	Chile	387
22	Thailand	965	45	Austria	382
23	Argentina	930		Hong Kong	382

Note: For a list of 183 countries with their GDPs, see pages 250–53.
a Includes overseas departments. b 2012 c IMF coverage.

Regional GDP

$bn, 2014		*% annual growth 2009–14*	
World	77,302	World	3.9
Advanced economies	47,044	Advanced economies	1.8
G7	35,624	G7	1.8
Euro area (18)	13,391	Euro area (18)	0.6
Other Asia	14,922	Other Asia	7.6
Latin America & Caribbean	5,800	Latin America & Caribbean	3.6
Other Europe & CIS	4,414	Other Europe & CIS	3.3
Middle East, N. Africa, Afghanistan & Pakistan	3,453	Middle East, N. Africa, Afghanistan & Pakistan	3.8
Sub-Saharan Africa	1,670	Sub-Saharan Africa	5.2

Regional purchasing power

GDP, % of total, 2014		*$ per person, 2014*	
World	100.0	World	15,200
Advanced economies	43.1	Advanced economies	44,590
G7	32.2	G7	46,250
Euro area (18)	12.1	Euro area (18)	39,360
Other Asia	29.5	Other Asia	9,200
Latin America & Caribbean	8.7	Latin America & Caribbean	15,490
Other Europe & CIS	8.0	Other Europe & CIS	18,910
Middle East, N. Africa, Afghanistan & Pakistan	7.6	Middle East, N. Africa, Afghanistan & Pakistan	12,900
Sub-Saharan Africa	3.1	Sub-Saharan Africa	3,720

Regional population

% of total (7.2bn), 2014		*No. of economies[c], 2014*	
World	100.0	World	189
Advanced economies	14.7	Advanced economies	37
G7	10.6	G7	7
Euro area (18)	4.7	Euro area (18)	18
Other Asia	48.8	Other Asia	29
Latin America & Caribbean	8.5	Latin America & Caribbean	32
Other Europe & CIS	6.4	Other Europe & CIS	24
Middle East, N. Africa, Afghanistan & Pakistan	9.0	Middle East, N. Africa, Afghanistan & Pakistan	22
Sub-Saharan Africa	12.6	Sub-Saharan Africa	45

Regional international trade

Exports of goods & services *% of total, 2014*		*Current-account balances* *$bn, 2014*	
World	100.0	World	367
Advanced economies	62.0	Advanced economies	170
G7	33.4	G7	-291
Euro area (18)	25.3	Euro area (18)	313
Other Asia	17.2	Other Asia	195
Latin America & Caribbean	5.2	Latin America & Caribbean	-165
Other Europe & CIS	7.0	Other Europe & CIS	0
Middle East, N. Africa, Afghanistan & Pakistan	6.6	Middle East, N. Africa, Afghanistan & Pakistan	221
Sub-Saharan Africa	2.0	Sub-Saharan Africa	-55

Living standards

Highest GDP per person
$, 2013

1	Monaco	173,377	31	Hong Kong	38,124
2	Liechtenstein	152,933	32	New Caledonia	37,862
3	Luxembourg	110,665	33	Israel	36,051
4	Norway	100,898	34	Italy	35,686
5	Qatar	93,714	35	Guadeloupe[a]	30,038
6	Macau	91,376	36	Martinique[a]	30,037
7	Bermuda	85,302	37	Spain	29,882
8	Switzerland	84,748	38	Guam[bc]	28,700
9	Australia	67,463	39	Puerto Rico	28,529
10	Sweden	60,381	40	Réunion[a]	26,908
11	Denmark	59,819	41	South Korea	25,977
12	Channel Islands	56,608	42	Saudi Arabia	25,962
13	Singapore	55,182	43	Cyprus	25,249
14	United States	53,042	44	Bahrain	24,689
15	Kuwait	52,197	45	Slovenia	23,295
16	Canada	51,964	46	French Polynesia	23,162
17	Netherlands	50,793	47	Malta	22,775
18	Austria	50,511	48	Bahamas	22,312
19	Ireland	50,478	49	Greece	21,966
20	Finland	49,151	50	Oman	21,929
21	Iceland	47,349	51	Taiwan	21,874
22	Belgium	46,930	52	Portugal	21,738
23	Germany	46,251	53	French Guiana[a]	20,649
24	United Arab Emirates	43,049	54	Equatorial Guinea	20,582
25	France	42,560	55	Czech Republic	19,858
26	New Zealand	41,824	56	Estonia	18,877
27	United Kingdom	41,781	57	Trinidad & Tobago	18,373
28	Andorra	41,015	58	Slovakia	18,049
29	Japan	38,634	59	Uruguay	16,351
30	Brunei	38,563	60	Chile	15,732

Lowest GDP per person
$, 2013

1	Somalia	133	17	Rwanda	639
2	Malawi	226	18	Uganda	657
3	Burundi	267	19	Afghanistan	665
4	Central African Rep.	333	20	Sierra Leone	679
5	Niger	415	21	Nepal	694
6	Liberia	454	22	Mali	715
7	Madagascar	463	23	Burkina Faso	761
8	Congo-Kinshasa	484	24	Benin	805
9	Gambia, The	489	25	Haiti	820
10	Ethiopia	505	26	Tanzania	913
11	Guinea	523	27	Zimbabwe	953
12	Eritrea	544	28	Bangladesh	958
13	Guinea-Bissau	564	29	Cambodia	1,007
14	Mozambique	605	30	Tajikistan	1,037
15	North Korea	621	31	South Sudan	1,045
16	Togo	636	32	Senegal	1,047

a 2011   b 2010   c Estimate.

Highest purchasing power
GDP per person in PPP (US = 100), 2013

1	Macau	268.8	35	Japan	68.3
2	Qatar	257.8	36	Italy	66.5
3	Luxembourg	171.7	37	New Zealand	65.5
4	Liechtenstein[a]	168.5		Puerto Rico	65.5
5	Kuwait[b]	158.1	39	Equatorial Guinea	63.7
6	Singapore	148.5	40	Spain	62.4
7	Monaco	148.4	41	South Korea	62.3
8	Brunei	135.3	42	Israel	61.3
9	Norway	121.4	43	Trinidad & Tobago	57.4
10	United Arab Emirates[b]	112.8	44	Malta	54.9
11	Switzerland	107.4	45	Czech Republic	54.7
12	Channel Islands	106.7	46	Slovenia	54.4
13	Saudi Arabia	101.1	47	Guam[d]	54.1
14	Hong Kong	100.3	48	Cyprus	53.2
15	Bermuda[b]	100.0	49	Portugal	52.4
	United States	100.0	50	Guadeloupe[c]	50.4
17	Netherlands	87.0		Martinique[c]	50.4
18	Ireland	86.1	52	Slovakia	50.0
19	Oman[b]	85.5	53	French Polynesia[b]	49.2
20	Austria	85.0	54	Estonia	48.7
21	Sweden	84.2	55	Greece	48.4
22	Bahrain	82.7	56	Lithuania	48.0
	Germany	82.7	57	Russia	47.6
24	Denmark	82.5	58	Réunion[c]	45.2
25	Taiwan	82.3	59	Poland	44.7
26	Australia	81.4	60	Hungary	44.0
27	Canada	80.6		Malaysia	44.0
28	Iceland	78.9	62	Bahamas	43.9
29	Belgium	78.4	63	Kazakhstan	43.8
30	Finland	74.9	64	Latvia	42.5
31	New Caledonia[b]	73.1	65	Argentina	42.2
32	United Kingdom	72.1	66	Chile	41.4
33	France	70.8	67	Croatia	40.3
34	Andorra[c]	70.1	68	Libya	39.7

Lowest purchasing power
GDP per person in PPP (US = 100), 2013

1	Somalia[d]	1.13	13	Guinea-Bissau	2.65
2	Central African Rep.	1.14	14	Madagascar	2.67
3	Burundi	1.45	15	Rwanda	2.78
4	Malawi	1.47	16	Sierra Leone	2.91
5	Congo-Kinshasa	1.53	17	Mali	3.10
6	Liberia	1.66	18	Gambia, The	3.13
7	Niger	1.73	19	Uganda	3.16
8	Mozambique	2.08	20	Burkina Faso	3.18
9	Eritrea	2.25	21	Haiti	3.21
10	Guinea	2.36	22	Benin	3.38
11	Ethiopia	2.60	23	North Korea	3.39
12	Togo	2.62	24	Zimbabwe	3.45

a 2009   b 2012   c 2011   d 2010

The quality of life

Human development index[a]
Highest, 2013

1	Norway	94.4	31	Qatar	85.1
2	Australia	93.3	32	Cyprus	84.5
3	Switzerland	91.7	33	Estonia	84.0
4	Netherlands	91.5	34	Saudi Arabia	83.6
5	United States	91.4	35	Lithuania	83.4
6	Germany	91.1		Poland	83.4
7	New Zealand	91.0	37	Andorra	83.0
8	Canada	90.2		Slovakia	83.0
9	Singapore	90.1	39	Malta	82.9
10	Denmark	90.0	40	United Arab Emirates	82.7
11	Ireland	89.9	41	Chile	82.2
12	Sweden	89.8		Portugal	82.2
13	Iceland	89.5	43	Hungary	81.8
14	United Kingdom	89.2	44	Bahrain	81.5
15	Hong Kong	89.1		Cuba	81.5
	South Korea	89.1	46	Kuwait	81.4
17	Japan	89.0	47	Croatia	81.2
18	Liechtenstein	88.9	48	Latvia	81.0
19	Israel	88.8	49	Argentina	80.8
20	France	88.4	50	Uruguay	79.0
21	Austria	88.1	51	Bahamas	78.9
	Belgium	88.1		Montenegro	78.9
	Luxembourg	88.1	53	Belarus	78.6
24	Finland	87.9	54	Romania	78.5
25	Slovenia	87.4	55	Libya	78.4
26	Italy	87.2	56	Oman	78.3
27	Spain	86.9	57	Russia	77.8
28	Czech Republic	86.1	58	Bulgaria	77.7
29	Greece	85.3	59	Barbados	77.6
30	Brunei	85.2	60	Malaysia	77.3

Human development index[a]
Lowest, 2013

1	Niger	33.7	13	Liberia	41.2
2	Congo-Kinshasa	33.8	14	Malawi	41.4
3	Central African Rep.	34.1	15	Ethiopia	43.5
4	Chad	37.2	16	Gambia, The	44.1
5	Sierra Leone	37.4	17	Ivory Coast	45.2
6	Eritrea	38.1	18	Afghanistan	46.8
7	Burkina Faso	38.8	19	Haiti	47.1
8	Burundi	38.9	20	Sudan	47.3
9	Guinea	39.2		Togo	47.3
10	Mozambique	39.3	22	Benin	47.6
11	Guinea-Bissau	39.6	23	Uganda	48.4
12	Mali	40.7	24	Senegal	48.5

a GDP or GDP per person is often taken as a measure of how developed a country is, but its usefulness is limited as it refers only to economic welfare. The UN Development Programme combines statistics on average and expected years of schooling and life expectancy with income levels (now GNI per person, valued in PPP US$). The HDI is shown here scaled from 0 to 100; countries scoring over 80 are considered to have very high human development, 70–79 high, 55–69 medium and those under 55 low.

Social progress index[a]

Highest, 2015

1	Norway	88.4		13	Austria	84.5
2	Sweden	88.1		14	Germany	84.0
3	Switzerland	88.0		15	Japan	83.2
4	Iceland	87.6		16	United States	82.9
5	New Zealand	87.1		17	Belgium	82.8
6	Canada	86.9		18	Portugal	81.9
7	Finland	86.8		19	Slovenia	81.6
8	Denmark	86.6		20	Spain	81.2
9	Netherlands	86.5		21	France	80.8
10	Australia	86.4		22	Czech Republic	80.6
11	Ireland	84.7		23	Estonia	80.5
	United Kingdom	84.7		24	Uruguay	79.2

Gini coefficient[b]

Highest 2003–12 | | | | *Lowest 2003–12* | | |

1	Namibia	63.9		1	Sweden	25.0
2	South Africa	63.1		2	Ukraine	25.6
3	Haiti	59.2		3	Norway	25.8
4	Zambia	57.5		4	Slovakia	26.0
5	Honduras	57.0		5	Belarus	26.5
6	Bolivia	56.3		6	Finland	26.9
	Central African Rep.	56.3		7	Romania	27.4
8	Colombia	55.9		8	Afghanistan	27.8
	Guatemala	55.9		9	Bulgaria	28.2
10	Brazil	54.7		10	Germany	28.3
11	Suriname	52.9		11	Montenegro	28.6
12	Lesotho	52.5		12	Kazakhstan	29.0
13	Paraguay	52.4		13	Austria	29.2

Economic freedom index[c]

Highest, 2015

1	Hong Kong	89.6		14	Taiwan	75.1
2	Singapore	89.4		15	Lithuania	74.7
3	New Zealand	82.1		16	Germany	73.8
4	Australia	81.4		17	Netherlands	73.7
5	Switzerland	80.5		18	Bahrain	73.4
6	Canada	79.1			Finland	73.4
7	Chile	78.5		20	Japan	73.3
8	Estonia	76.8		21	Luxembourg	73.2
9	Ireland	76.6		22	Georgia	73.0
10	Mauritius	76.4		23	Sweden	72.7
11	Denmark	76.3		24	Czech Republic	72.5
12	United States	76.2		25	United Arab Emirates	72.4
13	United Kingdom	75.8		26	Iceland	72.0

a Ranks countries' performance on basic human needs, well-being and opportunity,
  where 100 = maximum, published by the Social Progress Imperative.
b The lower its value, the more equally household income is distributed.
c Ranks countries on the basis of indicators of how government intervention can
  restrict the economic relations between individuals, published by the Heritage
  Foundation. Scores are from 80–100 (free) to 0–49.9 (repressed) (see Glossary).

Economic growth

Highest economic growth
Average annual % increase in real GDP, 2003–13

1	Qatar	14.1	28	Kazakhstan	6.9
2	Macau	13.6	29	Monaco[a]	6.7
3	Azerbaijan	12.4	30	Belarus	6.5
4	Turkmenistan	11.5		Sri Lanka	6.5
5	Ethiopia	10.9		Singapore	6.5
6	Angola	10.6	33	Peru	6.4
7	China	10.2		Tanzania	6.4
8	Iraq	10.1		Vietnam	6.4
9	Mongolia	9.9	36	Congo-Kinshasa	6.3
10	Afghanistan	8.7	37	Equatorial Guinea	6.2
	Myanmar	8.7	38	Bangladesh	6.1
12	Panama	8.6	39	Burkina Faso	6.0
13	Uzbekistan	8.1		Saudi Arabia	6.0
14	Cambodia	7.9	41	Argentina	5.9
15	Laos	7.8		Armenia	5.9
	Rwanda	7.8		Indonesia	5.9
	Zambia	7.8		Georgia	5.9
18	Chad	7.7	45	Cuba	5.8
	India	7.7		Papua New Guinea	5.8
	Sierra Leone	7.7	47	Venezuela	5.7
21	Nigeria	7.6	48	Jordan	5.6
22	Timor-Leste	7.5		Mauritania[b]	5.6
23	Ghana	7.4	50	Malawi	5.5
	Mozambique	7.4		Uruguay	5.5
25	Liberia	7.2	52	Philippines	5.4
	Tajikistan	7.2		Syria	5.4
27	Uganda	7.0	54	Bahrain[c]	5.2

Lowest economic growth
Average annual % change in real GDP, 2003–13

1	South Sudan[d]	-8.4		Finland	1.0
2	Central African Rep.	-1.6		Hungary	1.0
	Greece	-1.6	22	France	1.1
4	Puerto Rico	-1.4		Netherlands	1.1
5	Libya	-0.5	24	Germany	1.2
6	Bermuda[e]	-0.3		United Kingdom	1.2
	Italy	-0.3	26	Cyprus	1.3
8	Portugal	-0.2		Ireland	1.3
9	Jamaica	0.2	28	Belgium	1.4
10	Zimbabwe	0.4		Haiti	1.4
11	Denmark	0.5		Slovenia	1.4
12	Bahamas	0.6	31	Austria	1.5
13	Brunei	0.7	32	Norway	1.6
	Croatia	0.7	33	Eritrea	1.7
15	Japan	0.8		United States	1.7
	North Korea[f]	0.8	35	El Salvador	1.8
	Spain	0.8	36	Sweden	1.9
18	Euro area	0.9	37	Canada	2.0
19	Barbados	1.0		New Zealand	2.0

a 2003–08 b 2003–11 c 2002–10 d 2008–13 e 2003–12 f 2003–10

Highest economic growth
Average annual % increase in real GDP, 1993–2003

1	Equatorial Guinea	27.6		10	Vietnam	7.2
2	Bosnia & Herz.[a]	18.7		11	Angola	6.9
3	Liberia	14.1		12	Estonia[b]	6.8
4	China	9.4			Uganda	6.8
	Myanmar	9.4		14	Albania	6.4
6	Ireland	7.7			Laos	6.4
7	Cambodia	7.5		16	India	6.1
8	Armenia	7.4		17	Burkina Faso	6.0
9	Mozambique	7.3				

Lowest economic growth
Average annual % change in real GDP, 1993–2003

1	Iraq[c]	-3.4		11	Papua New Guinea	0.3
2	Moldova	-3.0			Turkmenistan	0.3
3	Ukraine	-2.6		13	Jamaica[d]	0.4
4	Congo-Kinshasa	-1.6		14	Montenegro[c]	0.6
5	Burundi	-1.4		15	Russia	0.7
6	Venezuela	-0.9		16	Argentina	0.8
7	Tajikistan	-0.7		17	Japan	0.9
8	Zimbabwe	-0.6			Uruguay	0.9
9	North Korea	-0.5		19	Kyrgyzstan	1.1
10	Guinea-Bissau	0.0			Macedonia	1.1

Highest services growth
Average annual % increase in real terms, 2005–13

1	Liberia[e]	20.6		10	China	11.9
2	Nigeria	18.6		11	Mongolia	11.8
3	Qatar	16.5		12	Ethiopia	10.8
4	Macau[e]	14.4		13	Uzbekistan	9.9
5	Ghana	14.3		14	Equatorial Guinea	9.1
6	Azerbaijan	13.8		15	Timor-Leste[e]	8.9
7	Angola	13.4		16	Uganda	8.7
8	Afghanistan	13.3		17	Armenia	8.6
9	Yemen	13.1			Tajikistan	8.6

Lowest services growth
Average annual % change in real terms, 2005–13

1	Puerto Rico	-15.7			Hungary	0.4
2	Greece	-1.6		11	Denmark	0.6
3	Latvia[f]	-0.8		12	Suriname	0.8
4	Bahamas	-0.2		13	Barbados[e]	0.9
	Bermuda[e]	-0.2			Japan[e]	0.9
	Italy	-0.2		15	Germany	1.0
7	Jamaica[g]	0.1		16	France	1.1
8	Portugal	0.2			Netherlands	1.1
9	Croatia	0.4				

a 1994–2003   b 1995–2003   c 1997–2003   d 1993–2001   e 2005–12
f 2005–10   g 2006–13
Note: Rankings of highest and lowest industrial growth 2005–13 can be found on page 48 and highest and lowest agricultural growth 2005–13 on page 51.

Trading places

Biggest exporters
% of total world exports (goods, services and income), 2013

1	Euro area (17)	14.47	22	Singapore	1.33
2	United States	11.43	23	Brazil	1.30
3	China	10.39	24	Thailand	1.26
4	Germany	7.15	25	Turkey	1.13
5	Japan	4.03	26	Malaysia	1.11
6	France	3.68	27	Poland	1.10
7	United Kingdom	3.55	28	Sweden	1.04
8	South Korea	3.14	29	Austria	0.98
9	Netherlands	2.88	30	Indonesia	0.95
10	Italy	2.68	31	Ireland	0.75
11	Canada	2.57	32	Norway	0.74
12	Russia	2.33	33	Czech Republic	0.72
13	India	2.25	34	Denmark	0.70
14	Switzerland	2.01	35	Hong Kong	0.69
15	Spain	1.96	36	Vietnam	0.66
16	Mexico	1.95	37	South Africa	0.54
17	Belgium	1.91	38	Hungary	0.52
18	United Arab Emirates	1.62	39	Finland	0.45
19	Taiwan	1.56		Qatar	0.45
20	Australia	1.39	41	Iran	0.43
21	Saudi Arabia	1.35		Slovakia	0.43

Most trade dependent
Trade[a] as % of GDP, 2013

1	Slovakia	84.6
2	United Arab Emirates	78.3
3	Vietnam	74.6
4	Lithuania	71.0
5	Hungary	70.3
6	Equatorial Guinea	69.0
7	Mauritania	68.5
8	Singapore	67.3
9	Malaysia	64.8
10	Estonia	63.8
11	Czech Republic	63.6
12	Belgium	62.2
13	Netherlands	60.7
14	Slovenia	59.0
15	Lesotho	58.5
16	Thailand	57.4
17	Puerto Rico	57.1
18	Bulgaria	57.1
19	Taiwan	56.0
20	Oman	55.4
21	Malawi	54.7
22	Congo-Brazzaville	54.3

Least trade dependent
Trade[a] as % of GDP, 2013

1	Bermuda	9.4
2	Syria	10.5
3	Brazil	10.7
4	United States	11.6
5	Sudan	11.9
6	Argentina	12.5
7	Central African Rep.	13.0
8	Macau	13.0
9	Burundi	14.1
10	Pakistan	14.3
11	Myanmar	14.7
12	Cuba	14.9
13	Japan	15.0
14	French Polynesia	15.1
15	Nigeria	15.2
16	Colombia	15.5
17	Ethiopia	15.7
18	Uganda	15.8
19	Egypt	16.0
20	Australia	16.2
	Venezuela	16.2

Notes: The figures are drawn wherever possible from balance of payment statistics so have differing definitions from statistics taken from customs or similar sources. For Hong Kong and Singapore, only domestic exports and retained imports are used. Euro area data exclude intra-euro area trade.

a Average of imports plus exports of goods.

Biggest traders of goods[a]
% of world, 2014

	Exports			Imports	
1	China	12.4	1	United States	12.7
2	United States	8.6	2	China	10.3
3	Germany	8.0	3	Germany	6.4
4	Japan	3.6	4	Japan	4.3
	Netherlands	3.6	5	France	3.6
6	France	3.1		United Kingdom	3.6
7	South Korea	3.0	7	Netherlands	3.1
8	Italy	2.8	8	South Korea	2.8
9	United Kingdom	2.7	9	Canada	2.5
10	Russia	2.6		Italy	2.5
11	Belgium	2.5	11	Belgium	2.4
	Canada	2.5		India	2.4
13	Mexico	2.1	13	Mexico	2.2
14	Saudi Arabia[b]	1.9	14	Spain	1.9
	United Arab Emirates[b]	1.9	15	Russia	1.6
16	India	1.7	16	Taiwan	1.4
	Spain	1.7		United Arab Emirates[b]	1.4
	Taiwan	1.7	18	Brazil	1.3
19	Australia	1.3		Turkey	1.3
	Switzerland	1.3	20	Australia[b]	1.2
				Thailand	1.2

Biggest earners from services and income
% of world exports of services and income, 2013

1	Euro area (17)	19.31	24	Australia	1.20
2	United States	17.65	25	Norway	1.08
3	Germany	6.47	26	Taiwan	0.92
4	United Kingdom	6.35	27	Thailand	0.80
5	France	5.54	28	Poland	0.73
6	China	4.82	29	Macau	0.68
7	Luxembourg	4.33	30	Malaysia	0.66
8	Japan	4.30	31	Turkey	0.62
9	Hong Kong	3.02	32	Brazil	0.59
10	Switzerland	2.84	33	Finland	0.53
11	Netherlands	2.72	34	Greece	0.50
12	Singapore	2.35		Israel	0.50
13	Spain	2.34	36	United Arab Emirates	0.47
14	Ireland	2.31	37	Hungary	0.46
15	Italy	2.25	38	Portugal	0.44
16	Belgium	2.13		Saudi Arabia	0.44
17	Canada	1.96	40	Mexico	0.38
18	India	1.92		Philippines	0.38
19	Sweden	1.64	42	Czech Republic	0.37
20	South Korea	1.61		Ukraine	0.37
21	Russia	1.35	44	Indonesia	0.31
22	Denmark	1.24	45	Malta	0.30
23	Austria	1.22	46	South Africa	0.28

a Individual countries only.   b Estimate.

Balance of payments: current account

Largest surpluses
$m, 2013

1	Euro area (17)	305,395	26	Philippines	11,384
2	Germany	251,791	27	Spain	10,668
3	China	182,807	28	Vietnam	9,471
4	Saudi Arabia	132,640	29	Angola	8,348
5	Netherlands	87,089	30	Israel	6,893
6	South Korea	81,148	31	Brunei	5,558
7	Switzerland	73,153	32	Hungary	5,497
8	Kuwait	69,783	33	Venezuela	5,327
9	United Arab Emirates	64,682	34	Oman	5,117
10	Qatar	62,418	35	Austria	4,439
11	Taiwan	55,257	36	Hong Kong	4,153
12	Singapore	54,084	37	Luxembourg	2,947
13	Norway	50,962	38	Timor-Leste[a]	2,746
14	Sweden	42,090	39	Slovenia	2,688
15	Russia	34,801	40	Trinidad & Tobago	2,572
16	Japan	34,068	41	Gabon[b]	2,566
17	Iran	27,963	42	Bahrain	2,560
18	Denmark	24,023	43	Bangladesh	2,366
19	Macau	22,363	44	Slovakia	2,026
20	Iraq	22,054	45	Botswana	1,769
21	Nigeria	20,148	46	Cuba[c]	1,437
22	Italy	20,122	47	Greece	1,409
23	Ireland	14,438	48	Bolivia	1,173
24	Azerbaijan	12,232	49	Portugal	1,160
25	Malaysia	11,732	50	Nepal	1,151

Largest deficits
$m, 2013

1	United States	-400,253	22	New Zealand	-5,932
2	United Kingdom	-114,210	23	Mozambique	-5,892
3	Brazil	-81,108	24	Ghana	-5,685
4	Turkey	-64,658	25	Panama	-4,920
5	Canada	-54,665	26	Kenya	-4,788
6	Australia	-50,227	27	Papua New Guinea	-4,750
7	India	-49,226	28	Tanzania	-4,703
8	France	-40,213	29	Argentina	-4,696
9	Mexico	-29,682	30	Sudan	-4,481
10	Indonesia	-29,102	31	Pakistan	-4,328
11	South Africa	-21,194	32	Tunisia	-3,879
12	Ukraine	-16,518	33	Zimbabwe	-3,432
13	Colombia	-12,330	34	Jordan	-3,359
14	Lebanon	-10,983	35	Mongolia	-3,192
15	Chile	-10,125	36	Uruguay	-2,924
16	Peru	-9,126	37	Congo-Kinshasa	-2,863
17	Morocco	-7,844	38	Ethiopia	-2,821
18	Belarus	-7,567	39	Serbia	-2,790
19	Poland	-6,988	40	Thailand	-2,678
20	Afghanistan	-6,706	41	Sri Lanka	-2,627
21	Egypt	-6,390	42	Costa Rica	-2,522

Note: Euro area data exclude intra-euro area trade. a 2012 b Estimate. c 2011

Largest surpluses as % of GDP
2013

1	Timor-Leste[a]	216.3		Oman	6.4
2	Macau	43.2	27	Swaziland	6.3
3	Kuwait	39.7	28	Ireland	6.2
4	Brunei	34.5		South Korea	6.2
5	Qatar	30.7	30	Nepal	6.0
6	Singapore	18.2	31	Iceland	5.8
7	Saudi Arabia	17.7	32	Slovenia	5.6
8	Azerbaijan	16.6	33	Vietnam	5.5
9	United Arab Emirates	16.1	34	Luxembourg	4.9
10	Bermuda	15.0	35	Philippines	4.2
11	Gabon[a]	13.3	36	Hungary	4.1
12	Botswana	12.0	37	Nigeria	3.9
13	Taiwan	10.8	38	Bolivia	3.8
14	Switzerland	10.7	39	Malaysia	3.7
15	Trinidad & Tobago	10.4	40	Malta	3.1
16	Netherlands	10.2	41	French Polynesia	2.6
17	Norway	9.9	42	Israel	2.4
18	Iraq	9.6	43	Cuba[b]	2.1
19	Bahrain	7.8		Paraguay	2.1
20	Iran	7.6		Slovakia	2.1
21	Sweden	7.3	46	China	2.0
22	Denmark	7.2	47	Bulgaria	1.8
23	Angola	6.7	48	Russia	1.7
	Germany	6.7	49	Bangladesh	1.6
25	Gambia, The[a]	6.4			

Largest deficits as % of GDP
2013

1	Mozambique	-37.7	22	Albania	-10.7
2	Afghanistan	-33.0		Nicaragua	-10.7
3	Papua New Guinea	-30.8	24	Belarus	-10.6
4	Mauritania	-30.3	25	Cambodia	-10.5
5	Mongolia	-27.7		Senegal	-10.5
6	Liberia	-27.5	27	Burkina Faso	-10.4
7	Zimbabwe	-25.4	28	Barbados	-10.3
8	Lebanon	-24.8	29	Jordan	-10.0
9	Kyrgyzstan	-23.3	30	Mauritius	-9.9
10	West Bank & Gaza[a]	-20.3	31	Burundi	-9.3
11	Bahamas	-19.2		Sierra Leone	-9.3
12	Guinea	-18.9		Ukraine	-9.3
13	New Caledonia	-17.9	34	Jamaica	-9.2
14	Niger	-15.5	35	Honduras	-8.9
15	Montenegro	-14.7	36	Congo-Kinshasa	-8.8
16	Fiji	-14.5	37	Kenya	-8.7
17	Togo	-13.1	38	Chad[a]	-8.3
18	Equatorial Guinea	-12.1		Tunisia	-8.3
19	Ghana	-11.8	40	Benin	-8.1
20	Panama	-11.5		Uganda	-8.1
21	Tanzania	-10.8	42	Armenia	-8.0

a 2012   b 2011

Official reserves[a]

$m, end-2014

1	China	3,900,039	16	Algeria	186,351
2	Japan	1,260,680	17	Thailand	157,163
3	Euro area (17)	745,742	18	France	143,977
4	Saudi Arabia	744,441	19	Italy	142,757
5	Switzerland	545,787	20	Turkey	127,422
6	Taiwan	436,096	21	Malaysia	115,959
7	United States	434,416	22	Indonesia	111,863
8	Russia	386,216	23	United Kingdom	107,728
9	Brazil	363,570	24	Poland	100,452
10	South Korea	362,835	25	Libya	93,615
11	Hong Kong	328,517	26	Israel	86,101
12	India	325,081	27	Philippines	79,629
13	Singapore	261,583	28	United Arab Emirates	78,424
14	Mexico	195,682	29	Iraq[b]	77,820
15	Germany	193,485	30	Denmark	75,392

Official gold reserves

Market prices, $m, end-2014

1	Euro area (17)	346,720	14	Saudi Arabia	10,382
2	United States	261,499	15	United Kingdom	9,975
3	Germany	108,805	16	Lebanon	9,222
4	Italy	78,829	17	Spain	9,053
5	France	78,300	18	Austria	9,002
6	Russia	38,844	19	Belgium	7,312
7	China	33,890	20	Philippines	6,279
8	Switzerland	33,437	21	Kazakhstan	6,166
9	Japan	24,602	22	Algeria	5,583
10	Netherlands	19,691	23	Thailand	4,900
11	India	17,932	24	Singapore	4,096
12	Turkey	17,011	25	Sweden	4,042
13	Portugal	12,298	26	South Africa	4,025

Workers' remittances

Inflows, $m, 2013

1	India	69,970	16	Lebanon	7,551
2	China	59,491	17	Italy	7,471
3	Philippines	26,700	18	Poland	6,984
4	France	23,336	19	Morocco	6,882
5	Mexico	23,022	20	Russia	6,751
6	Nigeria	20,890	21	Uzbekistan	6,633
7	Egypt	17,833	22	United States	6,623
8	Germany	15,204	23	South Korea	6,425
9	Pakistan	14,626	24	Sri Lanka	6,422
10	Bangladesh	13,857	25	Thailand	5,690
11	Belgium	11,105	26	Nepal	5,552
12	Vietnam	11,000	27	Guatemala	5,371
13	Ukraine	9,667	28	Dominican Rep.	4,486
14	Spain	9,584	29	Portugal	4,372
15	Indonesia	7,615	30	Colombia	4,119

a Foreign exchange, SDRs, IMF position and gold at market prices.   b 2013

Exchange rates

The Economist's Big Mac index

		Big Mac prices		Implied	Actual $	Under (-)/
		in local currency	in $	PPP[a] of the $	exchange rate	over (+) valuation against $, %
Countries with the most under-valued currencies, January 2015						
1	Ukraine	19.00	1.20	3.97	15.82	-75
2	Russia	89.00	1.36	18.58	65.23	-72
3	India[b]	116.25	1.89	24.27	61.62	-61
4	Malaysia	7.63	2.11	1.59	3.62	-56
5	South Africa	25.50	2.22	5.32	11.48	-54
6	Indonesia	27,939.00	2.24	5,833.00	12,480.00	-53
7	Egypt	16.93	2.30	3.53	7.35	-52
8	Hong Kong	18.80	2.43	3.92	7.75	-49
9	Poland	9.20	2.48	1.92	3.71	-48
	Taiwan	79.00	2.51	16.49	31.49	-48
11	Venezuela	132.00	2.53	27.56	52.10	-47
12	Sri Lanka	350.00	2.65	73.07	131.88	-45
13	China[c]	17.20	2.77	3.59	6.21	-42
14	Vietnam	60,000.00	2.81	12,526.10	21,380.00	-41
15	Czech Republic	70.45	2.92	14.71	24.13	-39
	Saudi Arabia	11.00	2.93	2.30	3.76	-39
17	Pakistan	300.00	2.98	62.63	100.74	-38
18	Thailand	99.00	3.04	20.67	32.61	-37
19	Hungary	860.00	3.17	179.54	271.39	-34
	Japan	370.00	3.14	77.24	117.77	-34
21	Argentina	28.00	3.25	5.85	8.61	-32
22	Peru	10.00	3.32	2.09	3.01	-31
23	Chile	2,100.00	3.35	438.41	627.49	-30
	Colombia	7,900.00	3.34	1,649.27	2,364.98	-30
	Mexico	49.00	3.35	10.23	14.63	-30
26	Singapore	4.70	3.53	0.98	1.33	-26
	UAE	13.00	3.54	2.71	3.67	-26
28	Philippines	163.00	3.67	34.03	44.41	-23
29	South Korea	4,100.00	3.78	855.95	1,083.30	-21
30	Turkey	9.25	3.96	1.93	2.33	-17
31	Costa Rica	2,150.00	4.01	448.85	536.09	-16
32	Euro area[d]	3.68	4.26	1.30[e]	1.16[e]	-11
33	Australia	5.30	4.32	1.11	1.23	-10
34	United Kingdom	2.89	4.37	1.66[f]	1.51[f]	-9
35	Israel	17.50	4.45	3.65	3.93	-7
36	New Zealand	5.90	4.49	1.23	1.31	-6
Countries with the most over-valued currencies, January 2015						
1	Switzerland	6.50	7.54	1.36	0.86	57
2	Norway	48.00	6.30	10.02	7.62	31
3	Denmark	34.50	5.38	7.20	6.42	12
4	Brazil	13.50	5.21	2.82	2.59	9
5	Sweden	40.70	4.97	8.50	8.19	4

a Purchasing-power parity: local price in the 41 countries listed divided by United States price ($4.79, average of four cities).
b Maharaja Mac. c Average of five cities. d Weighted average of prices in euro area.
e Dollars per euro. f Dollars per pound.

Public finance

Government debt
As % of GDP, 2014

1	Japan	230.0	16	Slovenia	82.9
2	Greece	182.3	17	Germany	79.0
3	Italy	146.9	18	Netherlands	77.8
4	Portugal	142.4	19	Israel	68.6
5	Spain	130.8	20	Finland	68.4
6	Belgium	119.2	21	Slovakia	60.1
7	Ireland	116.6	22	Denmark	58.9
8	France	114.1	23	Poland	55.7
9	United States	109.7	24	Czech Republic	51.9
10	Euro area (15)	108.2	25	Sweden	46.5
11	Austria	103.4	26	Switzerland	42.6
12	Hungary	96.7	27	New Zealand	41.1
13	United Kingdom	95.9	28	South Korea	36.7
14	Canada	93.9	29	Australia	36.2
15	Iceland	86.7	30	Norway	35.1

Government spending
As % of GDP, 2014

1	Finland	58.3	16	Germany	44.1
2	France	57.3	17	Luxembourg	44.0
3	Denmark	56.2	18	United Kingdom	43.9
4	Sweden	54.6	19	Spain	43.4
5	Belgium	54.1	20	Japan	42.2
6	Austria	51.8	21	New Zealand	41.9
7	Italy	51.1	22	Czech Republic	41.6
8	Portugal	50.1	23	Israel	41.4
9	Hungary	49.4	24	Poland	41.3
10	Euro area (15)	49.1	25	Slovakia	40.8
11	Slovenia	48.6	26	Canada	39.8
12	Greece	47.5	27	Estonia	38.7
13	Netherlands	47.0	28	Ireland	38.4
14	Norway	46.0		United States	38.4
15	Iceland	44.6	30	Australia	37.1

Tax revenue
As % of GDP, 2013

1	Denmark	48.6	14	Iceland	35.5
2	France	45.0	15	Czech Republic	34.1
3	Belgium	44.6	16	Greece	33.5
4	Finland	44.0	17	Portugal	33.4
5	Sweden	42.8	18	United Kingdom	32.9
6	Italy	42.6	19	Spain	32.6
7	Austria	42.5	20	New Zealand	32.1
8	Norway	40.8		Poland[a]	32.1
9	Luxembourg	39.3	22	Estonia	31.8
10	Hungary	38.9	23	Canada	30.6
11	Slovenia	36.8	24	Israel	30.5
12	Germany	36.7	25	Slovakia	29.6
13	Netherlands[a]	36.3	26	Japan[a]	29.5

Note: Includes only OECD countries.   a 2012

Democracy

Democracy index
Most democratic = 100, 2014

Most			Least		
1	Norway	87.8	1	Syria	28.3
2	Switzerland	85.9	2	Yemen	29.6
3	Sweden	85.8	3	Ivory Coast	34.0
4	Finland	85.5	4	Pakistan	35.9
5	Denmark	84.8	5	Togo	38.3
6	Netherlands	82.6	6	Bahrain	38.7
7	New Zealand	81.3	7	China	39.2
8	Germany	81.0	8	Egypt	39.3
9	Ireland	80.1	9	Nigeria	39.9
10	Belgium	79.8	10	Guinea	40.4
11	Austria	79.4	11	Burundi	41.0
12	Australia	78.9	12	Uganda	41.7
13	United Kingdom	78.4	13	Morocco	42.9
14	Canada	78.2	14	Burkina Faso	43.0
15	France	77.7	15	Mozambique	44.0
16	United States	76.9	16	Russia	44.4
17	Hong Kong	74.6		Zambia	44.4
18	Spain	74.3	18	Madagascar	45.2
19	Portugal	73.9	19	Venezuela	45.5
	Slovenia	73.9	20	Kyrgyzstan	45.7

Parliamentary seats
Lower or single house, seats per 100,000 population, April 2015

Most			Least		
1	Liechtenstein	69.2	1	India	0.05
2	Monaco	65.1	2	United States	0.14
3	Andorra	35.9	3	Pakistan	0.19
4	Iceland	19.8	4	Myanmar	0.20
5	Malta	16.5	5	China	0.22
6	Equatorial Guinea	14.4	6	Bangladesh	0.23
7	Montenegro	13.1		Indonesia	0.23
8	Luxembourg	11.8		Nigeria	0.23
9	Barbados	10.7	9	Brazil	0.26
10	Bahamas	10.5	10	Thailand	0.30

Women in parliament
Lower or single house, women as % of total seats, April 2015

1	Rwanda	63.8	12	Mozambique	39.6
2	Bolivia	53.1		Norway	39.6
3	Cuba	48.9	14	Belgium	39.3
4	Sweden	43.6	15	Nicaragua	39.1
5	Senegal	42.7	16	Timor-Leste	38.5
6	Finland	42.5	17	Denmark	38.0
7	Ecuador	41.6		Mexico	38.0
8	South Africa	41.5	19	Netherlands	37.3
9	Iceland	41.3	20	Angola	36.8
	Namibia	41.3	21	Slovenia	36.7
11	Spain	41.1	22	Germany	36.5

Inflation

Consumer price inflation

Highest, 2014, %

1	Venezuela[a]	62.2
2	Sudan[a]	36.9
3	Malawi	23.8
4	Belarus	18.1
5	Ghana[a]	15.5
	Iran	15.5
7	Central African Rep.	15.0
8	Mongolia	12.9
9	Eritrea	12.3
10	Ukraine	12.1
11	Argentina[b]	10.6
12	Egypt	10.1
13	Liberia[a]	9.9
14	Guinea	9.7
15	Nepal	9.0
16	Turkey	8.9
	Uruguay	8.9
18	Pakistan	8.6
19	Uzbekistan[a]	8.4
20	Sierra Leone	8.3
21	Yemen[a]	8.2
22	Nigeria	8.1

Lowest, 2014, %

1	Bulgaria	-1.6
2	Greece	-1.4
3	Benin[a]	-1.0
	Guinea-Bissau[a]	-1.0
5	Bosnia & Herz.[a]	-0.9
	Niger	-0.9
7	Montenegro	-0.7
	South Sudan	-0.7
9	Senegal[a]	-0.5
10	Burkina Faso	-0.3
	Cyprus	-0.3
	Hungary[a]	-0.3
13	Brunei[a]	-0.2
	Croatia	-0.2
	Portugal	-0.2
	Spain	-0.2
	Sweden	-0.2
	Zimbabwe	-0.2
19	Macedonia	-0.1
	Slovakia	-0.1
21	Poland[a]	0
	Switzerland	0

Highest average annual consumer price inflation, 2009–14, %

1	Venezuela[a]	34.9
2	Belarus	29.7
3	Sudan[a]	27.6
4	Iran	22.6
5	Malawi	17.4
6	Ethiopia	15.7
7	Guinea	14.7
8	Sierra Leone	13.6
9	South Sudan[c]	12.9
10	Eritrea[a]	12.6
11	Yemen[a]	11.9
12	Angola	10.8
	Mongolia	10.8
	Uzbekistan[a]	10.8
15	Nigeria	10.6
16	Pakistan	10.1
17	Tanzania[a]	9.9
18	Egypt	9.7
	Ghana[a]	9.7
20	Vietnam[a]	9.4
21	Nepal	9.3
22	Burundi[a]	9.2
23	Uganda	9.1

Lowest average annual consumer price inflation, 2009–14, %

1	Switzerland	0
2	Brunei[a]	0.1
3	Japan	0.4
	Niger	0.4
5	Ireland	0.5
6	Sweden	1.0
7	Morocco[a]	1.1
8	Burkina Faso	1.2
	Latvia[a]	1.2
	Senegal[a]	1.2
	United Arab Emirates	1.2
12	Taiwan	1.3
13	Bosnia & Herz.[a]	1.4
	Greece	1.4
15	Bulgaria	1.5
	Qatar	1.5
17	Bahamas[a]	1.6
	France	1.6
	Germany	1.6
	Guinea-Bissau[a]	1.6
	Portugal	1.6
	Slovenia	1.6

a Estimate.   b 2013   c 2011–14

Commodity prices

End 2014, % change on a year earlier			*2009–14, % change*		
1	Coffee	35.8	1	Beef (US)	88.5
2	Beef (Aus)	28.2	2	Beef (Aus)	86.0
3	Beef (US)	23.2	3	Hides	66.8
4	Cocoa	7.8	4	Wool (NZ)	66.6
5	Nickel	6.3	5	Timber	63.9
6	Rice	5.2	6	Coconut oil	62.8
7	Lamb	4.2	7	Lamb	25.8
8	Aluminium	4.0	8	Wool (Aus)	20.5
9	Zinc	2.6	9	Coffee	18.1
10	Wool (NZ)	2.2	10	Soya meal	17.3
11	Hides	2.0	11	Tin	14.6
12	Gold	-0.2	12	Wheat	11.3
13	Wheat	-0.5	13	Gold	9.0
14	Coconut oil	-1.6	14	Soyabeans	0.0
15	Corn	-3.7	15	Corn	-2.5
16	Wool (Aus)	-6.6	16	Palm oil	-11.1
17	Timber	-6.8	17	Cotton	-11.4
18	Sugar	-9.5	18	Cocoa	-11.8
19	Tea	-13.8	19	Copper	-12.4
20	Copper	-14.4	20	Zinc	-14.7
21	Soya oil	-15.3	21	Soya oil	-16.6
22	Soya meal	-15.6	22	Aluminium	-18.3
23	Tin	-15.8	23	Nickel	-21.6
24	Lead	-17.8	24	Lead	-23.3
25	Soyabeans	-20.9	25	Rubber	-30.0
26	Cotton	-21.9	26	Rice	-30.8

The Economist's house-price indicators

Q1 2015ª, % change on a year earlier			*Q1 2009–Q1 2015ª, % change*		
1	Ireland	16.2	1	Brazil	155.7
2	Turkey	16.0	2	Hong Kong	154.0
3	Hong Kong	11.9	3	Israel	69.5
4	South Africa	9.7	4	Greece	64.1
5	Sweden	8.6	5	Singapore	45.4
6	United Kingdom	7.9	6	South Africa	39.5
7	Brazil	7.4	7	Australia	38.5
8	India	7.1	8	Canada	34.9
9	Australia	7.0	9	Germany	32.9
10	Canada	5.2	10	United Kingdom	28.8
11	Mexico	5.1	11	Mexico	26.9
12	Israel	5.0	12	Sweden	26.8
13	Germany	4.6	13	Switzerland	22.7
14	United States	4.0	14	China	20.3
15	Netherlands	2.2	15	Belgium	14.7
16	South Korea	2.1	16	South Korea	13.6
17	Russia	1.6	17	United States	12.7
18	Belgium	0.8	18	France	4.1
19	Japan	0.6	19	Japan	3.3
20	Switzerland	0.5	20	Russia	0.8

a Or latest.

Debt

Highest foreign debt[a]
$bn, 2013

1	China	874.5	26	Israel	95.4
2	Russia	726.7	27	Colombia	92.0
3	Brazil	482.5	28	Vietnam	65.5
4	Mexico	443.0	29	Croatia	62.9
5	India	427.6	30	Philippines	60.6
6	South Korea	422.6	31	Iraq	59.5
7	Turkey	388.2	32	Peru	56.7
8	Poland	361.2	33	Pakistan	56.5
9	Indonesia	259.1	34	Bulgaria	53.0
10	Malaysia	213.1	35	Sudan	45.6
11	Hong Kong	172.0	36	Egypt	44.4
12	Taiwan	170.1	37	Latvia	41.0
13	United Arab Emirates	168.8	38	Morocco	39.3
14	Saudi Arabia	155.7	39	Belarus	39.1
15	Qatar	149.3	40	Serbia	36.4
16	Hungary	149.1	41	Kuwait	36.3
17	Kazakhstan	148.5	42	Lebanon	32.2
18	Ukraine	147.7	43	Lithuania	31.0
19	South Africa	139.8	44	Singapore	28.3
20	Argentina	136.3	45	Bangladesh	27.8
21	Thailand	135.4	46	Tunisia	25.8
22	Romania	134.0	47	Sri Lanka	25.2
23	Chile	130.7	48	Cuba	24.7
24	Venezuela	118.8	49	Angola	24.0
25	Czech Republic	114.4		Jordan	24.0

Highest foreign debt burden[a]
Total foreign debt as % of GDP, 2013

1	Zimbabwe	337.0	21	Laos	77.0
2	Mongolia	164.3	22	Qatar	73.5
3	Papua New Guinea	141.3	23	Jordan	71.4
4	Latvia	133.0	24	Romania	69.9
5	Hungary	111.7	25	Poland	69.8
6	Croatia	108.8	26	Sudan	68.6
7	Bulgaria	97.3	27	Lebanon	68.2
8	Jamaica	96.6	28	Malaysia	68.1
9	Kyrgyzstan	94.2	29	Lithuania	66.7
10	Mauritius	91.5	30	Kazakhstan	66.4
11	Nicaragua	89.5	31	Macedonia	64.4
12	Estonia	85.7	32	Hong Kong	62.6
13	Georgia	84.8	33	Gambia	58.6
14	Armenia	83.2	34	Bosnia & Herz.	58.3
15	Bhutan	83.1	35	Albania	58.1
16	Moldova	83.0	36	El Salvador	55.1
17	Mauritania	81.5	37	Tunisia	55.0
	Ukraine	81.5	38	Czech Republic	54.8
19	Balkans	81.4	39	Belarus	53.5
20	Serbia	80.0	40	Bahrain	52.3

a Foreign debt is debt owed to non-residents and repayable in foreign currency; the figures shown include liabilities of government, public and private sectors. Longer-established developed countries have been excluded.

Highest foreign debt[a]
As % of exports of goods and services, 2013

1	Sudan	452.2	15	Romania	159.7
2	Mongolia	358.0	16	Kazakhstan	159.2
3	Central African Rep.	356.8	17	Nicaragua	159.1
4	Burundi	277.6	18	Niger	155.7
5	Laos	271.1	19	Tanzania	150.7
6	Croatia	227.6	20	Ukraine	143.5
7	Zimbabwe	225.9	21	Armenia	140.9
8	Bhutan	212.2	22	Albania	139.8
9	Latvia	205.8	23	Syria	139.0
10	Jamaica	205.6	24	Chile	137.2
11	Turkey	181.1	25	Argentina	137.0
12	Ethiopia	167.4		Poland	137.0
13	Brazil	163.9	27	Macedonia	136.0
14	Serbia	162.7	28	Georgia	135.6

Highest debt service ratio[b]
Average, %, 2013

1	Zimbabwe	79.8	15	Sudan	27.2
2	Papua New Guinea	75.3	16	Mongolia	26.6
3	Mauritius	40.8	17	Venezuela	21.2
4	Ukraine	38.1	18	Chile	21.1
5	Serbia	37.8	19	Indonesia	18.7
6	Romania	36.9	20	Lithuania	18.6
7	Latvia	33.4	21	Jamaica	18.0
8	Kazakhstan	33.1	22	Georgia	17.6
9	Armenia	32.6	23	Pakistan	17.4
10	Croatia	30.7		Poland	17.4
11	Hungary	30.3	25	Cuba	16.6
12	Namibia	28.7	26	Costa Rica	16.4
	Turkey	28.7		Uruguay	16.4
14	Brazil	28.3	28	Macedonia	15.5

Household debt[c]
As % of gross disposable income, 2013

1	Denmark	310.2	13	Spain	131.9
2	Netherlands	281.8	14	Japan	129.2
3	Norway[d]	213.7	15	Finland	122.8
4	Ireland	213.2	16	United States	114.1
5	Australia	201.1	17	Greece	112.4
6	Switzerland[d]	186.4	18	Belgium	105.8
7	Sweden	169.2	19	France	104.2
8	Canada	165.6	20	Germany	93.9
9	South Korea[d]	163.8	21	Italy	90.9
10	United Kingdom	154.0	22	Austria	89.2
11	Luxembourg[d]	153.4	23	Estonia	85.1
12	Portugal	146.1	24	Czech Republic	69.4

b Debt service is the sum of interest and principal repayments (amortisation) due on outstanding foreign debt. The debt service ratio is debt service as a percentage of exports of goods, non-factor services, primary income and workers' remittances.
c OECD countries.   d 2012

Aid

Largest recipients of bilateral and multilateral aid
$m, 2013

1	Egypt	5,506	24	South Africa	1,293
2	Afghanistan	5,266	25	Ivory Coast	1,262
3	Vietnam	4,085	26	Haiti	1,171
4	Myanmar	3,935	27	Sudan	1,163
5	Ethiopia	3,826	28	Brazil	1,150
6	Syria	3,627	29	Zambia	1,142
7	Tanzania	3,430	30	Malawi	1,126
8	Kenya	3,236	31	Rwanda	1,081
9	Turkey	2,741	32	Burkina Faso	1,040
10	Bangladesh	2,669	33	Yemen	1,004
11	West Bank & Gaza	2,610	34	Somalia	992
12	Congo-Kinshasa	2,572	35	Senegal	983
13	Nigeria	2,529	36	Nepal	871
14	India	2,436	37	Colombia	852
15	Mozambique	2,314	38	Zimbabwe	811
16	Pakistan	2,174	39	Cambodia	805
17	Morocco	1,966	40	Ukraine	801
18	Uganda	1,693	41	Serbia	783
19	Iraq	1,541	42	Niger	773
20	South Sudan	1,447	43	Cameroon	737
21	Jordan	1,408	44	Tunisia	714
22	Mali	1,391	45	Bolivia	699
23	Ghana	1,331	46	Papua New Guinea	656

Largest recipients of bilateral and multilateral aid
$ per person, 2013

1	West Bank & Gaza	626.1	25	Kyrgyzstan	93.8
2	Kosovo	292.2	26	Swaziland	92.8
3	Timor-Leste	218.9	27	Rwanda	91.8
4	Jordan	218.0	28	Mali	90.9
5	Montenegro	204.9	29	Mozambique	89.6
6	Afghanistan	172.4		Papua New Guinea	89.6
7	Syria	158.8	31	Nicaragua	81.7
8	Lesotho	154.3	32	Zambia	78.6
9	Mongolia	150.9	33	Honduras	77.5
10	Georgia	145.8	34	Mauritania	74.9
11	Bosnia & Herz.	143.6	35	Myanmar	73.9
12	Lebanon	140.2	36	Kenya	73.0
13	South Sudan	128.1	37	Sierra Leone	72.8
14	Liberia	124.4	38	Tanzania	69.6
15	Macedonia	119.4	39	Senegal	69.5
16	Mauritius	114.4	40	Malawi	68.8
17	Namibia	113.6	41	Egypt	67.1
18	Haiti	113.5	42	Tunisia	65.6
19	Serbia	109.3	43	Bolivia	65.5
20	Albania	107.6	44	Benin	63.2
21	Moldova	105.2	45	Laos	62.2
22	Fiji	103.2	46	Ivory Coast	62.1
23	Armenia	98.4	47	Burkina Faso	61.4
24	Somalia	94.5	48	Guinea-Bissau	60.8

Largest bilateral and multilateral donors[a]
$m, 2013

1	United States	31,545		15	Switzerland	3,198
2	United Kingdom	17,881		16	Denmark	2,928
3	Germany	14,059		17	Belgium	2,281
4	Japan	11,786		18	Spain	2,199
5	France	11,376		19	South Korea	1,744
6	Sweden	5,831		20	Finland	1,435
7	Saudi Arabia	5,683		21	Austria	1,172
8	Norway	5,581		22	Ireland	822
9	Netherlands	5,435		23	Russia	610
10	United Arab Emirates	5,402		24	Portugal	484
11	Canada	4,911		25	Poland	474
12	Australia	4,851		26	New Zealand	461
13	Turkey	3,276		27	Luxembourg	431
14	Italy	3,253		28	Greece	305

Largest bilateral and multilateral donors[a]
% of GDP, 2013

1	United Arab Emirates	1.25		14	France	0.41
2	Norway	1.07		15	Germany	0.38
3	Sweden	1.02		16	Australia	0.34
4	Luxembourg	1.00		17	Austria	0.28
5	Denmark	0.85		18	Canada	0.27
6	Saudi Arabia	0.74		19	Iceland	0.26
7	United Kingdom	0.72			New Zealand	0.26
8	Netherlands	0.67		21	Japan	0.23
9	Finland	0.55			Portugal	0.23
10	Switzerland	0.47		23	Malta[b]	0.21
11	Belgium	0.45		24	United States	0.19
	Ireland	0.45		25	Italy	0.16
13	Turkey	0.42			Spain	0.16

Biggest changes to aid
$m, 2010–13

	Increases				Decreases	
1	Egypt	4,908		1	Haiti	-1,894
2	Myanmar	3,580		2	Indonesia	-1,339
3	Syria	3,492		3	China	-1,297
4	Turkey	1,693		4	Afghanistan	-1,161
5	Kenya	1,608			Congo-Brazzaville	-1,161
6	South Sudan	1,447		6	Congo-Kinshasa	-914
7	Bangladesh	1,254		7	Sudan	-896
8	Vietnam	1,145		8	Liberia	-883
9	Morocco	974		9	Pakistan	-839
10	Brazil	697		10	Iraq	-650
11	Peru	623		11	India	-371
12	Somalia	494		12	Ghana	-362
13	Tanzania	472		13	Philippines	-341
14	Nigeria	468		14	Azerbaijan	-222
15	Jordan	453		15	Nicaragua	-166

a China also provides aid, but does not disclose amounts.   b 2012

Industry and services

Largest industrial output
$bn, 2013

1	China	4,056	23	Switzerland	171
2	United States	3,185	24	Netherlands	170
3	Japan[a]	1,512	25	Thailand	165
4	Germany	1,030	26	Poland	155
5	Russia	655	27	Argentina	147
6	India	532	28	Qatar	141
7	Taiwan	504	29	Sweden	132
8	France	499	30	Colombia	129
9	United Kingdom	481	31	Malaysia	127
10	Brazil	476	32	Iraq	115
11	South Korea	459	33	Nigeria	113
12	Saudi Arabia	453	34	Austria	108
13	Italy	450	35	Belgium	106
14	Mexico	423	36	Egypt	102
15	Canada[b]	420	37	Puerto Rico	98
16	Indonesia	397		South Africa	98
17	Australia	392	39	Algeria	93
18	Spain	297	40	Chile	89
19	United Arab Emirates	237	41	Philippines	85
20	Turkey	194	42	Kazakhstan	80
21	Venezuela[b]	191	43	Angola	72
22	Norway	187		Romania	72

Highest growth in industrial output
Average annual % increase in real terms, 2005–13

1	Liberia[c]	24.3	11	Congo-Kinshasa	9.8
2	Timor-Leste	19.4	12	Togo	9.7
3	Laos	14.2	13	Niger	8.7
4	Azerbaijan	13.9	14	Bangladesh	8.5
5	Ethiopia	13.5	15	Cambodia	8.4
6	Qatar	12.6		Zambia	8.4
7	Panama	11.5	17	Sri Lanka	8.1
8	Ghana	11.0		Uganda	8.1
9	China	10.8	19	Tanzania	8.0
10	Rwanda	10.0	20	Malawi	7.9

Lowest growth in industrial output
Average annual % change in real terms, 2005–13

1	Greece	-7.5	12	Italy	-1.9
2	Bermuda[c]	-5.8	13	Denmark	-1.4
3	Barbados[c]	-3.5		United Kingdom	-1.4
4	Moldova	-3.2	15	Eritrea[e]	-1.3
5	Spain	-3.1		Norway	-1.3
6	Jamaica[c]	-2.9	17	Luxembourg	-1.2
7	Ireland	-2.8	18	Finland	-1.1
8	Latvia[d]	-2.4		Puerto Rico	-1.1
9	Croatia	-2.3			
10	Brunei	-2.0			
	Portugal	-2.0			

a 2012   b 2010   c 2005–12   d 2005–10   e 2005–09

Largest manufacturing output
$bn, 2013

1	China	2,941	21	Netherlands	93
2	United States[a]	1,966	22	Poland	88
3	Japan[a]	1,073	23	Sweden	84
4	Germany	745	24	Argentina	79
5	South Korea	370	25	Saudi Arabia	76
6	India	299	26	Malaysia	75
7	Italy	287	27	Austria	71
8	France	286	28	Belgium	67
9	Russia	268	29	Philippines	55
10	Brazil	250	30	Singapore	53
11	United Kingdom	231	31	Puerto Rico	48
12	Mexico	216	32	Czech Republic	47
13	Indonesia	206		Nigeria	47
14	Canada[b]	162	34	Colombia	43
15	Venezuela	154		South Africa	43
16	Thailand	128	36	Egypt	41
17	Turkey	126		Ireland	41
18	Switzerland	124	38	Denmark	40
19	Taiwan	121	39	Finland	38
20	Australia	104	40	United Arab Emirates	34

Largest services output
$bn, 2013

1	United States[a]	11,796	27	Austria	268
2	Japan[a]	4,323	28	Norway	264
3	China	4,259	29	Hong Kong	246
4	Germany	2,295	30	South Africa	223
5	France	1,977	31	Denmark	219
6	United Kingdom	1,888	32	Singapore	210
7	Italy	1,439	33	Colombia	196
8	Brazil	1,321	34	Greece	176
9	Russia	1,079		Thailand	176
10	Canada[b]	1,075	36	Finland	162
11	Australia	1,033		United Arab Emirates	162
12	Spain	940	38	Ireland	158
13	India	889	39	Malaysia	157
14	Mexico	749		Philippines	157
15	South Korea	704	41	Chile	155
16	Netherlands	583	42	Venezuela[b]	154
17	Switzerland	487	43	Portugal	153
18	Turkey	461	44	Kazakhstan	126
19	Sweden	372	45	Egypt	121
20	Belgium	360	46	Pakistan	120
21	Indonesia	346	47	Czech Republic	114
22	Argentina	334	48	Iraq	105
23	Taiwan	331	49	Ukraine	97
24	Poland	296	50	Romania	84
25	Nigeria	294	51	Algeria	81
26	Saudi Arabia	281	52	Bangladesh	80

a 2012   b 2010

Agriculture

Largest agricultural output
$bn, 2013

1	China	925	16	Argentina	36
2	India	311		Australia	36
3	United States[a]	199	18	Spain	35
4	Indonesia	125	19	Vietnam	32
5	Brazil	109	20	Philippines	31
6	Nigeria	108	21	Germany	29
7	Japan[a]	72		Malaysia	29
8	Russia	71	23	South Korea	28
9	Turkey	61	24	Bangladesh	23
10	Pakistan	56		Canada[b]	23
11	Thailand	46	26	Algeria	21
12	Italy	45		Colombia	21
13	France	43		Venezuela[b]	21
14	Mexico	42	29	Ethiopia	20
15	Egypt	38	30	Sudan	18

Most economically dependent on agriculture
% of GDP from agriculture, 2013

1	Sierra Leone	59.5	15	Togo[c]	30.8
2	Central African Rep.[a]	54.3	16	Kenya	29.5
3	Chad	51.5	17	Mozambique	29.0
4	Ethiopia	45.0	18	Sudan	28.1
5	Guinea-Bissau	43.7	19	Tajikistan	27.4
6	Mali[a]	42.3	20	Malawi	27.0
7	Burundi	39.8	21	Laos	26.5
8	Liberia[a]	38.8	22	Madagascar	26.4
9	Niger	37.2	23	Uganda	25.3
10	Benin	36.5	24	Pakistan	25.1
11	Nepal	35.1	25	Afghanistan	24.0
12	Tanzania	33.8	26	Burkina Faso	22.9
13	Cambodia	33.5		Cameroon	22.9
14	Rwanda	33.4	28	North Korea	22.4

Least economically dependent on agriculture
% of GDP from agriculture, 2013

1	Macau	0.0		Puerto Rico	0.8
	Singapore	0.0	15	Germany	0.9
3	Hong Kong	0.1	16	Japan	1.2
	Qatar	0.1	17	Oman	1.3
5	Luxembourg	0.3		United States	1.3
6	Kuwait	0.4	19	Austria	1.4
7	Trinidad & Tobago	0.6		Denmark	1.4
8	Brunei	0.7		Sweden	1.4
	Switzerland	0.7		Taiwan	1.4
	United Arab Emirates	0.7	23	Barbados	1.5
	United Kingdom	0.7		Canada	1.5
12	Belgium	0.8		Norway	1.5
	Bermuda	0.8	26	Ireland	1.6

a 2012   b 2010   c 2011

Highest growth in agriculture
Average annual % increase in real terms, 2005–13

1	Angola	11.1	10	Slovakia	6.6
2	Qatar	9.2	11	Estonia	6.4
3	Liberia[a]	9.1	12	Sudan[a]	6.2
4	Tajikistan	8.1		Uzbekistan	6.2
5	Puerto Rico	7.7	14	Mali[a]	6.0
6	Ethiopia	7.5	15	Mozambique	5.9
7	Morocco	6.8	16	Sierra Leone	5.8
8	Central African Rep.[a]	6.7	17	Nigeria	5.6
	Paraguay	6.7	18	Mongolia	5.3

Lowest growth in agriculture
Average annual % change in real terms, 2005–13

1	United Arab Emirates	-5.0	9	Moldova	-3.0
2	Czech Republic	-4.2	10	Hungary	-2.9
3	Greece	-4.1	11	Croatia	-2.6
4	Namibia	-3.7	12	Luxembourg	-2.4
5	Bahamas	-3.5	13	Malta	-2.3
	Hong Kong	-3.5	14	Barbados[a]	-2.1
7	Zimbabwe	-3.4		Serbia[a]	-2.1
8	Bulgaria	-3.2	16	Romania[a]	-2.0

Biggest producers
'000 tonnes, 2013

Cereals

1	China	551,147	6	Indonesia	89,792
2	United States	436,554	7	France	67,518
3	India	293,940	8	Canada	66,372
4	Brazil	101,073	9	Ukraine	63,129
5	Russia	90,379	10	Bangladesh	55,009

Meat

1	China	83,462	6	India	6,215
2	United States	42,642	7	Mexico	6,122
3	Brazil	26,011	8	France	5,560
4	Russia	8,544	9	Spain	5,424
5	Germany	8,201	10	Argentina	5,210

Fruit

1	China	151,838	6	Mexico	17,553
2	India	82,632	7	Italy	16,371
3	Brazil	37,774	8	Indonesia	16,003
4	United States	26,986	9	Philippines	15,887
5	Spain	17,699	10	Turkey	15,341

Vegetables

1	China	580,702	5	Iran	23,652
2	India	121,015	6	Egypt	19,591
3	United States	34,280	7	Russia	15,485
4	Turkey	28,281	8	Vietnam	14,976

a 2005–12

Commodities

Wheat

Top 10 producers, 2013-14
'000 tonnes

1	EU28	143,060
2	China	121,926
3	India	93,510
4	United States	58,105
5	Russia	52,091
6	Canada	37,530
7	Australia	26,929
8	Pakistan	24,000
9	Ukraine	22,278
10	Turkey	18,750

Top 10 consumers, 2013-14
'000 tonnes

1	China	123,330
2	EU28	114,600
3	India	93,740
4	Russia	34,550
5	United States	34,230
6	Pakistan	23,930
7	Egypt	18,890
8	Turkey	18,330
9	Iran	17,720
10	Ukraine	11,900

Rice[a]

Top 10 producers, 2013-14
'000 tonnes

1	China	142,530
2	India	106,540
3	Indonesia	36,300
4	Bangladesh	34,390
5	Vietnam	28,161
6	Thailand	20,460
7	Myanmar	11,957
8	Philippines	11,858
9	Brazil	8,300
10	Japan	7,832

Top 10 consumers, 2013-14
'000 tonnes

1	China	146,300
2	India	99,180
3	Indonesia	38,500
4	Bangladesh	34,900
5	Vietnam	22,000
6	Philippines	12,850
7	Thailand	10,875
8	Myanmar	10,450
9	Japan	8,250
10	Brazil	7,900

Sugar[b]

Top 10 producers, 2013
'000 tonnes

1	Brazil	37,500
2	India	22,970
3	EU28	15,910
4	China	13,130
5	Thailand	9,790
6	United States	7,410
7	Mexico	6,580
8	Pakistan	5,210
9	Russia	4,430
10	Australia	4,220

Top 10 consumers, 2013
'000 tonnes

1	India	22,580
2	EU28	18,520
3	China	14,630
4	Brazil	11,870
5	United States	10,280
6	Indonesia	5,840
7	Russia	5,630
8	Pakistan	4,610
9	Mexico	4,220
10	Egypt	3,080

Coarse grains[c]

Top 5 producers, 2013-14
'000 tonnes

1	United States	367,507
2	China	226,260
3	EU28	157,672
4	Brazil	82,790
5	India	42,880

Top 5 consumers, 2013-14
'000 tonnes

1	United States	305,349
2	China	222,065
3	EU28	159,454
4	Brazil	58,649
5	Mexico	40,650

Tea

Top 10 producers, 2013 '000 tonnes		Top 10 consumers, 2013 '000 tonnes	
1 China	1,924	1 China	1,614
2 India	1,209	2 India	1,001
3 Kenya	432	3 Turkey	228
4 Sri Lanka	340	4 Russia	159
5 Vietnam	214	5 Pakistan	127
6 Turkey	212	United States	127
7 Iran	160	7 Japan	119
8 Indonesia	148	8 United Kingdom	116
9 Argentina	105	9 Egypt	99
10 Japan	85	10 Iran	83

Coffee

Top 10 producers, 2013–14 '000 tonnes		Top 10 consumers, 2013 '000 tonnes	
1 Brazil	2,949	1 EU28	2,512
2 Vietnam	1,650	2 United States	1,405
3 Colombia	727	3 Brazil	1,209
4 Indonesia	700	4 Japan	446
5 Ethiopia	392	5 Indonesia	243
6 India	305	6 Russia	227
7 Honduras	274	7 Canada	211
8 Peru	260	8 Ethiopia	208
9 Mexico	235	9 Mexico	141
10 Uganda	220	10 Philippines	131

Cocoa

Top 10 producers, 2013–14 '000 tonnes		Top 10 consumers, 2012–13 '000 tonnes	
1 Ivory Coast	1,746	1 United States	775
2 Ghana	897	2 Germany	330
3 Indonesia	375	3 United Kingdom	225
4 Nigeria	248	4 France	220
5 Brazil	228	5 Russia	207
6 Ecuador	220	6 Brazil	198
7 Cameroon	211	7 Japan	166
8 Peru	76	8 Spain	108
9 Dominican Rep.	70	9 Canada	91
10 Colombia	49	10 Italy	87

a Milled.
b Raw.
c Includes: maize (corn), barley, sorghum, oats, rye, millet, triticale and other.

Copper

Top 10 producers[a], 2013		*Top 10 consumers[b], 2013*	
'000 tonnes		*'000 tonnes*	
1 Chile	5,776	1 China	9,830
2 China	1,707	2 United States	1,826
3 Peru	1,376	3 Germany	1,136
4 United States	1,240	4 Japan	996
5 Australia	996	5 South Korea	722
6 Zambia	839	6 Italy	552
7 Congo-Kinshasa	817	7 Russia	484
8 Russia	720	8 Turkey	453
9 Canada	632	9 Taiwan	437
10 Kazakhstan	538	10 Brazil	432

Lead

Top 10 producers[a], 2013		*Top 10 consumers[b], 2013*	
'000 tonnes		*'000 tonnes*	
1 China	3,048	1 China	4,467
2 Australia	711	2 United States	1,750
3 United States	343	3 South Korea	498
4 Peru	266	4 India	428
5 Mexico	253	5 Germany	392
6 Russia	143	6 United Kingdom	274
7 India	106	7 Spain	257
8 Bolivia	82	8 Japan	255
9 Turkey	78	9 Italy	235
10 Poland	74	10 Brazil	234

Zinc

Top 10 producers[a], 2013		*Top 10 consumers[c], 2013*	
'000 tonnes		*'000 tonnes*	
1 China	5,391	1 China	5,995
2 Australia	1,523	2 United States	939
3 Peru	1,351	3 India	640
4 India	817	4 South Korea	578
5 United States	788	5 Japan	498
6 Mexico	643	6 Germany	479
7 Canada	426	7 Russia	265
8 Bolivia	407	8 Brazil	249
9 Kazakhstan	361	9 Italy	245
10 Ireland	327	10 Turkey	234

Tin

Top 5 producers[a], 2013		*Top 5 consumers[b], 2013*	
'000 tonnes		*'000 tonnes*	
1 China	149.0	1 China	168.2
2 Indonesia	84.0	2 United States	29.2
3 Peru	23.7	3 Japan	28.3
4 Bolivia	19.3	4 Germany	18.0
5 Brazil	13.8	5 South Korea	14.5

Nickel

Top 10 producers[a], 2013 *'000 tonnes*		*Top 10 consumers[b], 2013* *'000 tonnes*	
1 Indonesia	811.5	1 China	909.2
2 Philippines	315.6	2 Japan	158.7
3 Russia	241.8	3 United States	122.6
4 Australia	234.0	4 South Korea	107.3
5 Canada	223.3	5 Germany	66.1
6 New Caledonia	150.4	6 Italy	59.4
7 China	98.4	7 Taiwan	52.7
8 Brazil	74.4	8 India	37.0
9 Cuba	62.0	9 South Africa	35.2
10 South Africa	51.2	10 Spain	31.8

Aluminium

Top 10 producers[d], 2013 *'000 tonnes*		*Top 10 consumers[e], 2013* *'000 tonnes*	
1 China	22,046	1 China	21,955
2 Russia	3,724	2 United States	4,632
3 Canada	2,967	3 Germany	2,083
4 United States	1,948	4 Japan	1,772
5 United Arab Emirates	1,848	5 India	1,534
6 Australia	1,778	6 South Korea	1,241
7 India	1,571	7 Brazil	988
8 Brazil	1,304	8 Turkey	867
9 Norway	1,155	9 United Arab Emirates	835
10 Bahrain	913	10 Italy	709

Precious metals

Gold [a] *Top 10 producers, 2013* *tonnes*		*Silver* [a] *Top 10 producers, 2013* *tonnes*	
1 China	428.2	1 Mexico	5,821
2 Australia	267.2	2 Peru	3,674
3 United States	230.0	3 China	3,673
4 Russia	208.8	4 Australia	1,840
5 South Africa	169.0	5 Russia	1,412
6 Peru	151.3	6 Poland	1,403
7 Canada	124.7	7 Bolivia	1,287
8 Mexico	119.8	8 Chile	1,174
9 Ghana	94.8	9 United States	1,050
10 Brazil	79.6	10 Kazakhstan	964

Platinum *Top 3 producers, 2013* *tonnes*		*Palladium* *Top 3 producers, 2013* *tonnes*	
1 South Africa	128.1	1 Russia	84.0
2 Russia	24.3	2 South Africa	73.1
3 United States/Canada	9.8	3 United States/Canada	28.9

a Mine production.   b Refined consumption.   c Slab consumption.
d Primary refined production.   e Primary refined consumption.

Rubber (natural and synthetic)

Top 10 producers, 2013
'000 tonnes

1	China	4,955
2	Thailand	4,309
3	Indonesia	3,292
4	EU28	2,531
5	United States	2,234
6	Japan	1,673
7	South Korea	1,493
8	Russia	1,482
9	Vietnam	949
10	Malaysia	928

Top 10 consumers, 2013
'000 tonnes

1	China	9,652
2	EU28	3,417
3	United States	2,611
4	Japan	1,664
5	India	1,433
6	Thailand	965
7	Brazil	935
8	Germany	826
9	Indonesia	813
10	Malaysia	765

Raw wool

Top 12 producers[a], 2013, '000 tonnes

1	China	471
2	Australia	361
3	New Zealand	165
4	United Kingdom	68
5	Iran	62
6	Morocco	56

7	Russia	55
8	Turkey	51
9	India	47
10	Argentina	45
11	Pakistan	44
12	South Africa	40

Cotton

Top 10 producers, 2013–14
'000 tonnes

1	China	6,929
2	India	6,770
3	United States	2,811
4	Pakistan	2,076
5	Brazil	1,705
6	Uzbekistan	940
7	Australia	890
8	Turkey	760
9	Turkmenistan	329
10	Argentina	302

Top 10 consumers, 2013–14
'000 tonnes

1	China	7,531
2	India	5,042
3	Pakistan	2,271
4	Turkey	1,400
5	Bangladesh	900
6	Brazil	871
7	United States	773
8	Vietnam	694
9	Indonesia	683
10	Mexico	412

Major oil seeds[b]

Top 5 producers, 2013–14
'000 tonnes

1	United States	98,540
2	Brazil	89,313
3	Argentina	56,498
4	China	49,260
5	India	33,630

Top 5 consumers, 2013–14
'000 tonnes

1	China	124,372
2	United States	58,915
3	EU28	50,135
4	Brazil	41,733
5	Argentina	40,529

Oil[c]

Top 10 producers, 2014
'000 barrels per day

1	United States	11,644
2	Saudi Arabia[d]	11,505
3	Russia	10,838
4	Canada	4,292
5	China	4,246
6	United Arab Emirates[d]	3,712
7	Iran[d]	3,614
8	Iraq[d]	3,285
9	Kuwait[d]	3,123
10	Mexico	2,784

Top 10 consumers, 2014
'000 barrels per day

1	United States	19,035
2	China	11,056
3	Japan	4,298
4	India	3,846
5	Brazil	3,229
6	Russia	3,196
7	Saudi Arabia[d]	3,185
8	South Korea	2,456
9	Canada	2,371
	Germany	2,371

Natural gas

Top 10 producers, 2014
Billion cubic metres

1	United States	728.3
2	Russia	578.7
3	Qatar[d]	177.2
4	Iran[d]	172.6
5	Canada	162.0
6	China	134.5
7	Norway	108.8
8	Saudi Arabia[d]	108.2
9	Algeria[d]	83.3
10	Indonesia	73.4

Top 10 consumers, 2014
Billion cubic metres

1	United States	759.4
2	Russia	409.2
3	China	185.5
4	Iran[d]	170.2
5	Japan	112.5
6	Saudi Arabia[d]	108.2
7	Canada	104.2
8	Mexico	85.8
9	Germany	70.9
10	United Arab Emirates[d]	69.3

Coal

Top 10 producers, 2014
Million tonnes oil equivalent

1	China	1,844.6
2	United States	507.8
3	Indonesia	281.7
4	Australia	280.8
5	India	243.5
6	Russia	170.9
7	South Africa	147.7
8	Colombia	57.6
9	Kazakhstan	55.3
10	Poland	55.0

Top 10 consumers, 2014
Million tonnes oil equivalent

1	China	1,962.4
2	United States	453.4
3	India	360.2
4	Japan	126.5
5	South Africa	89.4
6	Russia	85.2
7	South Korea	84.8
8	Germany	77.4
9	Indonesia	60.8
10	Poland	52.9

Oil reserves[c]

Top proved reserves, end 2014
% of world total

1	Venezuela[d]	17.5	5	Iraq[d]	8.8
2	Saudi Arabia[d]	15.7	6	Russia	6.1
3	Canada	10.2	7	Kuwait[d]	6.0
4	Iran[d]	9.3	8	United Arab Emirates[d]	5.8

a Greasy basis.   b Soybeans, sunflower seed, cottonseed, groundnuts and rapeseed.
c Includes crude oil, shale oil, oil sands and natural gas liquids.   d Opec member.

Energy

Largest producers
Million tonnes of oil equivalent, 2012

1	China	2,545	16	Algeria	180
2	United States	1,980	17	Nigeria	167
3	Russia	1,382	18	Kuwait	163
4	Saudi Arabia	692	19	Iraq	161
5	Canada	478	20	South Africa	157
6	Indonesia	407	21	Kazakhstan	156
7	India	397	22	Colombia	134
8	Iran	341	23	France	127
9	Australia	323	24	United Kingdom	122
10	Qatar	247	25	Germany	120
11	Brazil	244	26	Angola	98
12	Norway	239	27	Egypt	95
13	Mexico	218		Malaysia	95
14	United Arab Emirates	214	29	Libya	88
15	Venezuela	181	30	Ukraine	82

Largest consumers
Million tonnes of oil equivalent, 2012

1	China	2,647	16	Indonesia	161
2	United States	2,376	17	Spain	151
3	Russia	788	18	Australia	150
4	India	598	19	South Africa	142
5	Japan	508	20	Thailand	129
6	Germany	337	21	Turkey	126
7	Canada	334		Ukraine	126
8	Brazil	302	23	Taiwan	121
9	South Korea	288	24	Netherlands	101
10	France	267	25	Poland	98
11	Iran	241	26	United Arab Emirates	96
12	Saudi Arabia	233	27	Argentina	92
13	United Kingdom	216	28	Egypt	89
14	Mexico	194	29	Venezuela	84
15	Italy	179			

Energy efficiency[a]
GDP per unit of energy use, 2011

Most efficient			*Least efficient*		
1	Hong Kong	23.8	1	Trinidad & Tobago	1.8
2	Cuba	18.9	2	Congo-Kinshasa	1.9
3	Switzerland	17.0	3	Iceland	2.2
4	Colombia	16.9	4	Turkmenistan	2.3
5	Sri Lanka	16.2		Zimbabwe	2.3
6	Ireland	15.6	6	Mozambique	2.4
7	Dominican Rep.	15.5	7	Uzbekistan	2.7
8	Panama	15.0	8	Togo	3.0
	Peru	15.0		Ukraine	3.0
10	Congo-Brazzaville	14.2	10	Ethiopia	3.1
11	Gabon	14.0	11	Benin	4.3

a 2011 PPP $ per kg of oil equivalent.

Net energy importers
% of commercial energy use, 2012 or latest

Highest			Lowest		
1	Hong Kong	100	1	Congo-Brazzaville	-905
2	Lebanon	97	2	Gabon	-615
	Luxembourg	97	3	Angola	-579
	Singapore	97	4	Norway	-577
5	Cyprus	96	5	Qatar	-535
	Jordan	96	6	Mongolia	-435
	Moldova	96	7	Brunei	-388
	Morocco	96	8	Azerbaijan	-377
9	Japan	94	9	Kuwait	-375
	Malta	94	10	Colombia	-281
11	Ireland	90	11	Iraq	-253
12	Dominican Rep.	89	12	Algeria	-248

Largest consumption per person
Kg of oil equivalent, 2012

1	Virgin Islands (US)	55,448	12	Luxembourg	8,927
2	Qatar	21,808	13	Saudi Arabia	8,232
3	Trinidad & Tobago	17,053	14	Oman	7,746
4	Iceland	16,166	15	United States	7,571
5	Singapore	14,615	16	Australia	6,590
6	Kuwait	12,151	17	Netherlands	6,035
7	Bahrain	11,075	18	Belgium	5,821
8	United Arab Emirates	10,383	19	Sweden	5,786
9	Norway	9,681	20	South Korea	5,759
10	Canada	9,606	21	Finland	5,640
11	Brunei	9,200	22	Russia	5,504

Sources of electricity
% of total, 2012 or latest

Oil			Gas		
1	Benin	99.4	1	Bahrain	100.0
	Eritrea	99.4		Qatar	100.0
	Malta	99.4		Turkmenistan	100.0
4	Cyprus	96.4	4	Trinidad & Tobago	99.7
5	Lebanon	95.1	5	Brunei	99.0

Hydropower			Nuclear power		
1	Albania	100.0	1	France	76.6
	Paraguay	100.0	2	Slovakia	54.7
3	Mozambique	99.9	3	Belgium	52.1
	Nepal	99.9	4	Ukraine	46.3
5	Zambia	99.7	5	Hungary	45.9

Coal		
1	Botswana	100.0
2	Kosovo	97.8
3	Mongolia	95.1
4	South Africa	93.8
5	Estonia	85.3

Workers of the world

Labour-force participation
% of working-age population[a] working or looking for work, 2014 or latest

Highest			Lowest		
1	Tanzania	89.1	1	West Bank & Gaza	33.4
2	Madagascar	88.5	2	Timor-Leste	37.9
3	Equatorial Guinea	86.7	3	Moldova	40.7
	Qatar	86.7	4	Jordan	41.6
5	Zimbabwe	86.5	5	Iraq	42.3
6	Rwanda	85.9	6	Puerto Rico	42.6
7	Eritrea	84.8	7	Syria	43.6
8	Mozambique	84.2	8	Algeria	43.9
9	Ethiopia	83.7	9	Iran	45.1
10	Burkina Faso	83.4	10	Bosnia & Herz.	45.3
11	Nepal	83.3	11	Lebanon	47.6
12	Malawi	83.0		Tunisia	47.6
13	Burundi	82.6	13	Afghanistan	47.9
14	Cambodia	82.5	14	Yemen	48.8
15	Togo	81.0	15	Egypt	49.1
16	United Arab Emirates	79.9		Italy	49.1
17	Zambia	79.3	17	Montenegro	50.0
18	Central African Rep.	78.7	18	Morocco	50.5
19	Myanmar	78.6		Turkey	50.5
20	North Korea	78.0	20	Saudi Arabia	50.9
21	Laos	77.7	21	Croatia	51.3
22	Uganda	77.5	22	Hungary	51.9
23	Gambia, The	77.4	23	Malta	52.0
24	Botswana	76.7	24	South Africa	52.1
25	Senegal	76.5	25	Martinique	52.3
26	Peru	76.2	26	Serbia	52.4
	Vietnam	76.2	27	Libya	53.0
28	Bahamas	74.1	28	Greece	53.2

Most male workforce
*Highest % men in workforce
2013*

1	Qatar	88.8
2	Syria	87.8
3	Saudi Arabia	87.6
4	Oman	86.6
5	United Arab Emirates	85.4
6	Afghanistan	84.3
7	Algeria	84.1
	Iraq	84.1
9	Jordan	83.7
10	Iran	83.1
11	Bahrain	82.5
12	Yemen	80.7
13	Egypt	80.4
14	Pakistan	78.8
15	Lebanon	77.2
16	Kuwait	76.0

Most female workforce
*Highest % women in workforce
2013*

1	Mozambique	52.4
	Rwanda	52.4
3	Nepal	51.2
4	Burundi	51.1
5	Lithuania	50.9
6	Togo	50.8
7	Martinique	50.7
8	Malawi	50.5
9	Latvia	50.4
10	Laos	50.1
11	Cambodia	50.0
12	Moldova	49.9
	Sierra Leone	49.9
14	Ghana	49.8
	Ukraine	49.8
16	Estonia	49.7

a Aged 15 and over.

Highest rate of unemployment
% of labour force[a], 2013 or latest

1	Namibia	29.7	25	Georgia	14.6
2	Macedonia	29.0	26	Puerto Rico	14.3
	Réunion	29.0	27	Slovakia	14.2
4	Nigeria	28.5	28	Egypt	13.2
5	Bosnia & Herz.	27.5	29	Ireland	13.0
	Greece	27.5	30	Bulgaria	12.9
7	Guadeloupe	26.2	31	Jordan	12.6
8	Spain	26.1	32	Italy	12.2
9	South Africa	24.9	33	Latvia	11.9
10	Lesotho	24.4	34	Lithuania	11.8
11	West Bank & Gaza	24.1	35	Barbados	11.7
12	Martinique	22.8	36	Guam	11.5
13	Serbia	22.1	37	Iran	10.4
14	French Guiana	21.3	38	Poland	10.3
15	Montenegro	19.5	39	Hungary	10.2
16	Croatia	17.3	40	Slovenia	10.1
17	Armenia	16.2	41	France	9.9
	Bahamas	16.2	42	Algeria	9.8
	Portugal	16.2	43	Turkey	9.7
20	Cyprus	15.9	44	Costa Rica	9.3
21	Tunisia	15.8	45	Morocco	9.2
22	Albania	15.6	46	Colombia	8.9
23	Jamaica	15.2	47	Turkey	8.7
24	Dominican Rep.	15.0	48	Estonia	8.6

Highest rate of youth unemployment
% of labour force[a] aged 15–24, 2013 or latest

1	Bosnia & Herz.	60.4		Namibia	34.1
2	Greece	58.4	24	Jordan	33.7
3	Spain	57.3	25	Slovakia	33.5
4	Martinique	55.1	26	Lesotho	33.2
5	Réunion	54.4	27	Armenia	33.1
6	Guadeloupe	53.8	28	Tunisia	31.2
7	South Africa	53.6	29	Georgia	31.0
8	Macedonia	52.2	30	Dominican Rep.	29.9
9	Croatia	51.5	31	Syria	29.8
10	Libya	51.2		Yemen	29.8
11	Serbia	48.9	33	Belize	29.7
12	Mauritania	42.9		Bulgaria	29.7
13	Swaziland	42.4		Iran	29.7
14	Montenegro	41.3	36	Bahamas	28.9
15	Italy	39.7	37	Albania	28.7
16	Egypt	38.9		Saudi Arabia	28.7
17	Portugal	37.8	39	Bahrain	27.9
18	Cyprus	36.9	40	Puerto Rico	27.3
19	Jamaica	35.5	41	Poland	27.2
20	Gabon	35.2	42	Barbados	27.0
21	Botswana	34.1		Hungary	27.0
	Iraq	34.1	44	Ireland	26.7

a ILO definition.

NEET rates
Not in education, employment or training[a], 2013 or latest, % of total

1	Macedonia	32.1		15	Peru	17.9
2	El Salvador	30.4		16	Malawi	17.6
3	Jordan	30.0		17	Cyprus	17.3
4	Egypt	29.0		18	Latvia	17.1
	Liberia	29.0		19	Russia	15.7
6	Zambia	28.3		20	Estonia	15.3
7	Armenia	27.4		21	France	15.0
8	Benin	25.3		22	Lithuania	13.9
9	Bulgaria	24.7		23	United Kingdom[b]	14.2
10	Italy	23.9		24	Malta	11.9
11	Ireland	21.3		25	Vietnam	11.1
12	Romania	19.1		26	Togo	10.9
13	Croatia	18.8		27	Cambodia	8.7
14	Ukraine	18.7		28	Netherlands	6.2

Minimum wage
As a ratio of the median wage of full-time workers, 2013

1	Turkey	0.69			Latvia	0.48
2	Chile	0.68		16	Netherlands	0.47
3	France	0.63			United Kingdom	0.47
4	Slovenia	0.61		18	Slovakia	0.46
5	New Zealand	0.60		19	Greece	0.45
6	Israel	0.58		20	Canada	0.44
7	Portugal	0.56		21	Luxembourg	0.41
8	Australia	0.54			Spain	0.41
	Hungary	0.54		23	South Korea	0.40
10	Lithuania	0.52		24	Estonia	0.39
11	Belgium	0.50			Japan	0.39
	Poland	0.50		26	Mexico	0.37
	Romania	0.50			United States	0.37
14	Ireland	0.48		28	Czech Republic	0.36

Average hours worked
Per employee per week, 2013

1	Turkey	49.0		12	Iceland	39.0
2	Paraguay	46.8			Lithuania	39.0
3	Albania	43.3		14	Slovenia	38.9
4	South Africa	43.2		15	Czech Republic	38.8
5	Dominican Rep.	43.0			Estonia	38.8
6	Macedonia	41.7			Portugal	38.8
7	Romania	41.4			Slovakia	38.8
8	Croatia	40.1		19	Cyprus	38.6
9	Bulgaria	39.7			Hungary	38.6
	Poland	39.7		21	Greece	38.5
11	Latvia	39.2		22	Luxembourg	37.9

a Aged 15–29.   b Aged 16–24.

Business costs and foreign direct investment

Office rents

Rent, taxes and operating expenses, $ per sq. ft. per year, Q3 2014

1	London (West End), UK	273.63	10	Shanghai (Pudong), China	127.89
2	Hong Kong (Central)	250.61	11	New York (Midtown Manhattan), US	120.65
3	Beijing (Finance Street), China	197.75	12	San Francisco (Downtown), US	114.00
4	Beijing (CBD), China	189.39	13	Paris, France	113.95
5	Moscow, Russia	165.05	14	Singapore	112.91
6	New Delhi (Connaught Place, CBD), India	158.47	15	Shanghai (Puxi), China	112.14
7	Hong Kong (West Kowloon)	153.65	16	Mumbai (Bandra Kurla Complex), India	130.52
8	London (City), UK	152.67	17	Seoul (CBD), South Korea	102.55
9	Tokyo (Marunouchi Otemachi), Japan	136.46	18	Rio de Janeiro, Brazil	101.34

Employment costs

Hourly compensation costs in manufacturing[a], $, 2013

1	Norway	65.86	11	Netherlands	42.26
2	Switzerland	62.23	12	Ireland	41.98
3	Belgium	54.88	13	Italy	36.92
4	Sweden	51.10	14	United States	36.34
5	Denmark	51.07	15	Canada	36.33
6	Germany	48.98	16	United Kingdom	31.00
7	Australia	47.09	17	Japan	29.13
8	Finland	44.57	18	Spain	28.09
9	Austria	44.37	19	New Zealand	25.85
10	France	42.85	20	Singapore	23.95

Foreign direct investment[b]

Inflows, $m, 2013			*Outflows, $m, 2013*		
1	United States	187,528	1	United States	338,302
2	China	123,911	2	Japan	135,749
3	Russia	79,262	3	China	101,000
4	Hong Kong	76,633	4	Russia	94,907
5	Brazil	64,045	5	Hong Kong	91,530
6	Singapore	63,772	6	Switzerland	59,961
7	Canada	62,325	7	Germany	57,550
8	Australia	49,826	8	Canada	42,636
9	Spain	39,167	9	Netherlands	37,432
10	Mexico	38,286	10	Sweden	33,281
11	United Kingdom	37,101	11	Italy	31,663
12	Ireland	35,520	12	South Korea	29,172
13	Luxembourg	30,075	13	Singapore	26,967
14	India	28,199	14	Spain	26,035
15	Germany	26,721	15	Ireland	22,852
16	Netherlands	24,389	16	Luxembourg	21,626
17	Chile	20,258	17	United Kingdom	19,440
18	Indonesia	18,444	18	Norway	17,913

Note: CBD is Central Business District.
a Includes direct pay, social insurance expenditures, and labour-related taxes.
b Investment in companies in a foreign country.

Business creativity and research

Entrepreneurial activity
*Percentage of population aged 18-64 who are either a nascent entrepreneur[a]
or owner-manager of a new business*

Highest, 2014			Lowest, 2014		
1	Nigeria[b]	39.9	1	Suriname	2.1
	Zambia[b]	39.9	2	Hong Kong[c]	3.6
3	Cameroon	37.4	3	Japan	3.8
4	Uganda	35.5	4	Italy	4.4
5	Namibia[b]	33.3	5	Russia	4.7
6	Botswana	32.8	6	Tunisia[e]	4.8
7	Ecuador	32.6	7	Algeria[b]	4.9
8	Peru	28.8		Serbia[c]	4.9
9	Malawi[b]	28.1	9	France	5.3
10	Bolivia	27.4		Germany	5.3
11	Chile	26.8	11	Belgium	5.4
12	Ghana[b]	25.8	12	Denmark	5.5
13	Yemen[c]	24.0		Spain	5.5
14	Thailand	23.3	14	Finland	5.6
15	Burkina Faso	21.7	15	Norway	5.7
16	Angola	21.5	16	Malaysia	5.9
17	Guatemala	20.4	17	United Arab Emirates[f]	6.2
18	El Salvador	19.5	18	Slovenia	6.3
19	Jamaica	19.3	19	Ireland	6.5
20	Mexico	19.0	20	India	6.6
21	Colombia	18.6		Macedonia[b]	6.6
22	Philippines	18.4	22	Sweden	6.7
23	New Zealand[d]	17.6	23	South Korea[b]	6.9
24	Dominican Rep.[c]	17.5	24	South Africa	7.0

Brain drain[g]

Highest, 2014			Lowest, 2014		
1	Myanmar	1.7	1	Switzerland	5.8
2	Bulgaria	1.8		Qatar	5.8
	Serbia	1.8	3	United States	5.7
	Venezuela	1.8	4	Finland	5.6
5	Moldova	1.9		Norway	5.6
	Yemen	1.9	6	United Arab Emirates	5.5
7	Burundi	2.0	7	Hong Kong	5.3
8	Croatia	2.1	8	Singapore	5.2
9	Haiti	2.2	9	Germany	5.1
	Kyrgyzstan	2.2		Malaysia	5.1
11	Algeria	2.3	11	Luxembourg	5.0
	Lebanon	2.3		United Kingdom	5.0
	Mauritania	2.3	13	Canada	4.8
	Ukraine	2.3		Chile	4.8
15	Chad	2.4		Costa Rica	4.8
	Slovakia	2.4		Netherlands	4.8
				Sweden	4.8
			18	Bahrain	4.7

a An individual who has started a new firm which has not paid wages for over three months.
b 2013 c 2009 d 2005 e 2012 f 2011 g Scores: 1 = talented people leave
for other countries; 7 = they stay and pursue opportunities in the country.

Total expenditure on R&D

	% of GDP, 2013			$bn, 2013	
1	Israel	4.20	1	United States[a]	453.5
2	South Korea	4.15	2	China	191.2
3	Japan	3.47	3	Japan	170.9
4	Finland	3.31	4	Germany	109.5
5	Sweden	3.30	5	France	62.6
6	Denmark	3.06	6	South Korea	54.2
7	Taiwan	2.99	7	United Kingdom	43.5
8	Switzerland[a]	2.96	8	Australia[c]	32.7
9	Germany	2.94	9	Brazil[c]	30.0
10	Austria	2.81	10	Canada	29.9
	United States[a]	2.81	11	Italy	26.8
12	Slovenia	2.59	12	Russia	23.6
13	Venezuela[b]	2.37	13	Switzerland[a]	19.7
14	Belgium	2.28	14	Sweden	19.1
15	France	2.23	15	Spain	17.3
16	Australia[c]	2.18	16	India[a]	17.0
17	China	2.08	17	Netherlands	16.9
18	Singapore	2.00	18	Taiwan	15.3
19	Netherlands	1.98	19	Israel	12.2
20	Czech Republic	1.91	20	Austria	12.0
21	Iceland	1.88		Belgium	12.0
22	Estonia	1.74	22	Denmark	10.3
23	Norway	1.66	23	Finland	8.9
24	Ireland[a]	1.64	24	Norway	8.7
25	United Kingdom	1.63	25	Turkey	7.8
26	Canada	1.62		Venezuela[b]	7.8

Patents

	No. of patents granted by applicant's country of origin, average 2011–13			No. of patents in force by applicant's country of origin, per 100,000 people, 2013	
1	Japan	329,496	1	Japan	2,001
2	United States	225,040	2	Switzerland	1,633
3	China	141,571	3	South Korea	1,507
4	South Korea	111,208	4	Taiwan[a]	1,372
5	Germany	77,161	5	Luxembourg	1,214
6	Taiwan[d]	68,199	6	Sweden	849
7	France	39,459	7	Finland	841
8	Russia	23,315	8	United States	578
9	United Kingdom	19,848	9	Germany	572
10	Switzerland	19,161	10	Netherlands	543
11	Italy	17,142	11	Denmark	521
12	Netherlands	15,942	12	Austria	480
13	Canada	12,016	13	France	467
14	Sweden	11,809	14	Norway	431
15	Finland	6,135	15	Israel	399
16	Belgium	5,915	16	Belgium	301
17	Australia	5,884	17	Canada	273
18	Spain	5,382	18	Singapore	247

a 2012   b 2009   c 2011   d Average 2010–12.

Businesses and banks

Largest non-financial companies
By market capitalisation, $bn, end December 2014

1	Apple	United States	647.4
2	Exxon Mobil	United States	391.5
3	Microsoft	United States	382.9
4	Google	United States	358.4
5	PetroChina	China	305.4
6	Johnson & Johnson	United States	292.7
7	Walmart	United States	276.8
8	Alibaba	China	256.2
9	General Electric	United States	253.8
10	Novartis	Switzerland	251.5
11	Procter & Gamble	United States	246.1
12	China Mobile	China	238.0
13	Nestlé	Switzerland	236.7
14	Roche	Switzerland	233.9
15	Facebook	United States	218.2
16	Royal Dutch Shell	United Kingdom/Netherlands	216.0
17	Toyota Motor	Japan	215.6
18	Chevron	United States	212.1
19	Oracle	United States	197.5
20	Pfizer	United States	196.3
21	Verizon Communications	United States	194.1
22	Coca-Cola	United States	184.9
23	Anheuser-Busch	Belgium	182.7
24	Samsung Electronics	South Korea	178.8

Largest non-financial companies
By net profit, $bn, 2014

1	Vodafone	United Kingdom	76.7
2	Apple	United States	39.5
3	Exxon Mobil	United States	34.3
4	Gazprom	Russia	29.9
5	Samsung Electronics	South Korea	23.8
6	PetroChina	China	21.5
7	Microsoft	United States	21.4
8	Chevron	United States	20.7
9	Toyota Motor	Japan	19.1
10	China Mobile	China	19.0
11	Johnson & Johnson	United States	17.3
12	AT&T	United States	17.1
13	Verizon Communications	United States	16.9
14	Royal Dutch Shell	United Kingdom/Netherlands	16.1
15	Walmart	United States	15.8
16	Volkswagen	Germany	14.7
17	BHP Billiton	Australia/United Kingdom	13.8
18	General Electric	United States	13.3
19	Google	United States	13.1
20	IBM	United States	12.7
21	Total	France	12.1
22	Roche	Switzerland	11.9
23	Rosneft	Russia	11.5
24	Sinopec	China	11.1

Largest banks
By market capitalisation, $bn, end December 2014

1	Wells Fargo	United States	284.4
2	Industrial & Commercial Bank of China	China	271.0
3	JPMorgan Chase	United States	233.9
4	China Construction Bank	China	207.9
5	Agricultural Bank of China	China	191.3
6	Bank of America	United States	188.1
7	HSBC	United Kingdom	182.2
8	Bank of China	China	178.1
9	Citigroup	United States	163.9
10	Commonwealth Bank of Australia	Australia	113.4
11	Banco Santander	Spain	106.5
12	Royal Bank of Canada	Canada	99.6
13	TD Bank Group	Canada	88.2
14	Westpac Banking	Australia	84.5
15	Lloyds Banking Group	United Kingdom	84.4

By assets, $bn, end December 2014

1	Industrial & Commercial Bank of China	China	3,283
2	HSBC	United Kingdom	2,729
3	China Construction Bank	China	2,727
4	BNP Paribas	France	2,610
5	Agricultural Bank of China	China	2,600
6	JPMorgan Chase	United States	2,527
7	Bank of China	China	2,513
8	Mitsubishi UFJ	Japan	2,412
9	Barclays	United Kingdom	2,215
10	Bank of America	United States	2,124
11	Crédit Agricole	France	1,995
12	Citigroup	United States	1,883
13	Mizuho Financial	Japan	1,710
14	Royal Bank of Scotland	United Kingdom	1,697
15	Wells Fargo	United States	1,637

Largest sovereign-wealth funds
By assets, $bn, May 2015

1	Government Pension Fund, Norway	882
2	Abu Dhabi Investment Authority, UAE	773
3	SAMA Foreign Holdings, Saudi Arabia	757
4	China Investment Corporation	652
5	SAFE Investment Company, China[a]	568
6	Kuwait Investment Authority	548
7	Hong Kong Monetary Authority Investment Portfolio	400
8	Government of Singapore Investment Corporation	320
9	Qatar Investment Authority	256
10	China National Social Security Fund	236

Note: Countries listed refer to the company's domicile.
a Estimate.

Stockmarkets

Largest market capitalisation
$bn, end 2014

1	NYSE	19,351	20	BM&F BOVESPA		844
2	NASDAQ OMX	6,979	21	Singapore Exchange		753
3	Japan Exchange Group – Tokyo	4,378	22	Saudi Stock Exchange – Tadawul		483
4	London SE Group	4,013	23	Mexican Exchange		480
5	Shanghai SE	3,933	24	Bursa Malaysia		459
6	Euronext	3,319	25	Stock Exchange of Thailand		430
7	Hong Kong Exchanges	3,233	26	Indonesia SE		422
8	TMX Group	2,094	27	Moscow Exchange		386
9	Shenzhen SE	2,072	28	Philippine SE		262
10	Deutsche Börse	1,739	29	Santiago SE		233
11	BSE India	1,558	30	Borsa Istanbul		220
12	National Stock Exchange India	1,521	31	Oslo Bors		219
13	SIX Swiss Exchange	1,495	32	Tel Aviv SE		201
14	Australian SE[a]	1,289	33	Qatar SE		186
15	Korea Exchange[b]	1,213	34	Warsaw SE		169
16	NASDAQ OMX Nordic Exchange[c]	1197	35	Colombia SE		147
17	BME Spanish Exchanges	993	36	Irish SE		143
18	Johannesburg SE	934	37	Tehran SE		117
19	Taiwan SE Corp.	851	38	Abu Dhabi SE		114
			39	Wiener Börse		97
			40	Dubai Financial Market		88

Stockmarket gains and losses
$ terms, % change December 31st 2013 to December 29th 2014

Largest gains			Largest losses		
1	China (SSEA)	45.9	1	Russia (RTS)	-44.9
2	Pakistan (KSE)	31.4	2	Greece (Athex Comp)	-37.7
3	Egypt (Case 30)	28.3	3	Colombia (IGBC)	-28.2
4	India (BSE)	25.6	4	Hungary (BUX)	-25.8
5	Argentina (MERV)	19.4	5	Austria (ATX)	-24.5
6	Indonesia (JSX)	18.5	6	Czech Republic (PX)	-16.4
7	Turkey (BIST)	15.1	7	Norway (OSEAX)	-15.6
	US (NAScomp)	15.1	8	Poland (WIG)	-14.8
9	Thailand (SET)	15.0	9	Brazil (BVSP)	-13.8
10	US (S&P 500)	13.1	10	Malaysia (KLSE)	-11.3
11	China (SSEB, $ terms)	12.9	11	France (CAC 40)	-11.2
12	US (DJIA)	8.8	12	Italy (FTSE/MIB)	-10.8
13	Denmark (OMXCB)	6.5	13	Chile (IGPA)	-10.2
14	Saudi Arabia (Tadawul)	3.6	14	Mexico (IPC)	-9.9
15	Hong Kong (Hang Seng)	1.9	15	Euro area (EURO STOXX 50)	-9.4
16	Singapore (STI)	1.5	16	Euro area (FTSE Euro 100)	-9.2
17	Taiwan (TWI)	1.2	17	Sweden (OMXS30)	-9.0
16	Belgium (BEL 20)	0.2	18	Germany (DAX)	-8.1
			19	South Korea (KOSPI)	-7.9
				Spain (Madrid SE)	-7.9

a Includes investment funds.   b Includes Kosdaq.
c Copenhagen, Helsinki, Iceland, Stockholm, Tallinn, Riga and Vilnius stock exchanges.

Value traded[a]

$bn, 2014

1	NASDAQ OMX	31,044	18	Taiwan SE Corp.	694
2	NYSE	18,234	19	BM&F BOVESPA	648
3	BATS Global Markets – US	13,163	20	National Stock Exchange India	612
4	BATS Chi-x Europe	6,877	21	Saudi Stock Exchange – Tadawul	572
5	Shanghai SE	6,076	22	Borsa Istanbul	370
6	Shenzhen SE	5,912	23	Johannesburg SE	350
7	Japan Exchange Group - Tokyo	5,365	24	Stock Exchange of Thailand	321
8	London SE Group	4,021	25	Moscow Exchange	296
9	Euronext	2,938	26	Taipei Exchange	201
10	Hong Kong Exchanges	1,630		Singapore Exchange[e]	201
11	Deutsche Börse	1,464	28	Bursa Malaysia	151
12	TMX Group	1,349	29	Oslo Bors	142
13	Korea Exchange[b]	1,326		Mexican Exchange	142
14	BME Spanish Exchanges	1,321	31	BSE India	121
15	Australian SE[c]	852	32	Indonesia SE	117
16	SIX Swiss Exchange	846	33	Dubai Financial Market	105
17	NASDAQ OMX Nordic Exchange[d]	767	34	Warsaw SE	68

Number of listed companies[f]

End 2014

1	BSE India	5,542	20	Taipei Exchange	685
2	TMX Group	3,761	21	Deutsche Börse	670
3	Japan Exchange Group – Tokyo	3,470	22	Stock Exchange of Thailand	613
4	BME Spanish Exchanges	3,452	23	Indonesia SE	506
5	NASDAQ OMX	2,782	24	Tel Aviv SE	473
6	London SE Group	2,752	25	Johannesburg SE	380
7	NYSE	2,466	26	BM&F BOVESPA	363
8	Australian SE[c]	2,073	27	Tehran SE	315
9	Korea Exchange	1,864	28	Santiago SE	307
10	Hong Kong Exchanges	1,752	29	HoChiMinh SE	305
11	National Stock Exchange India	1,708	30	Colombo SE	294
12	Shenzhen SE	1,618	31	SIX Swiss Exchange	276
13	Euronext	1,055	32	Dhaka SE	274
14	Shanghai SE	995	33	Lima SE	263
15	Bursa Malaysia	905	34	Philippine SE	263
16	Warsaw SE	902	35	Moscow Exchange	257
17	Taiwan SE Corp.	880	36	Egyptian Exchange	247
18	NASDAQ OMX Nordic Exchange[d]	787	37	Athens Exchange	244
19	Singapore Exchange[g]	775	38	Amman SE	236
			39	Borsa Istanbul	227

Note: Figures are not entirely comparable due to different reporting rules and calculations. a Includes electronic and negotiated deals.   b Includes Kosdaq.   c Includes investment funds.   d Copenhagen, Helsinki, Iceland, Stockholm, Tallinn, Riga and Vilnius stock exchanges.   e Main board, Catalist and GlobalQuote. f Domestic and foreign.   g Main board and Catalist.

Transport: roads and cars

Longest road networks
Km, 2013 or latest

1	United States	6,623,177	26	Colombia	216,046
2	India	4,934,622	27	Malaysia	202,333
3	China	4,356,218	28	Hungary	201,486
4	Brazil	1,588,352	29	Philippines	197,515
5	Russia	1,481,114	30	Nigeria	197,277
6	Canada	1,409,003	31	Thailand	194,503
7	Japan	1,218,008	32	Ukraine	169,600
8	France	1,069,033	33	Peru	157,051
9	Australia	900,083	34	Belgium	156,302
10	South Africa	849,417	35	Egypt	145,438
11	Spain	666,949	36	Netherlands	140,231
12	Germany	643,424	37	Czech Republic	130,611
13	Sweden	587,840	38	Austria	124,119
14	Indonesia	508,000	39	Algeria	117,255
15	Italy	492,599	40	Greece	116,960
16	United Kingdom	420,540	41	Sri Lanka	114,093
17	Poland	412,685	42	Ghana	109,515
18	Turkey	388,666	43	South Korea	105,845
19	Mexico	378,923	44	Belarus	98,897
20	Iran	286,536	45	Kazakhstan	96,873
21	Pakistan	264,790	46	Venezuela	96,156
22	Saudi Arabia	253,790	47	Ireland	96,002
23	Argentina	229,915	48	New Zealand	94,546
24	Romania	229,210	49	Norway	94,401
25	Vietnam	221,033	50	Tanzania	86,472

Densest road networks
Km of road per km² land area, 2013 or latest

1	Monaco	38.1		Switzerland	1.7
2	Macau	24.3		United Kingdom	1.7
3	Malta	9.8	26	Italy	1.6
4	Bermuda	8.3	27	Austria	1.5
5	Bahrain	6.0		India	1.5
6	Singapore	5.4	29	Cyprus	1.4
7	Belgium	5.1		Ireland	1.4
8	Barbados	3.7	31	Estonia	1.3
9	Netherlands	3.4		Lithuania	1.3
10	Japan	3.2		Poland	1.3
11	Puerto Rico	3.0		Spain	1.3
12	Liechtenstein	2.5		Sweden	1.3
13	Hungary	2.2	36	Taiwan	1.2
14	France	2.0	37	Latvia	1.1
	Jamaica	2.0		Mauritius	1.1
	Luxembourg	2.0		South Korea	1.1
17	Guam	1.9	40	Portugal	1.0
	Hong Kong	1.9		Romania	1.0
	Slovenia	1.9	42	Greece	0.9
20	Germany	1.8		Israel	0.9
21	Czech Republic	1.7		Qatar	0.9
	Denmark	1.7		Slovakia	0.9
	Sri Lanka	1.7			

Most crowded road networks
Number of vehicles per km of road network, 2013 or latest

1	Monaco	427.3	26	Luxembourg	75.3
2	Hong Kong	314.6	27	Armenia	73.3
3	Singapore	245.4	28	Germany	72.2
4	Macau	238.0	29	Honduras	71.0
5	Kuwait	223.4	30	Portugal	69.5
6	South Korea	182.2	31	Dominican Rep.	65.7
7	Taiwan	168.4	32	Switzerland	65.5
8	Jordan	161.2	33	Netherlands	64.2
9	Israel	141.0	34	Croatia	62.4
10	El Salvador	130.2	35	Saudi Arabia	60.8
11	Bahrain	115.6	36	Brunei	60.1
12	Mauritius	111.8		Thailand	60.1
13	Guam	102.9	38	Bermuda	59.3
14	Guatemala	99.6	39	Malaysia	56.9
15	Malta	97.0	40	Greece	55.6
16	Puerto Rico	93.5	41	Poland	55.1
17	Mexico	93.2	42	Morocco	53.9
18	Italy	86.2	43	Venezuela	51.4
19	Sweden	85.4	44	Slovakia	49.7
20	United Kingdom	85.2	45	Moldova	49.2
21	Qatar	84.3	46	Ukraine	48.5
22	Barbados	83.9	47	Fiji	47.7
23	Bulgaria	79.5	48	Bahamas	47.3
24	Liechtenstein	77.3	49	Chile	46.6
25	Tunisia	75.5	50	Finland	46.4

Longest distance travelled
Average distance travelled per car per year, km, 2012

1	Chile	28,908	21	Finland	15,178
2	India	23,927	22	Kazakhstan	15,148
3	Peru	22,381	23	Morocco	14,986
4	Ecuador	21,925	24	Portugal	14,973
5	Azerbaijan	21,058	25	Indonesia	14,557
6	United States	19,885	26	Iceland	14,243
7	Singapore	18,647	27	China	14,170
8	Pakistan	18,412	28	Norway	13,829
9	Belgium	18,251	29	Switzerland	13,799
10	Ireland	17,798	30	Germany	13,794
11	Iran	17,792	31	Moldova	13,761
12	Russia	17,276	32	Latvia	13,691
13	Estonia	17,029	33	Czech Republic	13,397
14	Slovenia	17,019	34	France	13,391
15	Tunisia	16,320	35	Australia	13,117
16	Austria	16,276	36	New Zealand	13,095
17	Israel	16,125	37	Netherlands	13,053
18	Sweden	15,808	38	Japan	12,849
19	Canada	15,621	39	Croatia	12,824
20	Denmark	15,370	40	Hong Kong	12,798

Highest car ownership
Number of cars per 1,000 population, 2013

1	Monaco	894	26	Canada	456
2	Liechtenstein	757	27	Czech Republic	432
3	Luxembourg	709	28	Cyprus	431
4	Iceland	698	29	Portugal	429
5	New Zealand	636	30	Brunei	417
6	Puerto Rico	628	31	Ireland	405
7	Malta	625	32	United States	402
8	Italy	615	33	Barbados	398
9	Lithuania	578	34	Denmark	395
10	Finland	572	35	Bulgaria	390
11	Australia	546	36	Kuwait	381
12	Austria	539		Trinidad & Tobago	381
13	Switzerland	527	38	Guam	376
14	Germany	524	39	Saudi Arabia	352
15	Slovenia	510	40	Malaysia	350
16	Poland	507	41	Croatia	348
17	United Kingdom	499	42	Slovakia	331
18	Belgium	497	43	Lebanon	329
19	France	494	44	Bermuda	319
20	Norway	491	45	Japan	307
21	Spain	475	46	Belarus	305
22	Netherlands	473	47	Bahrain	303
23	Greece	464	48	South Korea	300
24	Sweden	463	49	Hungary	298
25	Estonia	459	50	Israel	295

Lowest car ownership
Number of cars per 1,000 population, 2013

1	Ethiopia	1		Pakistan	11
	Somalia	1	25	Cameroon	12
3	Bangladesh	2	26	Malawi	13
	Burundi	2	27	Kenya	15
	Chad	2	28	Ivory Coast	16
	Laos	2		Nicaragua	16
	Liberia	2		Senegal	16
8	Rwanda	3		Yemen	16
	Uganda	3	32	India	17
10	Congo-Kinshasa	4	33	Ghana	18
11	Gambia, The	5	34	Zambia	19
	Nepal	5	35	Vietnam	20
	Sierra Leone	5	36	Benin	21
14	Guinea	6		Congo-Brazzaville	21
	Myanmar	6		Cuba	21
	Niger	6	39	Sri Lanka	23
	Papua New Guinea	6	40	Bolivia	26
18	Eritrea	7		Cambodia	26
19	Burkina Faso	8	42	Afghanistan	27
	Philippines	8		Iraq	27
21	Mali	10	44	Guinea-Bissau	29
	Tanzania	10	45	Tajikistan	31
23	Mozambique	11	46	Syria	35

Vehicle production

Number produced, '000, 2013

Cars

1	China	18,084	16	Canada	965
2	Japan	8,189	17	Indonesia	925
3	Germany	5,440	18	Turkey	634
4	United States	4,369	19	Iran	631
5	South Korea	4,123	20	Malaysia	544
6	India	3,156	21	Argentina	507
7	Brazil	2,723	22	Poland	475
8	Russia	1,920	23	Belgium	466
9	Mexico	1,772	24	Romania	411
10	Spain	1,755	25	Italy	388
11	United Kingdom	1,510	26	Taiwan	291
12	France	1,458	27	South Africa	265
13	Czech Republic	1,128	28	Uzbekistan	247
14	Thailand	1,071	29	Hungary	220
15	Slovakia	975	30	Australia	171

Light vehicles

1	United States	6,698	6	Mexico	1,283
2	China	4,033	7	Brazil	989
3	Japan	1,441	8	India	743
4	Canada	1,415	9	Turkey	492
5	Thailand	1,386	10	Spain	409

Cars sold

New car registrations, '000, 2013

1	China	17,928	26	Austria	319
2	United States	7,585	27	Switzerland	308
3	Japan	4,562	28	Poland	290
4	Germany	2,952	29	Chile	287
5	Brazil	2,764	30	Sweden	270
6	Russia	2,649	31	Colombia	239
7	India	2,554	32	Algeria	223
8	United Kingdom	2,265	33	Egypt	220
9	France	1,790	34	Ukraine	213
10	Italy	1,305	35	Taiwan	212
11	South Korea	1,244	36	United Arab Emirates	207
12	Indonesia	880	37	Israel	200
13	Canada	756	38	Denmark	182
14	Spain	723	39	Czech Republic	165
15	Mexico	698	40	Kazakhstan	154
16	Iran	692	41	Norway	142
17	Argentina	684	42	Oman	140
18	Turkey	665	43	Peru	139
19	Thailand	664	44	Kuwait	125
20	Malaysia	577	45	Pakistan	121
21	Saudi Arabia	570	46	Morocco	108
22	Australia	566	47	Portugal	106
23	Belgium	486	48	Finland	103
24	South Africa	451	49	New Zealand	82
25	Netherlands	417	50	Iraq	78

Transport: planes and trains

Most air travel
Passengers carried, m, 2013

1	United States	743.1	16	Malaysia	46.3
2	China	352.8	17	Spain	45.8
3	United Kingdom	118.3	18	South Korea	41.1
4	Japan	105.9	19	Thailand	40.7
5	Germany	105.0	20	Mexico	38.8
6	Brazil	95.9	21	Hong Kong	34.2
7	Ireland	95.6	22	Netherlands	33.2
8	Indonesia	85.1	23	Singapore	30.6
9	India	75.3	24	Philippines	29.3
10	Turkey	74.4	25	Saudi Arabia	28.3
11	Canada	71.5	26	Switzerland	27.0
12	Australia	70.9	27	Italy	25.2
13	United Arab Emirates	69.2	28	Colombia	23.3
14	France	66.7	29	Iran	18.9
15	Russia	66.0	30	Qatar	18.7

Busiest airports

Total passengers, m, 2014

1	Atlanta, Hartsfield	96.6
2	Beijing, Capital	86.0
3	London, Heathrow	73.5
4	Tokyo, Haneda	73.2
5	Dubai Intl.	71.0
6	Chicago, O'Hare	70.7
	Los Angeles, Intl.	70.7
8	Dallas, Ft Worth	63.5
	Paris, Charles de Gaulle	63.5
10	Hong Kong, Intl.	63.2
11	Frankfurt, Main	59.6
12	Istanbul, Ataturk	57.1
13	Jakarta, Soekarno-Hatta	56.4
14	Amstersdam, Schipol	55.1
15	Guangzhou Baiyun, Intl	54.7

Total cargo, m tonnes, 2014

1	Hong Kong, Intl.	4.42
2	Memphis, Intl.	4.26
3	Shanghai, Pudong Intl.	3.20
4	Seoul, Incheon	2.56
5	Anchorage, Intl.	2.50
6	Dubai, Intl.	2.36
7	Louisville, Standiford Fld.	2.29
8	Frankfurt, Main	2.13
	Tokyo, Narita	2.13
10	Taiwan, Taoyuan Intl.	2.10
11	Miami, Intl.	2.00
12	Paris, Charles de Gaulle	1.88
	Singapore, Changi	1.88
14	Beijing, Capital	1.84
	Los Angeles, Intl.	1.84

Average daily aircraft movements, take-offs and landings, 2014

1	Chicago, O'Hare	2,409	13	Amsterdam, Schiphol	1,231
2	Atlanta, Hartsfield	2,319	14	Toronto, Pearson Intl.	1,188
3	Dallas, Ft Worth	1,846	15	Istanbul, Ataturk	1,185
4	Los Angeles, Intl.	1,735	16	San Francisco	1,183
5	Beijing, Capital	1,583	17	Phoenix, Skyharbor Intl.	1,179
6	Denver, Intl.	1,560	17	Philadelphia, Intl.	1,151
7	Charlotte/Douglas, Intl.	1,498	19	Tokyo, Haneda	1,150
8	Las Vegas, McCarran Intl.	1,433	20	Minneapolis, St Paul	1,146
9	Houston, George Bush Intercontinental	1,384	21	New York, JFK	1,139
10	London, Heathrow	1,296	22	Guangzhou Bayyun, Intl.	1,117
11	Frankfurt, Main	1,294	23	Mexico City, Intl.	1,113
12	Paris, Charles de Gaulle	1,293	24	Miami	1,098
			25	Detroit, Metro	1,096

Longest railway networks
'000 km, 2013 or latest

1	United States	228.2	21	Sweden	9.8
2	Russia	84.2	22	Turkey	9.7
3	China	66.3	23	Czech Republic	9.5
4	India	64.5	24	Iran	8.4
5	Canada	64.3	25	Hungary	7.9
6	South Africa	40.3	26	Pakistan	7.8
7	Germany	33.4	27	Finland	5.9
8	Australia	32.8	28	Belarus	5.5
9	France	30.0		Chile	5.5
10	Brazil	29.8	30	Thailand	5.3
11	Mexico	26.7	31	Egypt	5.2
12	Argentina	25.0	32	Austria	5.0
13	Ukraine	21.6	33	Algeria	4.7
14	Japan	20.1		Indonesia	4.7
15	Poland	19.0	35	Sudan	4.3
16	Italy	17.1	36	Norway	4.2
17	Spain	17.0		Uzbekistan	4.2
18	United Kingdom	16.4	38	Bulgaria	4.0
19	Kazakhstan	14.3	39	Serbia	3.8
20	Romania	10.8	40	South Korea	3.7

Most rail passengers
Km per person per year, 2013 or latest

1	Switzerland	2,307	13	Germany	977
2	Japan	1,912	14	Belarus	947
3	France	1,301	15	Slovakia	902
4	Austria	1,280	16	Taiwan	826
5	Denmark	1,190	17	India	809
6	Kazakhstan	1,095	18	Luxembourg	758
7	Ukraine	1,074	19	Finland	751
8	United Kingdom	1,063	20	Czech Republic	659
9	Mongolia	1,030	21	Sweden	644
10	Netherlands	1,019	22	Italy	643
11	Russia	1,012	23	China	593
12	Belgium	1,004	24	Hungary	580

Most rail freight
Million tonne-km per year, 2013 or latest

1	United States	2,524,585	13	Belarus	43,818
2	China	2,518,310	14	Poland	33,256
3	Russia	2,222,388	15	France	31,616
4	India	625,723	16	Mongolia	23,561
5	Canada	352,535	17	Iran	22,604
6	Brazil	267,700	18	Uzbekistan	22,482
7	Ukraine	237,722	19	Japan	20,255
8	Kazakhstan	235,846	20	Austria	15,143
9	South Africa	113,342	21	Latvia	14,991
10	Germany	104,259	22	Slovakia	14,072
11	Mexico	69,185	23	Lithuania	13,344
12	Australia	59,649	24	Argentina	12,111

Transport: shipping

Merchant fleets
Number of vessels, by country of domicile, January 2014

1	China	5,405	11	Turkey	1,547
2	Japan	4,022	12	Netherlands	1,234
3	Greece	3,826	13	United Kingdom	1,233
4	Germany	3,699	14	Denmark	955
5	Singapore	2,120	15	Taiwan	862
6	United States	1,927	16	Vietnam	859
7	Norway	1,864	17	Italy	851
8	Russia	1,734	18	India	753
9	Indonesia	1,598	19	United Arab Emirates	716
10	South Korea	1,568	20	Hong Kong	610

Shipbuilding
Deliveries[a], '000 dwt, 2014

1	China	36,633	11	Norway	168
2	South Korea	26,121	12	India	127
3	Japan	22,628	13	Netherlands	118
4	Philippines	2,861	14	Germany	117
5	Taiwan	651	15	Indonesia	86
6	Vietnam	526	16	Russia	63
7	Brazil	408	17	Singapore	55
8	United States	316	18	Poland	54
9	Romania	290	19	Malaysia	42
10	Turkey	171	20	Italy	39

Order books, % of world total by gross tonnage[b], by country of ownership, May 2015

1	China	44.95	11	Iran	0.15
2	South Korea	27.67	12	Netherlands	0.10
3	Japan	19.05	13	Norway	0.09
4	Philippines	2.33	14	Argentina	0.08
5	Brazil	2.07	15	Germany	0.07
6	Romania	1.15	17	Russia	0.06
7	Vietnam	0.66		Turkey	0.06
8	Taiwan	0.60	18	Bangladesh	0.05
9	United States	0.39		Indonesia	0.05
10	Croatia	0.25	20	Italy	0.03

Busiest ports
Cargo volume, million TEU[c], 2013

1	Shanghai, China	33.62	9	Jebel Ali, Dubai, United Arab Emirates	13.64
2	Singapore	32.60			
3	Shenzhen, China	23.28	10	Tianjin, China	13.01
4	Hong Kong	22.35	11	Rotterdam, Netherlands	11.62
5	Busan, South Korea	17.69	12	Dalian, China	10.86
6	Ningbo-Zhoushan, China	17.33	13	Port Klang, Malaysia	10.35
7	Qingdao, China	15.52	14	Kaohsiung, Taiwan	9.94
8	Guangzhou Harbor, China	15.31	15	Hamburg, Germany	9.30
			16	Antwerp, Belgium	8.59

a Sea-going propelled merchant ships of 100 gross tons and above.
b Sea-going cargo-carrying vessels. c Twenty-foot equivalent unit.

Tourism

Most tourist arrivals
Number of arrivals, '000, 2013

1	France	84,726	21	Netherlands	12,783
2	United States	69,768	22	South Korea	12,176
3	Spain	60,661	23	Singapore	11,899
4	China	55,686	24	Croatia	10,955
5	Italy	47,704	25	Hungary	10,675
6	Turkey	37,795	26	Japan	10,364
7	Germany	31,545	27	Morocco	10,046
8	United Kingdom	31,169	28	South Africa	9,537
9	Russia	30,792	29	Egypt	9,174
10	Thailand	26,547	30	Bahrain	9,163
11	Malaysia	25,715	31	Czech Republic	9,004
12	Hong Kong	25,661	32	Switzerland	8,967
13	Austria	24,813	33	Indonesia	8,802
14	Ukraine	24,671	34	Denmark	8,557
15	Mexico	24,151	35	Ireland	8,260
16	Greece	17,920	36	Portugal	8,097
17	Canada	16,590	37	Romania	8,019
18	Poland	15,800	38	Taiwan	8,016
19	Macau	14,268	39	Belgium	7,684
20	Saudi Arabia	13,380	40	Vietnam	7,572

Biggest tourist spenders
$m, 2013

1	China	128.6	13	Japan	21.8
2	United States	104.7	14	South Korea	21.6
3	Germany	91.4	15	Hong Kong	21.2
4	United Kingdom	57.6	16	Netherlands	20.1
5	Russia	53.5	17	Norway	18.5
6	France	42.9	18	Saudi Arabia	17.7
7	Canada	35.2		United Arab Emirates	17.7
8	Australia	28.6	20	Sweden	17.6
9	Italy	27.0	21	Spain	16.4
10	Brazil	25.0	22	Switzerland	16.1
11	Singapore	24.2	23	Taiwan	12.3
12	Belgium	21.9	24	Malaysia	12.2

Largest tourist receipts
$m, 2013

1	United States	139.5	13	Austria	20.1
2	Spain	60.4	14	Singapore	19.0
3	France	56.1	15	India	18.4
4	China	51.7	16	Canada	17.7
5	Macau	51.6	17	Switzerland	16.5
6	Italy	43.9	18	Greece	15.9
7	Thailand	42.1	19	Netherlands	15.6
8	Germany	41.2	20	Japan	14.9
9	United Kingdom	40.6	21	South Korea	14.3
10	Hong Kong	38.9	22	Mexico	13.8
11	Australia	31.0	23	Belgium	13.5
12	Turkey	28.0	24	Taiwan	12.7

Education

Primary enrolment
Number enrolled as % of relevant age group

Highest			Lowest		
1	Gabon	165	1	Eritrea	42
2	Madagascar	145	2	Sudan	70
3	Malawi	141	3	Niger	71
4	Angola	140	4	Syria	74
5	Burundi	134	5	Mali	84
	Rwanda	134		Senegal	84
	Sierra Leone	134	7	Nigeria	85
	Togo	134	8	South Sudan	86
9	Nepal	133	9	Burkina Faso	87
10	China	128		Gambia, The	87
11	Cambodia	125	11	Bermuda	88
	Timor-Leste	125	12	Macedonia	89
13	Argentina	124		Turkmenistan	89
	Benin	124	14	Puerto Rico	90
15	Laos	121		Tanzania	90

Highest secondary enrolment
Number enrolled as % of relevant age group

1	Australia	136		South Africa	111
2	Spain	131	13	France	110
3	Netherlands	130	14	Costa Rica	109
4	Denmark	125		Greece	109
5	New Zealand	120	16	Finland	108
6	Ireland	119		Liechtenstein	108
7	Saudi Arabia	116	18	Argentina	107
8	Portugal	113		Belgium	107
9	Iceland	112		Estonia	107
	Qatar	112	21	Brunei	106
11	Norway	111		Lithuania	106

Highest tertiary enrolment[a]
Number enrolled as % of relevant age group

1	Greece	117	11	Argentina	80
2	South Korea	98		Denmark	80
3	Finland	94		New Zealand	80
	United States	94	14	Ukraine	79
5	Belarus	93	15	Estonia	77
6	Australia	86		Netherlands	77
	Slovenia	86	17	Russia	76
8	Puerto Rico	85	18	Chile	74
	Spain	85		Lithuania	74
10	Iceland	81		Norway	74

Notes: Latest available year 2010–14. The gross enrolment ratios shown are the actual number enrolled as a percentage of the number of children in the official primary age group. They may exceed 100 when children outside the primary age group are receiving primary education.

a Tertiary education includes all levels of post-secondary education including courses leading to awards not equivalent to a university degree, courses leading to a first university degree and postgraduate courses.

Least literate
% adult population

1	Niger	15.5	15	Bangladesh	58.8
2	Guinea	25.3	16	Togo	60.4
3	Afghanistan	31.7	17	Malawi	61.3
4	Mali	33.6	18	Papua New Guinea	62.9
5	Central African Rep.	36.8	19	Rwanda	65.9
6	Chad	37.3	20	Yemen	66.4
7	Ivory Coast	41.0	21	Morocco	67.1
8	Sierra Leone	44.5	22	Tanzania	67.8
9	Gambia, The	52.0	23	Eritrea	70.5
10	Senegal	52.1	24	Angola	70.6
11	Pakistan	54.7	25	Cameroon	71.3
12	Guinea-Bissau	56.7	26	Ghana	71.5
13	Nepal	57.4	27	Uganda	73.2
14	Timor-Leste	58.3	28	Sudan	73.4

Top universities[a]
2014

1	Harvard, US	13	Cornell, US
2	Stanford, US	14	California, San Diego, US
3	Massachusetts Institute of Technology, US	15	Washington, US
4	California, Berkeley, US	16	Pennsylvania, US
5	Cambridge, UK	17	The Johns Hopkins, Baltimore, US
6	Princeton, US	18	California, San Francisco, US
7	California Institute of Technology, US	19	Swiss Federal Institute of Technology Zurich
8	Columbia, US	20	University College London, UK
9	Chicago, US	21	Tokyo, Japan
	Oxford, UK	22	Imperial College London, UK
11	Yale, US		Michigan – Ann Arbor, US
12	California, Los Angeles, US		

Education spending
% of GDP[b]

Highest			Lowest		
1	Cuba	12.8	1	South Sudan	0.7
2	Timor-Leste	9.4	2	Myanmar	0.8
3	Denmark	8.7	3	Central African Rep.	1.2
4	Namibia	8.5	4	Congo-Kinshasa	1.6
5	Moldova	8.3		Monaco	1.6
6	Ghana	8.2	6	Sri Lanka	1.7
7	Malta	7.8	7	Georgia	2.0
	Swaziland	7.8		Zimbabwe	2.0
9	Thailand	7.6	9	Armenia	2.3
10	Iceland	7.4		Chad	2.3
	New Zealand	7.4	11	Azerbaijan	2.4
12	Cyprus	7.2	12	Guinea	2.5
13	Costa Rica	6.9		Pakistan	2.5

a Based on academic peer review, employer review, faculty/student ratio, research strength and international factors.   b Latest year 2010–14.

Life expectancy

Highest life expectancy
Years, 2015–20

1	Monaco[a]	89.6	25	Germany	81.4
2	Japan	84.3	26	Belgium	81.3
3	Hong Kong	84.2		Lebanon	81.3
4	Switzerland	83.2		Luxembourg	81.3
5	Australia	83.1		Macau	81.3
	Italy	83.1	30	Finland	81.2
	Singapore	83.1		United Kingdom	81.2
8	Spain	82.8	32	Virgin Islands (US)	81.1
9	Andorra[a]	82.7	33	Bermuda[a]	81.0
	Iceland	82.7		Channel Islands	81.0
11	South Korea	82.6		Chile	81.0
12	France	82.5	36	Costa Rica	80.9
	Israel	82.5	37	Portugal	80.8
14	Martinique	82.4	38	Réunion	80.7
	Sweden	82.4	39	Cyprus	80.6
16	Canada	82.1	40	Malta	80.5
	Norway	82.1	41	Slovenia	80.3
18	Guadeloupe	81.9	42	Cuba	80.1
19	Austria	81.8	43	Denmark	80.0
	New Zealand	81.8		Guam	80.0
21	Liechtenstein[a]	81.7	45	Taiwan[a]	79.8
	Netherlands	81.7	46	Puerto Rico	79.6
23	Greece	81.5		United States	79.6
	Ireland	81.5	48	Brunei	79.4

Highest male life expectancy
Years, 2015–20

1	Monaco[a]	85.7	9	Andorra[a]	80.5
2	Hong Kong	81.2	10	Sweden	80.4
3	Australia	80.9	11	Italy	80.3
	Iceland	80.9	12	Canada	80.0
5	Japan	80.8		New Zealand	80.0
	Switzerland	80.8		Norway	80.0
7	Israel	80.6	15	Netherlands	79.8
	Singapore	80.6			

Highest female life expectancy
Years, 2015–20

1	Monaco[a]	93.6	11	Australia	85.4
2	Japan	87.7	12	Guadeloupe	85.0
3	Hong Kong	87.2	13	Andorra[a]	84.9
4	Spain	86.0	14	Iceland	84.5
5	France	85.9		Sweden	84.5
	South Korea	85.9	16	Finland	84.4
7	Italy	85.7		Liechtenstein[a]	84.4
8	Switzerland	85.6	18	Austria	84.3
9	Martinique	85.5		Bermuda[a]	84.3
	Singapore	85.5			

a 2014 estimates.

Lowest life expectancy
Years, 2015–20

1	Sierra Leone	46.8	26	Congo-Brazzaville	60.4
2	Swaziland	48.7	27	Niger	60.5
3	Lesotho	50.4	28	Uganda	60.8
4	Botswana	50.5	29	Zambia	61.3
5	Congo-Kinshasa	51.3	30	Ghana	61.9
6	Mozambique	51.8	31	Liberia	62.1
7	Ivory Coast	52.4	32	Mauritania	62.2
8	Central African Rep.	52.8	33	Zimbabwe	62.5
9	Chad	53.1	34	Afghanistan	62.6
10	Angola	53.7	35	Sudan	62.9
11	Nigeria	54.2	36	Kenya	63.1
12	Equatorial Guinea	55.0		Papua New Guinea	63.1
13	Guinea-Bissau	55.4		Tanzania	63.1
14	Burundi	55.9	39	Yemen	63.9
15	Somalia	56.5	40	Senegal	64.2
16	Mali	56.8	41	Haiti	64.3
17	Malawi	56.9	42	Gabon	64.9
18	Cameroon	57.0	43	Eritrea	65.1
19	Guinea	57.3	44	Namibia	65.3
20	South Africa	57.7	45	Ethiopia	65.9
	South Sudan	57.7		Myanmar	65.9
22	Togo	57.9	47	Rwanda	66.0
23	Burkina Faso	58.1	48	Turkmenistan	66.1
24	Gambia, The	59.8	49	Madagascar	66.6
25	Benin	60.1			

Lowest male life expectancy
Years, 2015–20

1	Sierra Leone	46.5	11	Equatorial Guinea	53.6
2	Congo-Kinshasa	49.5	12	Burundi	53.8
	Swaziland	49.5		Guinea-Bissau	53.8
4	Lesotho	50.3	14	Nigeria	53.9
5	Central African Rep.	50.7	15	Somalia	54.9
6	Botswana	51.2	16	South Africa	55.7
	Mozambique	51.2	17	Cameroon	55.9
8	Ivory Coast	51.6	18	Guinea	56.5
9	Angola	52.2		South Sudan	56.5
	Chad	52.2	20	Malawi	56.6

Lowest female life expectancy
Years, 2015–20

1	Sierra Leone	47.0	10	Central African Rep.	54.9
2	Swaziland	47.7	11	Angola	55.2
3	Botswana	49.4	12	Equatorial Guinea	56.5
4	Lesotho	50.2	13	Mali	56.8
5	Mozambique	52.3	14	Guinea-Bissau	56.9
6	Congo-Kinshasa	53.2	15	Malawi	57.1
7	Ivory Coast	53.4	16	Burundi	58.0
8	Chad	54.0	17	Guinea	58.1
9	Nigeria	54.6			

Death rates and infant mortality

Highest death rates
Number of deaths per 1,000 population, 2015–20

1	Ukraine	17.0	49	Finland	10.0
2	Sierra Leone	16.2		Kazakhstan	10.0
3	Bulgaria	16.1		Macedonia	10.0
4	Latvia	16.0	52	Burkina Faso	9.9
5	Russia	15.6	53	Togo	9.8
6	Belarus	15.5	54	Niger	9.6
7	Botswana	15.4	55	Austria	9.5
8	Swaziland	14.9		North Korea	9.5
9	Lesotho	14.7	57	Sweden	9.4
10	Congo-Kinshasa	14.4	58	Congo-Brazzaville	9.3
	Moldova	14.4		United Kingdom	9.3
12	Lithuania	14.1		Uruguay	9.3
13	Estonia	13.9	61	Channel Islands	9.2
14	Hungary	13.6	62	Armenia	9.1
15	Central African Rep.	13.3		Benin	9.1
16	South Africa	13.2		France	9.1
17	Ivory Coast	13.1		Gambia, The	9.1
	Mozambique	13.1		Malta	9.1
19	Chad	12.8	67	Barbados	9.0
	Croatia	12.8		Monaco[a]	9.0
	Romania	12.8		Netherlands	9.0
22	Serbia	12.7		Spain	9.0
23	Angola	12.6	71	Myanmar	8.7
24	Equatorial Guinea	12.1	72	Ghana	8.5
25	Nigeria	12.0		Mauritius	8.5
26	Georgia	11.8		Zambia	8.5
	Guinea-Bissau	11.8	75	Mauritania	8.4
28	Burundi	11.6		Uganda	8.4
	Mali	11.6		United States	8.4
30	Germany	11.5	78	Gabon	8.3
31	Somalia	11.2		Haiti	8.3
32	Montenegro	11.0		Switzerland	8.3
33	Bosnia & Herz.	10.9		Thailand	8.3
	Greece	10.9	82	Cuba	8.2
35	Poland	10.8		Martinique	8.2
36	Czech Republic	10.7		Puerto Rico	8.2
	Guinea	10.7		Virgin Islands (US)	8.2
	Japan	10.7	86	Bermuda[a]	8.1
39	Cameroon	10.6		Liberia	8.1
	Slovakia	10.6		Norway	8.1
41	Italy	10.5		Zimbabwe	8.1
	Malawi	10.5	90	India	8.0
	Portugal	10.5		Sudan	8.0
	South Sudan	10.5	92	Canada	7.8
45	Trinidad & Tobago	10.4		Luxembourg	7.8
46	Slovenia	10.3		Tanzania	7.8
47	Belgium	10.1		Turkmenistan	7.8
	Denmark	10.1			

Note: Both death and, in particular, infant mortality rates can be underestimated in certain countries where not all deaths are officially recorded.   a 2014 estimate.

Highest infant mortality
Number of deaths per 1,000 live births, 2015–20

1	Sierra Leone	106.8	23	Pakistan	58.7
2	Congo-Kinshasa	102.0	24	Swaziland	57.9
3	Angola	87.7	25	Congo-Brazzaville	56.5
4	Chad	86.8	26	Zambia	56.4
5	Guinea-Bissau	86.1	27	Liberia	52.2
6	Central African Rep.	83.5	28	Tajikistan	51.7
7	Burundi	80.1		Yemen	51.7
8	Malawi	78.2	30	Gambia, The	51.5
9	Equatorial Guinea	77.1	31	Sudan	51.3
10	Mali	76.2	32	Uganda	50.2
11	Somalia	70.9	33	Lesotho	50.1
12	South Sudan	67.5	34	Ghana	47.5
13	Guinea	67.1	35	Kenya	46.3
	Mauritania	67.1	36	Myanmar	45.4
15	Cameroon	65.3	37	Niger	45.3
	Nigeria	65.3		Papua New Guinea	45.3
17	Ivory Coast	65.1		Senegal	45.3
18	Benin	64.3	40	Turkmenistan	43.3
	Mozambique	64.3	41	Tanzania	42.9
20	Burkina Faso	61.1	42	Rwanda	42.6
21	Togo	59.7	43	Ethiopia	42.5
22	Afghanistan	59.1	44	Uzbekistan	40.4

Lowest death rates
No. deaths per 1,000 pop., 2015–20

1	United Arab Emirates	1.1
2	Qatar	1.4
3	Bahrain	2.4
4	Oman	2.6
5	Kuwait	2.8
6	Saudi Arabia	3.3
7	Brunei	3.5
	West Bank & Gaza	3.5
9	French Guiana	3.7
10	Jordan	3.8
11	Syria	3.9
12	Libya	4.3
13	Costa Rica	4.4
14	Honduras	4.5
	Nicaragua	4.5
16	Lebanon	4.6
17	Mexico	4.7
18	Ecuador	4.9
	Guam	4.9
	Guatemala	4.9
	Iraq	4.9
	Macau	4.9
	Malaysia	4.9

Lowest infant mortality
No. deaths per 1,000 live births, 2015–20

1	Singapore	1.5
2	Iceland	1.6
3	Hong Kong	1.7
4	Luxembourg	1.8
	Monaco[a]	1.8
6	Japan	1.9
7	Finland	2.1
	Sweden	2.1
9	Italy	2.3
	Norway	2.3
11	Czech Republic	2.4
	Ireland	2.4
	Portugal	2.4
14	Albania	2.5
	Bermuda[a]	2.5
	Slovenia	2.5
17	South Korea	2.6
18	Austria	2.7
	Germany	2.7
20	Belgium	2.8
	France	2.8
	Spain	2.8
23	Israel	2.9

a 2014 estimate.

Death and disease

Diabetes

*% of population aged 20–79,
2014 age-standardised estimate[a]*

1	French Polynesia	24.4
2	Saudi Arabia	23.9
3	Kuwait	23.1
4	Bahrain	21.9
5	Mauritius	21.2
6	Guam	20.1
	New Caledonia	20.1
8	Qatar	19.8
9	United Arab Emirates	19.0
10	Sudan	17.9
11	Malaysia	17.6
12	Egypt	16.6
13	Réunion	15.4
14	Lebanon	14.9
15	Turkey	14.8
16	Oman	14.5

Malaria

*Deaths per 100,000 population,
2012*

1	Chad	136
2	Central African Rep.	116
3	Niger	110
4	Nigeria	108
	Sierra Leone	108
6	Congo-Kinshasa	105
7	Congo-Brazzaville	104
8	Guinea	103
9	Burkina Faso	101
10	Angola	99
11	Guinea-Bissau	95
12	Mali	87
13	Togo	83
14	Gambia, The	82
15	Benin	79
16	Zambia	78

Cancer

*Deaths per 100,000 population,
2012 age-standardised estimate[a]*

1	Mongolia	161.0
2	Hungary	152.1
3	Armenia	150.3
4	Serbia	147.8
5	Uruguay	144.8
6	Zimbabwe	142.7
7	Macedonia	141.6
8	Kazakhstan	140.2
9	Montenegro	139.0
10	Croatia	136.7
11	Kenya	135.3
12	French Polynesia	134.4
13	Uganda	134.2
14	Poland	131.0
15	Timor-Leste	129.7
16	Lithuania	129.0
17	Latvia	128.8
	Turkey	128.8
19	New Caledonia	127.3
20	Romania	127.1
21	Slovakia	125.8
22	North Korea	125.5
23	Slovenia	125.4
24	Papua New Guinea	125.1

Tuberculosis

*Incidence per 100,000 population,
2012*

1	Sierra Leone	1,304
2	Swaziland	907
3	South Africa	857
4	Mauritania	794
5	Cambodia	764
6	Timor-Leste	758
7	Namibia	688
8	Somalia	581
9	Congo-Kinshasa	576
10	Gabon	563
11	Mozambique	553
12	Papua New Guinea	541
13	Congo-Brazzaville	530
14	Central African Rep.	520
15	Laos	514
16	North Korea	511
17	Liberia	495
18	Gambia, The	490
19	Myanmar	489
20	Angola	474
21	Philippines	461
22	Madagascar	442
23	Bangladesh	434
24	Zimbabwe	433

a Assumes that every country and region has the same age profile (the age profile of
   the world population has been used).
Note: Statistics are not available for all countries. The number of cases diagnosed and
reported depends on the quality of medical practice and administration and can be
under-reported in a number of countries.

Measles immunisation
Lowest % of children aged 12–23 months, 2013

1	Central African Rep.	25
2	South Sudan	30
3	Equatorial Guinea	42
4	Somalia	46
5	Chad	59
	Nigeria	59
7	Pakistan	61
	Syria	61
9	Ethiopia	62
	Guinea	62
11	Benin	63
	Iraq	63
	Madagascar	63
14	Congo-Brazzaville	65
	Haiti	65
16	South Africa	66
17	Niger	67
18	Guinea-Bissau	69

DPT[a] immunisation
Lowest % of children aged 12–23 months, 2013

1	Equatorial Guinea	3
2	Central African Rep.	23
3	Syria	41
4	Somalia	42
5	South Sudan	45
6	Chad	48
7	Nigeria	58
8	Vietnam	59
9	Guinea	63
10	South Africa	65
11	Haiti	68
	Iraq	68
	Papua New Guinea	68
14	Benin	69
	Congo-Brazzaville	69
16	Niger	70
17	Afghanistan	71

HIV/AIDS
Prevalence in adults aged 15–49, %, 2013

1	Swaziland	27.4
2	Lesotho	22.9
3	Botswana	21.9
4	South Africa	19.1
5	Zimbabwe	15.0
6	Namibia	14.3
7	Zambia	12.5
8	Mozambique	10.8
9	Malawi	10.3
10	Uganda	7.4
11	Kenya	6.0
12	Tanzania	5.0
13	Cameroon	4.3
14	Gabon	3.9
15	Central African Rep.	3.8
16	Guinea-Bissau	3.7
17	Bahamas	3.2
	Nigeria	3.2
19	Rwanda	2.9
20	Ivory Coast	2.7
21	Chad	2.5
	Congo-Brazzaville	2.5
23	Angola	2.4
24	Togo	2.3
25	South Sudan	2.2

AIDS
Deaths per 100,000 population, 2012

1	Lesotho	755
2	South Africa	449
3	Swaziland	443
4	Mozambique	305
5	Zimbabwe	288
6	Malawi	287
7	Botswana	282
8	Namibia	219
9	Zambia	215
10	Equatorial Guinea	194
11	Uganda	174
12	Tanzania	167
13	Cameroon	159
14	Ivory Coast	157
15	Gabon	143
16	Nigeria	142
17	Guinea-Bissau	136
18	Bahamas	134
19	Kenya	133
20	Congo-Brazzaville	119
	South Sudan	119
22	Chad	116
23	Togo	108
24	Haiti	73
25	Angola	60

a Diphtheria, pertussis and tetanus.

Health

Highest health spending
As % of GDP, 2013

1	United States	17.1
2	Netherlands	12.9
3	Moldova	11.8
	Sierra Leone	11.8
5	France	11.7
6	Lesotho	11.5
	Switzerland	11.5
8	Germany	11.3
9	Belgium	11.2
10	Rwanda	11.1
11	Austria	11.0
12	Canada	10.9
13	Denmark	10.6
	Serbia	10.6
15	Japan	10.3
16	Liberia	10.0
17	Costa Rica	9.9
18	Greece	9.8
	Uganda	9.8
20	Brazil	9.7
	New Zealand	9.7
	Portugal	9.7
	Sweden	9.7
24	Bosnia & Herz.	9.6
	Norway	9.6

Lowest health spending
As % of GDP, 2013

1	Timor-Leste	1.3
2	Myanmar	1.8
3	Laos	2.0
	Turkmenistan	2.0
5	Qatar	2.2
	South Sudan	2.2
7	Brunei	2.5
8	Oman	2.6
9	Pakistan	2.8
10	Kuwait	2.9
11	Eritrea	3.0
12	Indonesia	3.1
13	Saudi Arabia	3.2
	Sri Lanka	3.2
	United Arab Emirates	3.2
	Syria	3.3
17	Venezuela	3.4
18	Congo-Kinshasa	3.5
	Equatorial Guinea	3.5
20	Chad	3.6
21	Bangladesh	3.7
22	Angola	3.8
	Gabon	3.8
	Mauritania	3.8
25	Central African Rep.	3.9
	Nigeria	3.9

Highest pop. per doctor
2013 or latest[a]

1	Liberia	71,429
2	Malawi	52,632
	Niger	52,632
4	Ethiopia	45,455
	Sierra Leone	45,455
6	Tanzania	32,258
7	Somalia	28,571
8	Gambia, The	26,316
9	Mozambique	25,000
10	Guinea-Bissau	22,222
11	Burkina Faso	21,277
12	Togo	18,868
13	Rwanda	17,857
14	Papua New Guinea	17,241
15	Benin	16,949
	Senegal	16,949
17	Timor-Leste	13,699
18	Mali	12,048
	Zimbabwe	12,048
20	Congo-Brazzaville	10,526

Lowest pop. per doctor
2013 or latest[a]

1	Qatar	129
2	Monaco	140
3	Cuba	149
4	Greece	162
5	Spain	202
6	Belgium	205
7	Austria	207
8	Russia	232
9	Georgia	234
	Norway	234
11	Lithuania	243
12	Portugal	244
13	Switzerland	247
14	Belarus	255
	Sweden	255
16	Andorra	256
17	Germany	257
18	Argentina	259
	Bulgaria	259
20	Italy	266

a 2010–13

Obesity[a]

% of adult population aged 18 and over, 2014

Male

1	Qatar	40.0
2	Kuwait	35.5
3	United Arab Emirates	33.8
4	United States	32.6
5	Fiji	30.8
6	Bahrain	30.5
7	Saudi Arabia	29.9
8	Bahamas	29.7
9	Andorra	28.5
10	Australia	28.4
11	New Zealand	27.7
12	Oman	27.2
13	United Kingdom	26.9
14	Canada	26.8
15	Libya	26.6
	Luxembourg	26.6
17	Lebanon	26.3
18	Czech Republic	26.2
19	Ireland	25.9
20	Malta	24.6
	Norway	24.6
	Slovakia	24.6
	Slovenia	24.6
24	Barbados	24.4

Female

1	Qatar	49.7
2	Kuwait	45.9
3	United Arab Emirates	45.1
4	Bahrain	42.8
5	Bahamas	42.5
6	Fiji	42.3
7	Saudi Arabia	41.4
8	Libya	39.5
9	Jordan	38.6
10	Barbados	38.2
11	Trinidad & Tobago	38.0
12	Lebanon	37.7
	Oman	37.7
14	Egypt	37.5
15	South Africa	37.3
16	Turkey	35.8
17	Jamaica	35.7
18	United States	34.7
19	Tunisia	33.8
20	Papua New Guinea	33.4
21	Mexico	33.1
22	New Zealand	30.8
23	Andorra	30.5
24	United Kingdom	29.2

Food supply

Average per person per day, 2013 or latest

Highest calories available

1	Belgium	3,793
2	Austria	3,784
3	Turkey	3,680
4	United States	3,639
5	Israel	3,619
6	Ireland	3,591
7	Luxembourg	3,568
	Montenegro	3,568
9	Egypt	3,557
10	Germany	3,539
	Italy	3,539
12	France	3,524
13	Switzerland	3,487
14	Poland	3,485
15	Norway	3,484
16	Kuwait	3,471
17	Lithuania	3,463
18	Portugal	3,456
19	Greece	3,433
20	Canada	3,419

Lowest calories available

1	Zambia	1,930
2	Madagascar	2,052
3	Timor-Leste	2,083
4	Namibia	2,086
5	Afghanistan	2,090
6	Haiti	2,091
7	North Korea	2,094
8	Tajikistan	2,101
9	Chad	2,110
	Zimbabwe	2,110
11	Ethiopia	2,131
12	Rwanda	2,148
13	Congo-Kinshasa	2,195
14	Kenya	2,206
15	Tanzania	2,208
16	Yemen	2,223
17	Liberia	2,251
18	Bolivia	2,254
19	Swaziland	2,275
20	Uganda	2,279

a Defined as body mass index of 30 or more – see page 248.

Marriage and divorce

Highest marriage rates
Number of marriages per 1,000 population, 2013 or latest available year

1	Tajikistan	12.4	22	Macau	7.0
2	Egypt	11.2	23	Lithuania	6.9
3	Iran	10.9	24	Georgia	6.8
4	Jordan	10.3		Macedonia	6.8
	Kyrgyzstan	10.3		Moldova	6.8
6	Uzbekistan	10.1		Singapore	6.8
7	Guam	9.9		United States	6.8
8	Bahamas	9.8	29	Malta	6.7
9	Kazakhstan	9.7	30	Israel	6.6
10	Bermuda	9.6	31	South Korea	6.5
	China	9.6	32	Kuwait	6.4
12	West Bank & Gaza	9.4	33	French Polynesia	6.3
13	Azerbaijan	8.5	34	Montenegro	6.2
	Russia	8.5	35	Ukraine	6.1
15	Mauritius	8.3	36	Armenia	6.0
16	Albania	8.2	37	Latvia	5.7
17	Belarus	8.1	38	Guatemala	5.6
18	Turkey	7.9	39	Channel Islands[a]	5.5
19	Hong Kong	7.7		Costa Rica	5.5
20	Jamaica	7.5		Cuba	5.5
21	Cyprus	7.3	42	Australia	5.4

Lowest marriage rates
Number of marriages per 1,000 population, 2013 or latest available year

1	Qatar	1.9	22	Netherlands	4.2
2	French Guiana	2.5	23	Czech Republic	4.3
3	Peru	2.8		Dominican Rep.	4.3
	Uruguay	2.8	25	Canada	4.4
5	Bulgaria	2.9	26	Estonia	4.5
6	Argentina	3.1		Greece	4.5
7	Luxembourg	3.2		Ireland	4.5
	Martinique	3.2		United Kingdom	4.5
9	Portugal	3.3	30	Austria	4.6
10	New Caledonia	3.4		Iceland	4.6
	Slovenia	3.4		New Zealand	4.6
12	Guadeloupe	3.5	33	Germany	4.7
	Italy	3.5	34	Bosnia & Herz.	4.8
	Spain	3.5		Croatia	4.8
	Venezuela	3.5		Serbia	4.8
16	Belgium	3.6		Slovakia	4.8
	Hungary	3.6	38	Norway	4.9
18	Andorra	3.7	39	Liechtenstein	5.0
	Panama	3.7		Mexico	5.0
20	Chile	3.8			
	France	3.8			

Note: The data are based on latest available figures (no earlier than 2008) and hence will be affected by the population age structure at the time. Marriage rates refer to registered marriages only and, therefore, reflect the customs surrounding registry and efficiency of administration.   a Jersey and Guernsey only.

Highest divorce rates
Number of divorces per 1,000 population, 2013 or latest available year

1	Guam	4.6	23	Australia	2.2
2	Russia	4.5		Germany	2.2
3	Belarus	4.1		Hungary	2.2
4	Latvia	3.5		Spain	2.2
	Lithuania	3.5		Switzerland	2.2
6	Moldova	3.0	28	Canada	2.1
7	Cuba	2.9		Netherlands	2.1
8	Costa Rica	2.8		United Kingdom	2.1
	Denmark	2.8	31	Austria	2.0
	United States	2.8		France	2.0
11	Kazakhstan	2.7		Iran	2.0
12	Jordan	2.6		Kuwait	2.0
13	Belgium	2.5		Luxembourg	2.0
	Czech Republic	2.5		Macau	2.0
	Sweden	2.5		New Zealand	2.0
16	Estonia	2.4		Norway	2.0
	Finland	2.4		Slovakia	2.0
	Liechtenstein	2.4	40	Egypt	1.9
	Portugal	2.4		Singapore	1.9
20	Bermuda	2.3	42	China	1.8
	Cyprus	2.3		Dominican Rep.	1.8
	South Korea	2.3		Japan	1.8

Lowest divorce rates
Number of divorces per 1,000 population, 2013 or latest available year

1	Chile	0.1	19	Azerbaijan	1.2
2	Guatemala	0.3		Bahamas	1.2
3	Peru	0.4		Greece	1.2
4	Bosnia & Herz.	0.6		Mongolia	1.2
	Ireland	0.6		New Caledonia	1.2
	Uzbekistan	0.6		Slovenia	1.2
7	Montenegro	0.8	25	Albania	1.3
	Qatar	0.8		Croatia	1.3
9	Italy	0.9	27	Romania	1.5
	Jamaica	0.9		West Bank & Gaza	1.5
	Macedonia	0.9	29	Bulgaria	1.6
	Mexico	0.9		Georgia	1.6
	Tajikistan	0.9		Iceland	1.6
14	Armenia	1.0		Kyrgyzstan	1.6
	Serbia	1.0		Mauritius	1.6
16	Malta	1.1		Turkey	1.6
	Panama	1.1	35	Israel	1.7
	Ukraine	1.1		Poland	1.7

Households, living costs and giving

Number of households
Biggest, m, 2013

1	China	438.9	21	Turkey	20.3
2	India	257.8	22	Ethiopia	20.0
3	United States	122.5	23	Spain	18.5
4	Indonesia	63.3	24	South Korea	18.2
5	Brazil	60.3	25	Ukraine	17.8
6	Russia	55.7	26	South Africa	14.9
7	Japan	52.7	27	Canada	13.6
8	Germany	41.0		Poland	13.6
9	Bangladesh	35.8	29	Argentina	12.9
10	Nigeria	35.7	30	Colombia	12.8
11	Pakistan	31.1	31	Kenya	10.2
12	Mexico	29.8	32	Australia	8.5
13	France	28.8	33	Netherlands	7.6
14	United Kingdom	26.8		Peru	7.6
15	Italy	26.2		Taiwan	7.6
16	Vietnam	25.3	36	Venezuela	7.5
17	Iran	22.6	37	Romania	7.1
18	Egypt	21.9	38	Malaysia	6.9
19	Philippines	21.8		Morocco	6.9
20	Thailand	21.7	40	Algeria	6.6

Average household size, people

Biggest, 2013 or latest

1	Senegal	9.6
2	Guinea	8.8
3	Angola	8.6
4	Gambia, The	8.3
5	Chad	8.0
	Equatorial Guinea	8.0
7	Gabon	7.9
8	Mauritania	7.8
9	Oman	7.0
10	Guinea-Bissau	6.9
11	Congo-Kinshasa	6.8
	Kuwait	6.8
	Pakistan	6.8
14	Yemen	6.7
15	Iraq	6.5
16	Tajikistan	6.4
	Turkmenistan	6.4
18	Libya	6.2
19	Bahrain	5.9
	Saudi Arabia	5.9

Smallest, 2013 or latest

1	Germany	2.0
2	Denmark	2.1
	Finland	2.1
4	Estonia	2.2
	France	2.2
	Netherlands	2.2
	Norway	2.2
	Switzerland	2.2
9	Austria	2.3
	Belgium	2.3
	Italy	2.3
	Latvia	2.3
	Sweden	2.3
14	Belarus	2.4
	Bermuda	2.4
	Bulgaria	2.4
	Czech Republic	2.4
	Hungary	2.4
	Japan	2.4
	Lithuania	2.4
	Slovakia	2.4
	Slovenia	2.4
	United Kingdom	2.4

a The cost of living index shown is compiled by the Economist Intelligence Unit for use by companies in determining expatriate compensation: it is a comparison of the cost of maintaining a typical international lifestyle in the country rather than a comparison of the purchasing power of a citizen of the country. The index is based on typical urban prices an international executive and family will face abroad. The prices

Cost of living[a]

December 2014, US = 100

Highest

1	Singapore	129
2	France	126
3	Norway	124
4	Australia	120
5	Switzerland	116
6	Denmark	115
7	Hong Kong	113
	South Korea	113
9	Finland	109
	Japan	109
	United Kingdom	109
12	New Zealand	105
13	Austria	103
	Israel	103
	New Caledonia	103
16	Ireland	100
	United States	100
18	Spain	95
19	Italy	94
20	Belgium	93
	Sweden	93
22	Canada	92
23	Germany	91
	Iceland	91
25	Netherlands	87

Lowest

1	Pakistan	44
2	Venezuela	45
3	India	48
4	Iran	49
	Syria	49
6	Nepal	51
7	Algeria	52
8	Romania	54
	Ukraine	54
10	Kazakhstan	55
	Panama	55
	Saudi Arabia	55
13	Oman	58
14	Sri Lanka	59
15	Kuwait	60
	Nigeria	60
	Zambia	60
18	Paraguay	61
	Qatar	61
	South Africa	61
21	Uzbekistan	62
22	Bahrain	63
	Egypt	63
	Hungary	63
25	Serbia	64

World Giving Index[b]

Top givers, % of population, 2014

1	Myanmar	64		16	Austria	48
	United States	64		17	Denmark	47
3	Canada	60		18	Iran	46
	Ireland	60		19	Jamaica	45
5	New Zealand	58		20	Nigeria	44
6	Australia	56			Thailand	44
7	Malaysia	55		22	Cyprus	43
	United Kingdom	55			Finland	43
9	Sri Lanka	54			Guatemala	43
	Trinidad & Tobago	54			Turkmenistan	43
11	Netherlands	53		26	Dominican Rep.	42
12	Indonesia	51			Germany	42
13	Iceland	50			Uzbekistan	42
14	Kenya	49		29	Philippines	41
	Malta	49			Syria	41

are for products of international comparable quality found in a supermarket or department store. Prices found in local markets and bazaars are not used unless the available merchandise is of the specified quality and the shopping area itself is safe for executive and family members. New York City prices are used as the base, so United States = 100.

b Three criteria are used to assess giving: in the previous month those surveyed either gave money to charity, gave time to those in need or helped a stranger.

Telephones, computers and the internet

Telephones
Telephone lines per 100 population, 2013

1	Monaco	123.8	16	Andorra	48.7
2	Bermuda	110.2	17	Canada	48.1
3	Virgin Islands (US)	71.3	18	Japan	48.0
4	Taiwan	71.2	19	Greece	47.9
5	Hong Kong	63.1	20	Belarus	47.8
6	South Korea	61.6	21	Slovenia	47.7
7	France	60.8	22	Australia	44.3
8	Germany	58.9	23	Ireland	44.0
9	Switzerland	56.9	24	Portugal	42.7
10	Malta	53.9	25	Netherlands	42.5
11	United Kingdom	52.9	26	United States	42.2
12	Barbados	52.3	27	Belgium	41.4
13	Iceland	51.0	28	Spain	41.3
14	Luxembourg	50.5	29	New Zealand	41.1
15	Liechtenstein	49.6			

Mobile telephones
Subscribers per 100 population, 2013

1	Macau	304.1	18	Estonia	159.7
2	Hong Kong	237.4	19	Italy	158.8
3	Latvia	228.4	20	Austria	156.2
4	Gabon	214.8	21	Singapore	155.9
5	Kuwait	190.3	22	Oman	154.7
6	Kazakhstan	184.7	23	Uruguay	154.6
7	Saudi Arabia	184.2	24	Russia	152.8
8	Mali	181.2	25	Qatar	152.6
9	United Arab Emirates	171.9	26	Lithuania	151.3
10	Finland	171.6	27	Poland	149.1
11	Bahrain	165.9	28	Luxembourg	148.6
12	Libya	165.0	29	Costa Rica	146.0
13	Panama	163.0	30	South Africa	145.6
14	Argentina	162.5	31	Bulgaria	145.2
15	Suriname	161.1	32	Trinidad & Tobago	144.9
16	Botswana	160.6	33	Malaysia	144.7
17	Montenegro	160.0	34	Bermuda	144.3

Computers
Units sold per '000 population, 2013

1	Hong Kong	336.6	14	Singapore	165.6
2	United States	322.5	15	Taiwan	159.4
3	Norway	297.0	16	Germany	150.7
4	Australia	296.5	17	Chile	146.9
5	United Arab Emirates	278.2	18	New Zealand	140.7
6	Denmark	232.7	19	Spain	134.4
7	Canada	205.9	20	Belgium	132.7
8	Sweden	192.7	21	Malaysia	127.4
9	France	188.0	22	Saudi Arabia	125.9
10	United Kingdom	184.0	23	Israel	123.6
11	Switzerland	180.3	24	Finland	109.3
12	Netherlands	170.5	25	Portugal	105.2
13	Austria	167.8	26	Russia	105.1

Internet users
Per 100 population, 2013

1	Iceland	96.6	26	Austria	80.6
2	Bermuda	95.3	27	Estonia	80.0
3	Norway	95.1		Taiwan	80.0
4	Sweden	94.8	29	Ireland	78.3
5	Denmark	94.6	30	Slovakia	77.9
6	Andorra	94.0	31	Kuwait	75.5
	Netherlands	94.0	32	Latvia	75.2
8	Liechtenstein	93.8	33	Barbados	75.0
	Luxembourg	93.8	34	Hong Kong	74.2
10	Finland	91.5	35	Czech Republic	74.1
11	Monaco	90.7	36	Puerto Rico	73.9
12	Bahrain	90.0	37	Singapore	73.0
13	United Kingdom	89.8	38	Slovenia	72.7
14	United Arab Emirates	88.0	39	Hungary	72.6
15	Switzerland	86.7	40	Bahamas	72.0
16	Japan	86.3	41	Spain	71.6
17	Canada	85.8	42	Israel	70.8
18	Qatar	85.3	43	Lebanon	70.5
19	South Korea	84.8	44	Lithuania	68.5
20	United States	84.2	45	Bosnia & Herz.	67.9
21	Germany	84.0	46	Malaysia	67.0
22	Australia	83.0	47	Croatia	66.8
23	New Zealand	82.8	48	Chile	66.5
24	Belgium	82.2		Oman	66.5
25	France	81.9	50	Macau	65.8

Broadband
Fixed-broadband subscribers per 100 population, 2013

1	Bermuda	61.4	23	New Zealand	29.2
2	Monaco	44.7	24	Japan	28.9
3	Switzerland	42.5	25	Macau	26.8
4	Liechtenstein	40.7	26	Estonia	26.5
5	Denmark	40.2	27	Greece	26.2
6	Netherlands	40.1	28	Austria	26.1
7	France	38.8	29	Singapore	26.0
8	Norway	38.1	30	Israel	25.9
9	South Korea	38.0	31	Spain	25.8
10	United Kingdom	35.8	32	Australia	25.0
11	Iceland	35.2		Slovenia	25.0
12	Andorra	35.0	34	Hungary	24.9
13	Germany	34.6	35	Ireland	24.2
14	Belgium	34.4		Taiwan	24.2
15	Luxembourg	33.3	37	Barbados	23.8
16	Canada	33.2		Portugal	23.8
17	Malta	32.8	39	Latvia	23.5
18	Sweden	32.6	40	Italy	22.3
19	Finland	30.8	41	Lithuania	22.0
	Hong Kong	30.8	42	Croatia	21.5
21	Belarus	29.8	43	Uruguay	21.1
22	United States	29.3	44	Cyprus	19.9

Arts and entertainment

Music sales

Total including downloads, $m, 2014

1	United States	4,898
2	Japan	2,628
3	Germany	1,405
4	United Kingdom	1,335
5	France	843
6	Australia	376
7	Canada	343
8	South Korea	266
9	Brazil	247
10	Italy	235
11	Netherlands	205
12	Sweden	189
13	Spain	181
14	Mexico	130
15	Norway	120
16	Austria	115
17	Belgium	111
18	Switzerland	108
19	China	105
20	India	100
21	Denmark	98
22	Poland	79
23	Russia	73
24	South Africa	70
25	Finland	65
26	Argentina	64
27	Taiwan	58
28	New Zealand	52
29	Turkey	48
30	Thailand	43

$ per person, 2014

1	Norway	23.5
2	United Kingdom	21.0
3	Japan	20.7
4	Sweden	19.5
5	Denmark	17.5
6	Germany	17.3
7	Australia	16.7
8	United States	15.4
9	Austria	14.0
10	Switzerland	13.4
11	France	12.7
12	Finland	12.2
13	Netherlands	12.1
14	New Zealand	11.8
15	Belgium	10.7
16	Canada	9.8
17	Ireland	8.5
18	South Korea	5.4
19	Hong Kong	5.1
20	Italy	3.8
	Spain	3.8
22	Taiwan	2.5
23	Singapore	2.4
24	Greece	2.1
	Poland	2.1
26	Czech Republic	2.0
27	Croatia	1.8
28	Hungary	1.7
29	Argentina	1.5
	Slovakia	1.5

Book publishing

New titles per million population, 2013

1	United Kingdom	2,875
2	Slovenia	1,831
	Taiwan	1,831
4	Spain	1,626
5	Georgia	1,547
6	Czech Republic	1,509
7	Norway	1,275
8	Australia	1,176
9	Germany	1,156
10	France	1,008
11	Italy[a]	1,002
12	United States	959
13	Hungary	920
14	South Korea[a]	795

15	Finland	793
16	Austria	757
17	Russia	699
18	Malaysia[a]	639
19	Argentina	614
20	Japan	613
21	Turkey[a]	561
22	New Zealand[a]	479
23	Poland	353
24	China	325
25	Colombia	229
26	Mexico	200
27	Indonesia	119
28	Brazil	104

a 2012

Cinema attendances

Total visits, m, 2013

1	India	2,920.7
2	United States	1,339.0
3	China	487.1
4	Mexico	228.7
5	France	193.6
6	Russia	177.1
7	South Korea	165.6
8	United Kingdom	165.5
9	Brazil	164.2
10	Japan	155.9
11	Germany	129.7
12	Italy	106.7
13	Australia	84.2
14	Spain	78.2
15	Malaysia	65.6
16	Philippines	51.1
17	Turkey	50.4
18	Argentina	46.9
19	Colombia	45.1
20	Indonesia	43.0
21	Poland	36.3
22	Peru	34.6
23	Venezuela	32.1
24	Netherlands	30.8
25	Singapore	29.4
26	Thailand	24.4
27	Iran	22.0
28	South Africa	21.4
29	Chile	21.2
30	Belgium	20.9

Visits per person, 2013

1	Iceland[a]	5.0
2	Singapore	4.5
3	United States	4.2
4	Australia	3.6
5	South Korea	3.3
6	Ireland	3.2
7	France	3.0
8	Luxembourg[a]	2.6
	United Kingdom	2.6
10	Denmark	2.4
	Norway	2.4
12	India	2.3
13	Malaysia	2.2
14	Estonia	2.0
	Malta[a]	2.0
16	Belgium	1.9
	Mexico	1.9
	United Arab Emirates	1.9
19	Austria	1.8
	Italy	1.8
	Netherlands	1.8
22	Belarus	1.7
	Israel	1.7
	Spain	1.7
	Sweden	1.7
	Switzerland	1.7
27	Germany	1.6
28	Finland	1.4

Top Oscar winners

		Awards	Nominations
1	*Ben-Hur* (1959)	11	12
	Titanic (1997)	11	14
	The Lord of the Rings: The Return of the King (2003)	11	11
4	*West Side Story* (1961)	10	11
5	*Gigi* (1958)	9	9
	The Last Emperor (1987)	9	9
	The English Patient (1996)	9	12
8	*Gone With the Wind* (1939)	8	13
	From Here to Eternity (1953)	8	13
	On the Waterfront (1954)	8	12
	My Fair Lady (1964)	8	12
	Cabaret[b] (1972)	8	10
	Gandhi (1982)	8	11
	Amadeus (1984)	8	11
	Slumdog Millionaire (2008)	8	10

a 2012   b Did not win best picture award.

The press

Daily newspapers
Copies per '000 population, 2013

1	Luxembourg[a]	670	16	Germany	214
2	Hong Kong	527	17	Denmark	191
3	Liechtenstein[a]	500	18	United Kingdom	188
4	Kuwait[a]	417	19	Canada	160
5	Japan	370	20	Moldova[a]	159
6	Switzerland	355	21	Belarus	155
7	Austria	352	22	Taiwan	153
8	Iceland[a]	323	23	Macedonia	147
	Norway	323	24	Estonia	143
10	Finland	305		France	143
11	Sweden	269		United States	143
12	Singapore	260	27	Latvia	138
13	Malta[a]	250	28	Israel	137
14	South Korea	246	29	Belgium	136
15	Netherlands	228			

Press freedom[b]
Scores, 1 = best, 100 = worst, 2014

Most free			Least free		
1	Finland	7.52	1	Eritrea	84.86
2	Norway	7.75	2	North Korea	83.25
3	Denmark	8.24	3	Turkmenistan	80.83
4	Netherlands	9.22	4	Syria	77.29
5	Sweden	9.47	5	China	73.55
6	New Zealand	10.06	6	Vietnam	72.63
7	Austria	10.85	7	Sudan	72.34
8	Canada	10.99	8	Iran	72.32
9	Jamaica	11.18	9	Somalia	72.31
10	Estonia	11.19	10	Laos	71.25
11	Ireland	11.20	11	Cuba	70.21
12	Germany	11.47	12	Yemen	66.36
13	Czech Republic	11.62	13	Equatorial Guinea	66.23
14	Slovakia	11.66	14	Uzbekistan	61.14
15	Belgium	11.98	15	Sri Lanka	60.28
16	Costa Rica	12.26	16	Saudi Arabia	59.41
17	Namibia	12.50	17	Bahrain	58.69
18	Poland	12.71	18	Azerbaijan	58.41
19	Luxembourg	13.61	19	Rwanda	56.57
20	Switzerland	13.85	20	Kazakhstan	53.46
21	Iceland	13.87	21	Pakistan	50.46
22	Ghana	15.50	22	Egypt	50.17
23	Uruguay	15.94	23	Belarus	47.98
24	Cyprus	16.52	24	Iraq	47.76
25	Australia	17.03	25	Swaziland	47.28
26	Portugal	17.11	26	Libya	45.99
27	Liechtenstein	17.67	27	Singapore	45.87
28	Latvia	18.12	28	Russia	44.97

a 2012   b Based on data for deaths and violence against journalists, and attacks on organisations, plus 87 questions on topics such as media independence, monopolies, legal status and censorship, answered by journalists and media experts.

Nobel prize winners: 1901–2014

Peace (two or more)

1	United States	19
2	United Kingdom	12
3	France	9
4	Sweden	5
5	Belgium	4
	Germany	4
7	Austria	3
	Norway	3
	South Africa	3
	Switzerland	3
11	Argentina	2
	Egypt	2
	India	2
	Israel	2
	Russia	2

Economics[a]

1	United States	37
2	United Kingdom	9
3	France	2
	Norway	2
	Sweden	2
6	Denmark	1
	Germany	1
	Israel	1
	Netherlands	1
	Russia	1

Literature (three or more)

1	France	16
2	United States	12
3	United Kingdom	11
4	Germany	8
5	Sweden	7
6	Italy	5
	Spain	5
8	Norway	3
	Poland	3
	Russia	3

Medicine (three or more)

1	United States	55
2	United Kingdom	25
3	Germany	15
4	France	8
5	Sweden	7
6	Switzerland	6
7	Austria	5
	Denmark	5

Physics

1	United States	53
2	United Kingdom	21
3	Germany	19
4	France	10
5	Japan	6
	Netherlands	6
	Russia	6
8	Sweden	4
	Switzerland	4
10	Austria	3
	Italy	3
12	Canada	2
	Denmark	2
14	Australia	1
	Belgium	1
	China	1
	India	1
	Ireland	1
	Pakistan	1
	Poland	1

Chemistry

1	United States	48
2	United Kingdom	23
3	Germany	16
4	France	7
5	Switzerland	6
6	Japan	5
	Sweden	5
8	Canada	4
9	Israel	3
10	Argentina	1
	Austria	1
	Belgium	1
	Czech Republic	1
	Denmark	1
	Finland	1
	Italy	1
	Netherlands	1
	Norway	1
	Russia	1

a Since 1969.
Notes: Prizes by country of residence at time awarded. When prizes have been shared in the same field, one credit given to each country.

Sports champions

World Cup winners and finalists

Men's football	Winner	Runner-up
1 Brazil	5	2
2 Germany	4	4
3 Italy	4	2
4 Argentina	2	3
5 Uruguay	2	0
6 France	1	1
7 England	1	0
Spain	1	0
9 Netherlands	0	3
10 Czechoslovakia[a]	0	2
Hungary	0	2
12 Sweden	0	1

Women's football	Winner	Runner-up
1 Germany	2	1
United States	2	1
3 Norway	1	1
4 Japan	1	0
5 Brazil	0	1
Sweden	0	1
China	0	1

Men's cricket	Winner	Runner-up
1 Australia	5	2
2 India	2	1
West Indies	2	1
4 Sri Lanka	1	2
5 Pakistan	1	1
6 England	0	3
7 New Zealand	0	1

Men's rugby	Winner	Runner-up
1 Australia	2	1
New Zealand	2	1
3 South Africa	2	0
4 England	1	2
5 France	0	3

Men's tennis[b]	Winner	Runner-up
1 United States	32	29
2 Australia	28	20
3 Great Britain	9	10
4 France	9	8
5 Sweden	7	5
6 Spain	5	4
7 Czech Republic[c]	3	2
Germany	3	2
9 Russia	2	3
10 Italy	1	6
11 Croatia	1	0

Note: Data to May 2015. a Until 1993. b Davis Cup. c One title as Czechoslovakia.

Olympic winter games

Medals won, 2014	Gold	Silver	Bronze
1 Russia	13	11	9
2 Norway	11	5	10
3 Canada	10	10	5
4 United States	9	7	12
5 Netherlands	8	7	9
6 Germany	8	6	5
7 Switzerland	6	3	2
8 Belarus	5	0	1
9 Austria	4	8	5
10 France	4	4	7
11 Poland	4	1	1
12 China	3	4	2
13 South Korea	3	3	2
14 Sweden	2	7	6
15 Czech Republic	2	4	2
16 Slovenia	2	2	4
17 Japan	1	4	3
18 Finland	1	3	1
19 United Kingdom	1	1	2
20 Ukraine	1	0	1
21 Slovakia	1	0	0
22 Italy	0	2	6
23 Latvia	0	2	2
24 Australia	0	2	1
25 Croatia	0	1	0

Overall medals won, 1924–2014	Gold	Silver	Bronze
1 Norway	118	111	100
2 United States	96	102	83
3 Germany	86	84	58
4 Soviet Union (1952–88)	78	57	59
5 Canada	62	55	53
6 Austria	59	78	81
7 Sweden	50	40	54
8 Switzerland	50	40	48
9 Russia	49	40	35
10 Finland	42	62	57
11 East Germany (1968–88)	39	36	35
12 Netherlands	37	38	35
13 Italy	37	34	43
14 France	31	31	45
15 South Korea	26	17	10
16 China	12	22	19
17 West Germany (1968–88)	11	15	13
18 Japan	10	15	18
19 United Kingdom	10	4	12
20 Unified Team[a] (1992)	9	6	8

a Former Soviet states of Armenia, Belarus, Kazakhstan, Russia, Ukraine and Uzbekistan.

Vices

Beer drinkers
Retail sales, litres per person, 2013

1	Czech Republic	145.4
2	Germany	113.3
3	Austria	108.4
4	Estonia	102.4
5	Poland	98.7
6	Romania	95.6
7	Ireland	94.3
8	Lithuania	89.3
9	Luxembourg[a]	85.7
10	Belgium	82.4
11	Finland	81.4
12	Slovenia	81.1
13	Australia	79.5
14	Croatia	78.7
15	Latvia	77.2
16	United States	76.8
17	Bulgaria	75.9
18	United Kingdom	73.9
19	Slovakia	73.6
20	Hungary	72.8
21	Spain	71.6
22	Canada	67.6
23	Russia	67.3
24	Serbia	67.2

Smokers
Av. ann. consumption of cigarettes per person per day, 2013

1	Lebanon	8.0
2	Belarus	7.4
3	Russia	6.8
4	Serbia	6.4
5	Slovenia	5.5
6	Czech Republic	5.4
	Macedonia	5.4
8	China	5.1
	Moldova	5.1
10	South Korea	4.9
11	Ukraine	4.7
12	Bosnia & Herz.	4.6
13	Greece	4.5
14	Bulgaria	4.4
15	Austria	4.3
	Georgia	4.3
	Kuwait	4.3
	Taiwan	4.3
19	Japan	4.2
20	Estonia	3.9
21	Azerbaijan	3.7
	Switzerland	3.7
23	Armenia	3.6
	Belgium	3.6

Gambling losses[b]
Total, $bn, 2014

1	United States	148.4
2	China[c]	99.1
3	Japan	31.3
4	Italy	23.2
5	United Kingdom	22.9
6	Australia	19.8
7	Germany	14.4
8	Canada	13.5
9	France	12.8
10	Spain	11.4
11	Singapore	9.1
12	South Korea	7.9
13	Argentina	3.1
14	Netherlands	3.0
15	Malaysia	2.9
	Sweden	2.9
17	Brazil	2.8
18	Turkey	2.7
19	South Africa	2.6
20	Finland	2.4

Per person, $, 2014

1	Australia	1,105
2	Singapore	1,065
3	United States	614
4	New Zealand	581
5	Finland	554
6	Ireland	488
7	Norway	472
8	Italy	451
9	Canada	444
10	United Kingdom	443
11	Sweden	372
12	Switzerland	338
13	Denmark	327
14	Luxembourg	325
15	Spain	313
16	Japan	292
17	Greece	250
18	France	245
19	Austria	234
20	Netherlands	220

a 2012   b Data according to H2 Gambling Capital – May 2015.
c Includes Macau and Hong Kong.

Crime and punishment

Murders
Homicides per 100,000 pop., 2012 or latest

1	Honduras	91.0
2	Venezuela	53.6
3	Virgin Islands (US)	52.6
4	El Salvador	41.5
5	Jamaica	39.1
6	Lesotho	38.0
7	Guatemala	34.6
8	Colombia	30.7
	South Africa	30.7
10	Bahamas	29.7
11	Trinidad & Tobago	28.3
12	Brazil	26.5
13	Puerto Rico	26.5
14	Dominican Rep.	22.0
15	Mexico	21.5
16	Namibia	17.5
17	Swaziland	17.4
18	Panama	17.2
19	Botswana	15.4
20	South Sudan	14.4

Robberies
Per 100,000 pop., 2012 or latest

1	Belgium	1,737
2	Argentina	975
3	Mexico	618
4	Costa Rica	522
5	Brazil	493
6	Nicaragua	488
7	Chile	468
8	Uruguay	454
9	Trinidad & Tobago	332
10	Panama	264
11	Peru	255
12	Honduras	248
13	Paraguay	224
14	Spain	207
15	Barbados	196
16	France	194
17	Portugal	175
18	Colombia	173
19	Bolivia	137
20	Kazakhstan	125

Prisoners
Total prison pop., 2015 or latest

1	United States	2,217,000
2	China	1,657,812
3	Russia	673,818
4	Brazil	581,507
5	India	411,992
6	Thailand	308,093
7	Mexico	255,638
8	Iran	225,624
9	Indonesia	167,163
10	Turkey	165,033
11	South Africa	157,824
12	Vietnam	142,636
13	Colombia	116,760
14	Philippines	110,925
15	United Kingdom	94,953
16	Ethiopia	93,044
17	Poland	78,139
18	Pakistan	74,944
19	Morocco	72,816
20	Peru	71,913
21	Ukraine	71,811
22	Bangladesh	71,606
23	France	66,761
24	Spain	65,604
25	Argentina	64,288
26	Taiwan	62,327
27	Egypt	62,000

Per 100,000 pop., 2015 or latest

1	United States	698
2	Virgin Islands (US)	542
3	Turkmenistan	522
4	Cuba	510
5	Rwanda	492
6	Russia	468
7	Thailand	457
8	El Salvador	447
9	Guam	422
10	Bermuda	411
11	Panama	392
12	Bahamas	379
13	Trinidad & Tobago	362
14	Costa Rica	352
15	Belarus	335
	Puerto Rico	335
17	Barbados	318
18	Lithuania	315
19	Iran	290
	South Africa	290
21	Brazil	289
	Swaziland	289
23	Uruguay	282
24	Kazakhstan	275
25	Mongolia	274
26	Taiwan	266
27	Latvia	264

War and peace

Defence spending

As % of GDP, 2014

1	Afghanistan	14.6	13	Bahrain		3.9
2	Oman	12.0		Iran		3.9
3	Saudi Arabia	10.4		Myanmar		3.9
4	South Sudan	8.8	16	Jordan		3.5
5	Iraq	8.1	17	Brunei		3.4
6	Libya[a]	7.1		Colombia		3.4
7	Israel	6.6		Morocco		3.4
8	Algeria	5.3		Namibia		3.4
9	Angola	5.2		Russia		3.4
10	Congo-Brazzaville	5.1		Singapore		3.4
11	Armenia	4.2	23	United States		3.3
	Yemen	4.2	24	Mali		3.0

Defence spending

$bn, 2014

			Per person, $, 2014		
1	United States	596.9	1	Oman	2,989
2	China[b]	129.4	2	Saudi Arabia	2,956
3	Saudi Arabia	80.8	3	Israel	2,575
4	Russia	70.0	4	United States	1,822
5	United Kingdom	61.8	5	Singapore	1,799
6	France	53.1	6	Kuwait	1,765
7	Japan	47.7	7	Brunei	1,356
8	India	45.2	8	Norway	1,355
9	Germany	43.9	9	Bahrain	1,016
10	South Korea	34.4	10	Australia	1,000
11	Brazil	31.9	11	United Kingdom	970
12	Italy	24.3	12	Denmark	864
13	Australia	22.5	13	France	801
14	Israel	20.1	14	Libya	776
15	Iraq	18.9	15	Sweden	725

Armed forces

'000, 2015[c]

		Regulars	Reserves			Regulars	Reserves
1	China	2,333	510	16	Colombia	297	34
2	United States	1,433	855	17	Taiwan	290	1,657
3	India	1,346	1,155	18	Saudi Arabia	277	0
4	North Korea	1,190	600	19	Mexico	267	87
5	Russia	771	2,000	20	Japan	247	56
6	South Korea	655	4,500	21	Sudan	244	0
7	Pakistan	644	0	22	France	215	28
8	Iran	523	350	23	Morocco	196	150
9	Turkey	511	379	24	South Sudan	185	0
10	Vietnam	482	5,000	25	Germany	182	45
11	Egypt	439	479	26	Afghanistan	179	0
12	Myanmar	406	0	27	Iraq	178	0
13	Indonesia	396	400	28	Israel	177	465
14	Thailand	361	200	29	Italy	176	18
15	Brazil	318	1,340	30	Sri Lanka	161	6

a 2013   b Official budget only at market exchange rates.   c Estimates.

Arms exporters
$m, 2014

1	United States	10,194
2	Russia	5,971
3	France	1,978
4	United Kingdom	1,704
5	Germany	1,200
6	Spain	1,110
7	China	1,083
8	Israel	824
9	Italy	786
10	Ukraine	664
11	Netherlands	561
12	Sweden	394
13	Switzerland	350
14	Turkey	274
15	Canada	234
16	South Korea	153
17	Norway	127
18	Jordan	114
19	Australia	104
20	Finland	84

Arms importers
$m, 2014

1	India	4,243
2	Saudi Arabia	2,629
3	Turkey	1,550
4	China	1,357
5	Indonesia	1,200
6	Vietnam	1,058
7	Taiwan	1,039
8	United Arab Emirates	1,031
9	Australia	842
10	Oman	738
11	Singapore	717
12	Pakistan	659
13	Azerbaijan	640
14	Iraq	627
15	Morocco	594
16	Kuwait	591
17	United States	581
18	South Korea	530
19	Algeria	463
20	Japan	436

Global Peace Index[a]

Most peaceful, 2015

1	Iceland	1.148
2	Denmark	1.150
3	Austria	1.198
4	New Zealand	1.221
5	Switzerland	1.275
6	Finland	1.277
7	Canada	1.287
8	Japan	1.322
9	Australia	1.329
10	Czech Republic	1.341
11	Portugal	1.344
12	Ireland	1.354
13	Sweden	1.360
14	Belgium	1.368
15	Slovenia	1.378
16	Germany	1.379
17	Norway	1.393
18	Poland	1.430
19	Netherlands	1.432
20	Spain	1.451
21	Hungary	1.463
22	Slovakia	1.478
23	Singapore	1.490
24	Mauritius	1.503

Least peaceful, 2015

1	Syria	3.645
2	Iraq	3.444
3	Afghanistan	3.427
4	South Sudan	3.383
5	Central African Rep.	3.332
6	Somalia	3.307
7	Sudan	3.295
8	Congo-Kinshasa	3.085
9	Pakistan	3.049
10	North Korea	2.977
11	Russia	2.954
12	Nigeria	2.910
13	Ukraine	2.845
14	Libya	2.819
15	Israel	2.781
16	Yemen	2.751
17	Colombia	2.720
18	Lebanon	2.623
19	Mexico	2.530
20	India	2.504
21	Venezuela	2.493
22	Philippines	2.462
23	Chad	2.429
24	Rwanda	2.420

a Ranks 162 countries using 22 indicators which gauge the level of safety and security in society, the extent of domestic or international conflict and the degree of militarisation.

Space

Space budgets
$m, 2013

					% of GDP, 2013	
1	United States	39,332		1	Russia	0.25
2	China	6,111		2	United States	0.23
3	Russia	5,265		3	France	0.10
4	Japan	3,597		4	China	0.07
5	France	2,713			Japan	0.07
6	Germany	1,687		6	India	0.06
7	Italy	1,223			Italy	0.06
8	India	1,159		8	Belgium	0.05
9	Canada	474			Germany	0.05
10	United Kingdom	367		10	Argentina	0.03
11	South Korea	318			Canada	0.03
12	Spain	273			Finland	0.03
13	Belgium	271			Israel	0.03
14	Switzerland	197			Luxembourg	0.03
15	Brazil	183			Norway	0.03
16	Sweden	162			Sweden	0.03
17	Argentina	140			Switzerland	0.03
18	Norway	134		18	Austria	0.02
19	Netherlands	121			Denmark	0.02
20	Israel	100			Estonia	0.02
21	Austria	80			Netherlands	0.02
22	Finland	65			Spain	0.02
23	Turkey	59			South Korea	0.02
24	Denmark	52		24	Ireland	0.01
25	Indonesia	50			United Kingdom	0.01

Civil space budgets, % of government civil R&D, 2013 or latest

1	United States	16.7		9	Netherlands	3.5
2	France	10.4			Spain	3.5
3	Belgium	8.9		11	Taiwan	2.9
4	Italy	8.8		12	Estonia	2.8
5	Canada	7.9			Russia	2.8
6	Japan	6.5		14	Poland	2.5
7	Germany	4.8		15	Ireland	2.4
8	United Kingdom	3.9			South Korea	2.4

Orbital launches

2014		Commercial	Non-commercial[a]	Total	2005–14
1	Russia	4	28	32	287
2	United States	11	12	23	176
3	China	0	16	16	122
4	Europe	6	5	11	70
5	Japan	0	4	4	28
6	India	1	3	4	25
7	Multinational[b]	1	0	1	22
8	Israel	0	1	1	3
9	Iran	0	0	0	6
10	North Korea	0	0	0	3
	South Korea	0	0	0	3

a Government and non-profit launches. b Sea Launch.

Environment

Biggest emitters of carbon dioxide
Million tonnes, 2011

1	China	8,126.7	26	United Arab Emirates	228.7
2	United States	5,483.2	27	Kazakhstan	206.9
3	India	1,752.7	28	Singapore	205.4
4	Russia	1,710.0	29	Egypt	199.4
5	Japan	1,200.3	30	Malaysia	195.7
6	Germany	784.4	31	Argentina	194.6
7	South Korea	650.5	32	Venezuela	171.1
8	Iran	594.5	33	Pakistan	142.0
9	Canada	551.6	34	Belgium	140.1
10	Saudi Arabia	551.4	35	Vietnam	135.1
11	United Kingdom	488.3	36	Algeria	122.1
12	Brazil	476.6	37	Iraq	120.0
13	South Africa	471.5	38	Uzbekistan	117.1
14	Indonesia	450.1	39	Kuwait	100.5
15	Mexico	446.2	40	Czech Republic	94.4
16	Australia	426.5	41	Hong Kong	94.3
17	Italy	411.6	42	Greece	92.1
18	France	374.3	43	Romania	89.5
19	Spain	318.2	44	Philippines	83.3
20	Taiwan	311.3	45	Nigeria	83.1
21	Poland	308.1	46	Qatar	81.5
22	Ukraine	298.1	47	Chile	78.5
23	Turkey	294.9	48	Israel	74.4
24	Thailand	293.4	49	Colombia	70.6
25	Netherlands	239.7	50	Austria	69.3

Largest amount of carbon dioxide emitted per person
Tonnes, 2011

1	Virgin Islands (US)	130.0	23	Guam	12.7
2	Netherlands Antilles	52.7	24	New Caledonia	12.4
3	United Arab Emirates	44.4	25	Kazakhstan	12.0
4	Qatar	44.1		Russia	12.0
5	Trinidad & Tobago	42.5	27	Bahamas	11.6
6	Singapore	39.2	28	Iceland	11.5
7	Kuwait	38.7	29	Turkmenistan	11.0
8	Montenegro	25.5	30	Greenland	10.7
9	Bahrain	24.9	31	Israel	10.0
10	Luxembourg	23.1	32	Finland	9.8
11	Brunei	21.7	33	Germany	9.6
12	Saudi Arabia	21.1		South Africa	9.6
13	Australia	19.6	35	Japan	9.4
14	Malta	18.4	36	Czech Republic	9.3
15	Oman	17.7	37	Norway	8.9
16	United States	17.6	38	New Zealand	8.8
17	Canada	16.2	39	Bermuda	8.6
18	Netherlands	14.4		Greece	8.6
19	Belgium	13.4	41	Austria	8.4
	Taiwan	13.4	42	Denmark	8.2
21	South Korea	13.3	43	Poland	8.0
22	Hong Kong	13.2		Slovenia	8.0

Most polluted capital cities
Annual mean particulate matter concentration[a], micrograms per cubic metre
2012 or latest

1	Delhi, India	286	12	Accra, Ghana	98
2	Kabul, Afghanistan[b]	260	13	Mexico City, Mexico	93
3	Dhaka, Bangladesh	180	14	Tehran, Iran	91
4	Dakar, Senegal	179	15	Muscat, Oman	82
5	Abu Dhabi, United Arab Emirates	170	16	Sofia, Bulgaria	65
6	Doha, Qatar	168	17	Colombo, Sri Lanka	64
7	Ulaanbaatar, Mongolia	148	18	Beirut, Lebanon	63
8	Cairo, Egypt	135		Lima, Peru	63
9	Amman, Jordan	128	20	Ankara, Turkey	58
10	Beijing, China	121		Ho Chi Minh City, Vietnam	58
11	Kathmandu, Nepal	114	22	Manila, Philippines	49
				Seoul, South Korea	49

Renewable sources of energy[c]
As % of electricity production, 2012

1	Denmark	47.6	15	Lithuania[d]	14.9
2	El Salvador[d]	31.3	16	Philippines[d]	14.6
3	Portugal	30.2	17	Italy[d]	12.4
4	Iceland	29.7	18	Estonia	12.0
5	Guatemala[d]	27.1		Netherlands	12.0
6	Kenya[d]	23.3	20	Belgium	11.8
7	Spain	22.5	21	Sweden	10.8
8	Nicaragua[d]	22.4	22	United Kingdom	10.0
9	New Zealand	20.0	23	Chile	9.3
10	Germany	18.9		Uruguay[d]	9.3
11	Costa Rica[d]	18.7	25	Poland	9.1
12	Italy	16.3	26	Greece	8.1
13	Ireland	16.2	27	United Kingdom[d]	7.9
14	Finland	16.0			

Lowest access to electricity
% of population, 2010

1	South Sudan	1.5	16	Congo-Kinshasa	15.2
2	Chad	3.5	17	Mali	16.6
3	Liberia	4.1	18	Lesotho	17.0
4	Burundi	5.3	19	Mauritania	18.2
5	Malawi	8.7	20	Zambia	18.5
6	Niger	9.3	21	Guinea	20.2
7	Central African Rep.	9.5	22	Ethiopia	23.0
8	Rwanda	10.8		Kenya	23.0
9	Sierra Leone	12.1	24	North Korea	26.0
10	Burkina Faso	13.1	25	Benin	27.9
11	Madagascar	14.3		Togo	27.9
12	Papua New Guinea	14.5	27	Sudan	29.0
13	Uganda	14.6	28	Equatorial Guinea	29.1
14	Tanzania	14.8		Somalia	29.1
15	Mozambique	15.0	30	Gambia, The	31.0

a Particulates less than 10 microns in diameter.   b Recorded at ISAF HQ.
c Includes geothermal, solar, biofuels, but not hydroelectric.   d 2011

Largest forests

Sq km, 2012

1	Russia	8,092,100
2	Brazil	5,151,332
3	Canada	3,101,340
4	United States	3,047,876
5	China	2,123,873
6	Congo-Kinshasa	1,535,122
7	Australia	1,474,520
8	Indonesia	930,620
9	India	687,240
10	Peru	676,920
11	Mexico	644,916
12	Colombia	602,970
13	Angola	582,304
14	Bolivia	565,808
15	Sudan[a]	550,752
16	Zambia	491,348
17	Venezuela	456,998
18	Mozambique	385,992
19	Tanzania	326,212
20	Myanmar	311,538
21	Argentina	289,204
22	Papua New Guinea	284,416
23	Sweden	282,030
24	Japan	249,966
25	Central African Rep.	225,450
26	Congo-Brazzaville	223,870
27	Finland	221,570
28	Gabon	220,000
29	Malaysia	202,824
30	Cameroon	194,760

Most forest

% of land area, 2012

1	Suriname	94.6
2	Gabon	85.4
3	Finland	72.9
4	Brunei	71.4
5	Guinea-Bissau	71.2
6	Sweden	69.2
7	Japan	68.6
8	Congo-Kinshasa	67.7
9	Laos	67.6
10	Zambia	66.1
11	Congo-Brazzaville	65.6
12	Puerto Rico	64.2
13	South Korea	63.8
14	Papua New Guinea	62.8
15	Slovenia	62.4
16	Malaysia	61.7
17	Brazil	61.6
18	Equatorial Guinea	57.1
19	Virgin Islands (US)	56.9
20	Fiji	55.9
21	Cambodia	55.7
22	Colombia	54.3
	Latvia	54.3
24	Peru	52.9
25	Bolivia	52.2
26	Costa Rica	51.9
27	Estonia	51.8
	Venezuela	51.8
29	Bahamas	51.4
	Indonesia	51.4

Deforestation

Biggest % decrease in forested land, 1990–2012

1	Togo	-61.0	16	Armenia	-26.9
2	Nigeria	-52.3	17	El Salvador	-26.2
3	Mauritania	-44.1	18	Timor-Leste	-25.5
4	Burundi	-41.7	19	Guatemala	-25.3
5	Uganda	-40.8	20	Nepal	-24.5
6	Niger	-39.4	21	Cambodia	-24.0
7	Honduras	-39.1	22	Benin	-22.6
8	Ghana	-36.8	23	Sri Lanka	-22.1
9	Pakistan	-36.6	24	Indonesia	-21.5
10	Nicaragua	-34.1	25	Tanzania	-21.4
11	North Korea	-34.0	26	Myanmar	-20.6
12	Zimbabwe	-32.5	27	Somalia	-20.4
13	Ecuador	-31.5	28	Cameroon	-19.9
14	Ethiopia	-28.2	29	Burkina Faso	-19.2
15	Sudan	-27.9	30	Botswana	-19.0

a 2011

Number of species under threat
2014
Mammals

1	Indonesia	184	10	Colombia	54
2	Madagascar	114		Peru	54
3	Mexico	101	12	Vietnam	52
4	India	94	13	Ecuador	45
5	Brazil	82	14	Myanmar	44
6	China	73	15	Laos	43
7	Malaysia	70	16	Papua New Guinea	39
8	Australia	55			
	Thailand	55			

Fish

1	United States	236	10	Malawi	102
2	India	213	11	Thailand	96
3	Tanzania	175	12	Madagascar	87
4	Mexico	154		South Africa	87
5	Indonesia	145	14	Brazil	84
6	Turkey	126		Congo-Kinshasa	84
7	China	122	16	Greece	76
8	Cameroon	111	17	Philippines	74
9	Australia	106			

Plants

1	Ecuador	1,842	10	India	332
2	Malaysia	706	11	Peru	318
3	Brazil	509	12	Sri Lanka	287
4	China	501	13	United States	277
5	Tanzania	496	14	New Caledonia	259
6	Indonesia	408	15	Colombia	245
7	Cameroon	380	16	Philippines	232
8	Madagascar	374	17	Spain	214
9	Mexico	371	18	Jamaica	212

Biggest nationally protected land and marine area[a]
As % of total territorial area, 2012

1	Slovenia	54.9	16	New Caledonia	30.5
2	Venezuela	49.5	17	Congo-Brazzaville	30.4
3	Germany	49.0	18	Saudi Arabia	29.9
4	Namibia	42.6	19	Guatemala	29.8
5	Hong Kong	41.9	20	Brunei	29.6
6	Luxembourg	39.7	21	France	28.7
7	Zambia	37.8	22	Zimbabwe	27.2
8	Botswana	37.2	23	Guinea-Bissau	27.1
9	Ecuador	37.0	24	Guinea	26.8
10	Slovakia	36.1	25	Switzerland	26.3
11	Bulgaria	35.4	26	Brazil	26.0
12	Poland	34.8	27	Benin	25.5
13	Nicaragua	32.5	28	Spain	25.3
14	Tanzania	31.7	29	Belgium	24.5
15	Netherlands	31.5	30	Senegal	24.2

a Scientific reserves with limited access, national parks, nature reserves and protected landscapes.

Country profiles

ALGERIA

Area	2,381,741 sq km	Capital	Algiers
Arable as % of total land	3.2	Currency	Algerian dinar (AD)

People

Population	39.2m	Life expectancy: men	69.9 yrs
Pop. per sq km	16.5	women	73.3 yrs
Average annual growth		Adult literacy	...
in pop. 2015–20	1.5%	Fertility rate (per woman)	2.9
Pop. under 15	27.8%	Urban population	70.7%
Pop. over 60	7.4%		per 1,000 pop.
No. of men per 100 women	102.3	Crude birth rate	25
Human Development Index	71.7	Crude death rate	5.9

The economy

GDP	AD16,682bn	GDP per head	$5,360
GDP	$210bn	GDP per head in purchasing	
Av. ann. growth in real		power parity (USA=100)	25.1
GDP 2008–13	2.8%	Economic freedom index	48.9

Origins of GDP		Components of GDP	
	% of total		% of total
Agriculture	11	Private consumption	35
Industry, of which:	48	Public consumption	19
manufacturing	...	Investment	43
Services	42	Exports	33
		Imports	-30

Structure of employment

	% of total		% of labour force
Agriculture	10.8	Unemployed 2013	9.8
Industry	30.9	Av. ann. rate 2000–13	16.9
Services	58.4		

Energy

	m TOE		
Total output	179.9	Net energy imports as %	
Total consumption	55.9	of energy use	-248
Consumption per person			
kg oil equivalent	1,452		

Inflation and finance

Consumer price		av. ann. increase 2009–14	
inflation 2014	2.9%	Narrow money (M1)	13.8%
Av. ann. inflation 2009–14	4.7%	Broad money	13.4%
Treasury bill rate, Dec. 2014	0.35%		

Exchange rates

	end 2014		December 2014
AD per $	87.90	Effective rates	2010 = 100
AD per SDR	127.36	– nominal	95.10
AD per €	106.72	– real	106.71

Trade

Principal exports		Principal imports	
	$bn fob		*$bn cif*
Hydrocarbons	63.2	Capital goods	15.7
Semi-finished goods	1.6	Consumer goods	12.2
Raw materials	0.1	Semi-finished goods	10.8
Total incl. others	**65.5**	Food	9.6
		Total incl. others	**54.9**

Main export destinations		Main origins of imports	
	% of total		*% of total*
United States	11.5	China	12.4
Canada	11.0	France	11.4
France	8.1	Italy	10.3
Italy	8.0	Spain	9.3

Balance of payments, reserves and debt, $bn

Visible exports fob	64.3	Change in reserves	0.8
Visible imports fob	-54.9	Level of reserves	
Trade balance	9.5	end Dec.	201.4
Invisibles inflows	7.5	No. months of import cover	32.8
Invisibles outflows	-18.8	Official gold holdings, m oz	5.6
Net transfers	2.8	Foreign debt	5.2
Current account balance	0.9	– as % of GDP	2.5
– as % of GDP	0.4	– as % of total exports	7.3
Capital balance	0.3	Debt service ratio	0.7
Overall balance	0.1		

Health and education

Health spending, % of GDP	6.6	Education spending, % of GDP	4.3
Doctors per 1,000 pop.	1.2	Enrolment, %: primary	117
Hospital beds per 1,000 pop.	...	secondary	98
Improved-water source access,		tertiary	31
% of pop.	83.9		

Society

No. of households, m	6.6	Cost of living, Dec. 2014	
Av. no. per household	5.6	New York = 100	52
Marriages per 1,000 pop.	...	Cars per 1,000 pop.	90
Divorces per 1,000 pop.	...	Colour TV households, % with:	
Religion, % of pop.		cable	...
Muslim	97.9	satellite	93.1
Non-religious	1.8	Telephone lines per 100 pop.	8.0
Christian	0.2	Mobile telephone subscribers	
Hindu	<0.1	per 100 pop.	100.8
Jewish	<0.1	Broadband subs per 100 pop.	3.3
Other	<0.1	Internet users, % of pop.	16.5

ARGENTINA

Area	2,766,889 sq km	Capital	Buenos Aires
Arable as % of total land	14.4	Currency	Peso (P)

People

Population	41.4m	Life expectancy: men	73.6 yrs
Pop. per sq km	15.0	women	80.6 yrs
Average annual growth		Adult literacy	97.9
in pop. 2015–20	0.8%	Fertility rate (per woman)	2.3
Pop. under 15	24.2%	Urban population	91.8%
Pop. over 60	15.1%		*per 1,000 pop.*
No. of men per 100 women	95.8	Crude birth rate	19
Human Development Index	80.8	Crude death rate	7.7

The economy

GDP	P3,340bn	GDP per head	$14,720
GDP	$610bn	GDP per head in purchasing	
Av. ann. growth in real		power parity (USA=100)	42.2
GDP 2008–13	4.2%	Economic freedom index	44.1

Origins of GDP		**Components of GDP**	
	% of total		*% of total*
Agriculture	7	Private consumption	66
Industry, of which:	28	Public consumption	16
manufacturing	15	Investment	18
Services	65	Exports	15
		Imports	-15

Structure of employment

	% of total		*% of labour force*
Agriculture	0.7	Unemployed 2013	6.6
Industry	23.6	Av. ann. rate 2000–13	11.4
Services	75.7		

Energy

	m TOE		
Total output	77.9	Net energy imports as %	
Total consumption	91.6	of energy use	4
Consumption per person			
kg oil equivalent	2,230		

Inflation and finance

Consumer price		*av. ann. increase 2009–14*	
inflation 2014	10.6%	Narrow money (M1)	30.5%
Av. ann. inflation 2009–14	10.2%	Broad money	29.5%
Money market rate, Dec. 2014	21.83%		

Exchange rates

	end 2014		*December 2014*
P per $	8.51	Effective rates	*2010 = 100*
P per SDR	12.33	– nominal	...
P per €	10.33	– real	...

Trade

Principal exports		Principal imports	
	$bn fob		*$bn cif*
Processed agricultural products	29.0	Intermediate goods	20.0
Manufactures	28.5	Capital goods	12.2
Primary products	18.7	Fuels	11.3
Fuels	5.5	Consumer goods	7.5
Total	**81.7**	Total incl. others	**74.0**

Main export destinations		Main origins of imports	
	% of total		*% of total*
Brazil	20.2	Brazil	29.2
China	6.8	United States	15.2
United States	5.3	China	13.0
Chile	4.4	Germany	4.8

Balance of payments, reserves and debt, $bn

Visible exports fob	81.7	Change in reserves	-12.7
Visible imports fob	-70.5	Level of reserves	
Trade balance	11.1	end Dec.	30.5
Invisibles inflows	17.2	No. months of import cover	3.6
Invisibles outflows	-32.2	Official gold holdings, m oz	2.0
Net transfers	-0.9	Foreign debt	136.3
Current account balance	-4.7	– as % of GDP	21.8
– as % of GDP	-0.8	– as % of total exports	137.0
Capital balance	-3.4	Debt service ratio	14.0
Overall balance	-13.7		

Health and education

Health spending, % of GDP	7.3	Education spending, % of GDP	5.1
Doctors per 1,000 pop.	3.9	Enrolment, %: primary	124
Hospital beds per 1,000 pop.	4.7	secondary	107
Improved-water source access,		tertiary	80
% of pop.	98.7		

Society

No. of households, m	12.9	Cost of living, Dec. 2014	
Av. no. per household	3.2	New York = 100	68
Marriages per 1,000 pop.	3.1	Cars per 1,000 pop.	228
Divorces per 1,000 pop.	...	Colour TV households, % with:	
Religion, % of pop.		cable	64.8
Christian	85.2	satellite	14.4
Non-religious	12.2	Telephone lines per 100 pop.	23.3
Other	1.1	Mobile telephone subscribers	
Muslim	1.0	per 100 pop.	162.5
Jewish	0.5	Broadband subs per 100 pop.	14.4
Hindu	<0.1	Internet users, % of pop.	59.9

a Estimate.

AUSTRALIA

Area	7,682,300 sq km	Capital	Canberra
Arable as % of total land	6.1	Currency	Australian dollar (A$)

People

Population	23.3m	Life expectancy: men	80.9 yrs
Pop. per sq km	3.0	women	85.4 yrs
Average annual growth		Adult literacy	...
in pop. 2015–20	1.2%	Fertility rate (per woman)	1.9
Pop. under 15	19.1%	Urban population	89.4%
Pop. over 60	19.8%		per 1,000 pop.
No. of men per 100 women	99.1	Crude birth rate	13
Human Development Index	93.3	Crude death rate	6.7

The economy

GDP	A$1,521bn	GDP per head	$67,460
GDP	$1,560bn	GDP per head in purchasing	
Av. ann. growth in real		power parity (USA=100)	81.4
GDP 2008–13	2.4%	Economic freedom index	81.4

Origins of GDP		**Components of GDP**	
	% of total		% of total
Agriculture	2	Private consumption	55
Industry, of which:	27	Public consumption	18
manufacturing	7	Investment	28
Services	71	Exports	20
		Imports	-21

Structure of employment

	% of total		% of labour force
Agriculture	3.3	Unemployed 2013	5.7
Industry	21.1	Av. ann. rate 2000–13	5.4
Services	75.5		

Energy

	m TOE		
Total output	323.1	Net energy imports as %	
Total consumption	149.8	of energy use	-135
Consumption per person			
kg oil equivalent	6,590		

Inflation and finance

Consumer price		av. ann. increase 2009–14	
inflation 2014	2.5%	Narrow money (M1)	3.8%
Av. ann. inflation 2009–14	2.6%	Broad money	7.1%
Money market rate, Dec. 2014	2.50%	H'hold saving rate, 2014	9.8%

Exchange rates

	end 2014		December 2014
A$ per $	1.22	Effective rates	2010 = 100
A$ per SDR	1.77	– nominal	95.40
A$ per €	1.48	– real	96.30

Trade

Principal exports	$bn fob	Principal imports	$bn cif
Crude materials	98.2	Machinery & transport equip.	88.1
Fuels	65.2	Mineral fuels	40.7
Food	26.1	Miscellaneous manufactured	
Manufactured goods	14.0	articles	30.1
		Manufactured goods	25.7
Total incl. others	**240.1**	Total incl. others	**232.1**

Main export destinations	% of total	Main origins of imports	% of total
China	36.2	China	21.5
Japan	18.0	United States	11.5
South Korea	7.4	Japan	8.7
India	3.7	Singapore	6.0

Balance of payments, reserves and aid, $bn

Visible exports fob	254.2	Overall balance	5.5
Visible imports fob	-250.4	Change in reserves	3.7
Trade balance	3.8	Level of reserves	
Invisibles inflows	99.4	end Dec.	52.8
Invisibles outflows	-151.1	No. months of import cover	1.6
Net transfers	-2.3	Official gold holdings, m oz	2.6
Current account balance	-50.2	Aid given	4.8
– as % of GDP	-3.2	– as % of GDP	0.3
Capital balance	55.3		

Health and education

Health spending, % of GDP	9.0	Education spending, % of GDP	5.1
Doctors per 1,000 pop.	3.3	Enrolment, %: primary	105
Hospital beds per 1,000 pop.	3.9	secondary	136
Improved-water source access, % of pop.	100	tertiary	86

Society

No. of households, m	8.5	Cost of living, Dec. 2014	
Av. no. per household	2.7	New York = 100	120
Marriages per 1,000 pop.	5.4	Cars per 1,000 pop.	575
Divorces per 1,000 pop.	2.2	Colour TV households, % with:	
Religion, % of pop.		cable	24.9
Christian	67.3	satellite	33.7
Non-religious	24.2	Telephone lines per 100 pop.	44.3
Other	4.2	Mobile telephone subscribers	
Muslim	2.4	per 100 pop.	106.8
Hindu	1.4	Broadband subs per 100 pop.	25.0
Jewish	0.5	Internet users, % of pop.	83.0

AUSTRIA

Area	83,855 sq km	Capital	Vienna
Arable as % of total land	16.4	Currency	Euro (€)

People

Population	8.5m	Life expectancy: men	73.9 yrs
Pop. per sq km	101.4	women	84.3 yrs
Average annual growth		Adult literacy	...
in pop. 2015–20	0.4%	Fertility rate (per woman)	1.4
Pop. under 15	14.5%	Urban population	66.0%
Pop. over 60	23.7%		*per 1,000 pop.*
No. of men per 100 women	95	Crude birth rate	9
Human Development Index	88.1	Crude death rate	9.5

The economy

GDP	€323bn	GDP per head	$50,510
GDP	$428bn	GDP per head in purchasing	
Av. ann. growth in real		power parity (USA=100)	85.0
GDP 2008–13	0.4%	Economic freedom index	71.2

Origins of GDP		**Components of GDP**	
	% of total		*% of total*
Agriculture	1	Private consumption	54
Industry, of which:	28	Public consumption	20
manufacturing	18	Investment	23
Services	70	Exports	53
		Imports	-50

Structure of employment

	% of total		*% of labour force*
Agriculture	4.9	Unemployed 2013	4.9
Industry	26.2	Av. ann. rate 2000–13	4.4
Services	68.9		

Energy

	m TOE		
Total output	14.9	Net energy imports as %	
Total consumption	37.4	of energy use	62
Consumption per person			
kg oil equivalent	4,431		

Inflation and finance

Consumer price		*av. ann. increase 2009–14*	
inflation 2014	1.5%	Euro area:	
Av. ann. inflation 2009–14	2.3%	Narrow money (M1)	5.6%
Deposit rate, h'holds, Dec. 2014	0.54%	Broad money	2.0%
		H'hold saving rate, 2014	6.7%

Exchange rates

	end 2014		*December 2014*
€ per $	0.82	Effective rates	*2010 = 100*
€ per SDR	1.19	– nominal	100.30
		– real	102.10

Trade

Principal exports	
	$bn fob
Machinery & transport equip.	67.8
Chemicals & related products	22.2
Food, drink & tobacco	12.3
Raw materials	5.5
Total incl. others	**171.7**

Principal imports	
	$bn cif
Machinery & transport equip.	61.5
Mineral fuels & lubricants	22.5
Chemicals & related products	19.2
Food, drink & tobacco	12.9
Total incl. others	**179.1**

Main export destinations	
	% of total
Germany	30.1
Italy	6.5
France	4.7
United States	4.3
EU28	70.1

Main origins of imports	
	% of total
Germany	41.8
Italy	6.4
Switzerland	4.8
Czech Republic	4.2
EU28	76.6

Balance of payments, reserves and aid, $bn

Visible exports fob	163.6	Overall balance	0.5
Visible imports fob	-166.1	Change in reserves	-3.9
Trade balance	-2.6	Level of reserves	
Invisibles inflows	101.8	end Dec.	23.3
Invisibles outflows	-89.7	No. months of import cover	1.1
Net transfers	-5.1	Official gold holdings, m oz	9.0
Current account balance	4.4	Aid given	1.2
– as % of GDP	1.0	– as % of GDP	0.3
Capital balance	-5.7		

Health and education

Health spending, % of GDP	11.0	Education spending, % of GDP	5.8
Doctors per 1,000 pop.	4.8	Enrolment, %: primary	101
Hospital beds per 1,000 pop.	7.6	secondary	98
Improved-water source access,		tertiary	72
% of pop.	100		

Society

No. of households, m	3.7	Cost of living, Dec. 2014	
Av. no. per household	2.3	New York = 100	103
Marriages per 1,000 pop.	4.6	Cars per 1,000 pop.	547
Divorces per 1,000 pop.	2.0	Colour TV households, % with:	
Religion, % of pop.		cable	38.6
Christian	80.4	satellite	54.3
Non-religious	13.5	Telephone lines per 100 pop.	39.3
Muslim	5.4	Mobile telephone subscribers	
Other	0.5	per 100 pop.	156.2
Jewish	0.2	Broadband subs per 100 pop.	26.1
Hindu	<0.1	Internet users, % of pop.	80.6

BANGLADESH

Area	143,998 sq km	Capital	Dhaka
Arable as % of total land	59.0	Currency	Taka (Tk)

People

Population	156.6m	Life expectancy: men	71.5 yrs
Pop. per sq km	1,087.5	women	73.3 yrs
Average annual growth		Adult literacy	58.8
in pop. 2015–20	1.1%	Fertility rate (per woman)	2.2
Pop. under 15	30.0%	Urban population	34.3%
Pop. over 60	7.0%		per 1,000 pop.
No. of men per 100 women	103.2	Crude birth rate	20
Human Development Index	55.8	Crude death rate	5.4

The economy

GDP	Tk11,989bn	GDP per head	$960
GDP	$150bn	GDP per head in purchasing	
Av. ann. growth in real		power parity (USA=100)	5.6
GDP 2008–13	6.0%	Economic freedom index	53.9

Origins of GDP		**Components of GDP**	
	% of total		% of total
Agriculture	16	Private consumption	74
Industry, of which:	28	Public consumption	5
manufacturing	17	Investment	28
Services	56	Exports	20
		Imports	-27

Structure of employment

	% of total		% of labour force
Agriculture	...	Unemployed 2012	4.5
Industry	...	Av. ann. rate 2000–12	4.2
Services	...		

Energy

	m TOE		
Total output	21.3	Net energy imports as %	
Total consumption	27.3	of energy use	17
Consumption per person			
kg oil equivalent	177		

Inflation and finance

Consumer price		av. ann. increase 2009–14	
inflation 2014	7.0%	Narrow money (M1)	14.5%
Av. ann. inflation 2009–14	8.3%	Broad money	13.9%
Deposit rate, Dec. 2014	8.27%		

Exchange rates

	end 2014		December 2014
Tk per $	77.95	Effective rates	2010 = 100
Tk per SDR	112.93	– nominal	...
Tk per €	94.64	– real	...

Trade

Principal exports[a]		Principal imports[a]	
	$bn fob		$bn cif
Clothing	17.6	Fuels	4.6
Jute goods	0.7	Textiles & yarns	3.5
Fish & fish products	0.5	Iron & steel	2.5
Leather	0.5	Cotton	2.2
Total incl. others	25.8	Total incl. others	36.0

Main export destinations		Main origins of imports	
	% of total		% of total
United States	15.2	China	18.6
Germany	13.3	India	14.0
United Kingdom	8.5	Malaysia	5.3
France	5.2	Singapore	5.2

Balance of payments, reserves and debt, $bn

Visible exports fob	28.6	Change in reserves	5.3
Visible imports fob	-35.0	Level of reserves	
Trade balance	-6.4	end Dec.	18.1
Invisibles inflows	3.1	No. months of import cover	5.0
Invisibles outflows	-8.8	Official gold holdings, m oz	0.4
Net transfers	14.4	Foreign debt	27.8
Current account balance	2.4	– as % of GDP	18.5
– as % of GDP	1.6	– as % of total exports	61.0
Capital balance	3.1	Debt service ratio	3.6
Overall balance	5.2		

Health and education

Health spending, % of GDP	3.7	Education spending, % of GDP	...
Doctors per 1,000 pop.	0.4	Enrolment, %: primary	114
Hospital beds per 1,000 pop.	0.6	secondary	54
Improved-water source access,		tertiary	13
% of pop.	84.8		

Society

No. of households, m	35.8	Cost of living, Dec. 2014	
Av. no. per household	4.3	New York = 100	66
Marriages per 1,000 pop.	...	Cars per 1,000 pop.	2
Divorces per 1,000 pop.	...	Colour TV households, % with:	
Religion, % of pop. of pop.		cable	...
Muslim	89.8	satellite	...
Hindu	9.1	Telephone lines per 100 pop.	0.7
Other	0.9	Mobile telephone subscribers	
Christian	0.2	per 100 pop.	74.4
Jewish	<0.1	Broadband subs per 100 pop.	1.0
Non-religious	<0.1	Internet users, % of pop.	6.5

a Fiscal year ending June 30 2013.

BELGIUM

Area	30,520 sq km	Capital	Brussels
Arable as % of total land	26.5	Currency	Euro (€)

People

Population	11.1m	Life expectancy: men	78.8 yrs
Pop. per sq km	363.7	women	83.7 yrs
Average annual growth		Adult literacy	...
in pop. 2015–20	0.3%	Fertility rate (per woman)	1.8
Pop. under 15	17.0%	Urban population	97.9%
Pop. over 60	24.0%		per 1,000 pop.
No. of men per 100 women	96.2	Crude birth rate	11
Human Development Index	88.1	Crude death rate	10.1

The economy

GDP	€395bn	GDP per head	$46,930
GDP	$525bn	GDP per head in purchasing	
Av. ann. growth in real		power parity (USA=100)	78.4
GDP 2008–13	0.4%	Economic freedom index	68.8

Origins of GDP		Components of GDP	
	% of total		% of total
Agriculture	1	Private consumption	52
Industry, of which:	22	Public consumption	24
manufacturing	14	Investment	23
Services	77	Exports	83
		Imports	-81

Structure of employment

	% of total		% of labour force
Agriculture	1.2	Unemployed 2013	8.4
Industry	21.7	Av. ann. rate 2000–13	7.7
Services	77.1		

Energy

	m TOE		
Total output	12.4	Net energy imports as %	
Total consumption	64.8	of energy use	71
Consumption per person			
kg oil equivalent	5,821		

Inflation and finance

Consumer price		av. ann. increase 2009–14	
inflation 2014	0.5%	Euro area:	
Av. ann. inflation 2009–14	2.0%	Narrow money (M1)	5.6%
Treasury bill rate, Dec. 2014	-0.07%	Broad money	2.0%
		H'hold saving rate, 2014	10.1%

Exchange rates

	end 2014		December 2014
€ per $	0.82	Effective rates	2010 = 100
€ per SDR	1.19	– nominal	99.80
		– real	98.20

Trade

Principal exports		Principal imports	
	$bn fob		$bn cif
Chemicals & related products	134.6	Chemicals & related products	103.0
Machinery & transport equip.	93.1	Machinery & transport equip.	98.0
Mineral fuels & lubricants	59.1	Mineral fuels & lubricants	82.2
Food, drink & tobacco	40.4	Food, drink & tobacco	34.9
Total incl. others	**468.0**	Total incl. others	**452.0**

Main export destinations		Main origins of imports	
	% of total		% of total
Germany	16.9	Netherlands	20.5
France	15.7	Germany	13.5
Netherlands	12.3	France	10.6
United Kingdom	7.5	United States	6.7
EU28	70.1	EU28	66.4

Balance of payments, reserves and aid, $bn

Visible exports fob	321.1	Overall balance	-0.5
Visible imports fob	-331.3	Change in reserves	-3.8
Trade balance	-10.2	Level of reserves	
Invisibles inflows	177.4	end Dec.	26.9
Invisibles outflows	-155.8	No. months of import cover	0.7
Net transfers	-10.5	Official gold holdings, m oz	7.3
Current account balance	0.9	Aid given	2.3
– as % of GDP	0.2	– as % of GDP	0.5
Capital balance	-1.1		

Health and education

Health spending, % of GDP	11.2	Education spending, % of GDP	6.5
Doctors per 1,000 pop.	4.9	Enrolment, %: primary	103
Hospital beds per 1,000 pop.	6.5	secondary	107
Improved-water source access,		tertiary	71
% of pop.	100		

Society

No. of households, m	4.8	Cost of living, Dec. 2014	
Av. no. per household	2.3	New York = 100	93
Marriages per 1,000 pop.	3.6	Cars per 1,000 pop.	492
Divorces per 1,000 pop.	2.5	Colour TV households, % with:	
Religion, % of pop.		cable	74.2
Christian	64.2	satellite	5.9
Non-religious	29.0	Telephone lines per 100 pop.	41.4
Muslim	5.9	Mobile telephone subscribers	
Other	0.6	per 100 pop.	110.9
Jewish	0.3	Broadband subs per 100 pop.	34.4
Hindu	<0.1	Internet users, % of pop.	82.2

BRAZIL

Area	8,511,965 sq km	Capital	Brasília
Arable as % of total land	8.7	Currency	Real (R)

People

Population	200.4m	Life expectancy: men	71.6 yrs
Pop. per sq km	23.5	women	78.7 yrs
Average annual growth		Adult literacy	91.3
in pop. 2015–20	0.7%	Fertility rate (per woman)	1.8
Pop. under 15	24.1%	Urban population	85.7%
Pop. over 60	11.2%		per 1,000 pop.
No. of men per 100 women	97	Crude birth rate	15
Human Development Index	74.4	Crude death rate	6.7

The economy

GDP	R4,845bn	GDP per head	$11,210
GDP	$2,246bn	GDP per head in purchasing	
Av. ann. growth in real		power parity (USA=100)	28.4
GDP 2008–13	3.1%	Economic freedom index	56.6

Origins of GDP		**Components of GDP**	
	% of total		% of total
Agriculture	6	Private consumption	63
Industry, of which:	25	Public consumption	22
manufacturing	13	Investment	18
Services	69	Exports	13
		Imports	-15

Structure of employment

	% of total		% of labour force
Agriculture	15.4	Unemployed 2013	6.2
Industry	21.9	Av. ann. rate 2000–13	8.2
Services	62.7		

Energy

	m TOE		
Total output	244.0	Net energy imports as %	
Total consumption	302.4	of energy use	8
Consumption per person			
kg oil equivalent	1,522		

Inflation and finance

Consumer price		av. ann. increase 2009–14	
inflation 2014	6.3%	Narrow money (M1)	7.2%
Av. ann. inflation 2009–14	5.9%	Broad money	14.4%
Money market rate, Dec. 2014	11.58%		

Exchange rates

	end 2014		December 2014
R per $	2.66	Effective rates	2010 = 100
R per SDR	3.85	– nominal	75.17
R per €	3.23	– real	88.66

Trade

Principal exports		Principal imports	
	$bn fob		*$bn cif*
Primary products	113.0	Intermediate products &	
Manufactured products	92.9	raw materials	106.5
Semi-manufactured products	30.5	Capital goods	51.7
		Consumer goods	41.0
		Fuels & lubricants	40.6
Total incl. others	**242.0**	Total	**239.7**

Main export destinations		Main origins of imports	
	% of total		*% of total*
China	19.0	China	17.1
United States	10.3	United States	16.6
Argentina	8.1	Argentina	7.6
Netherlands	7.1	Netherlands	7.0

Balance of payments, reserves and debt, $bn

Visible exports fob	242.0	Change in reserves	-14.3
Visible imports fob	-239.6	Level of reserves	
Trade balance	2.4	end Dec.	358.8
Invisibles inflows	49.2	No. months of import cover	11.5
Invisibles outflows	-136.1	Official gold holdings, m oz	2.2
Net transfers	3.4	Foreign debt	482.5
Current account balance	-81.1	– as % of GDP	20.2
– as % of GDP	-3.6	– as % of total exports	163.9
Capital balance	74.2	Debt service ratio	28.3
Overall balance	-5.9		

Health and education

Health spending, % of GDP	9.7	Education spending, % of GDP	5.8
Doctors per 1,000 pop.	1.9	Enrolment, %: primary	...
Hospital beds per 1,000 pop.	2.3	secondary	...
Improved-water source access,		tertiary	...
% of pop.	97.5		

Society

No. of households, m	60.3	Cost of living, Dec. 2014	
Av. no. per household	3.3	New York = 100	79
Marriages per 1,000 pop.	...	Cars per 1,000 pop.	226
Divorces per 1,000 pop.	...	Colour TV households, % with:	
Religion, % of pop.		cable	11.3
Christian	88.9	satellite	16.9
Non-religious	7.9	Telephone lines per 100 pop.	22.5
Other	3.1	Mobile telephone subscribers	
Hindu	<0.1	per 100 pop.	135.3
Jewish	<0.1	Broadband subs per 100 pop.	10.1
Muslim	<0.1	Internet users, % of pop.	51.6

BULGARIA

Area	110,994 sq km	Capital	Sofia
Arable as % of total land	30.6	Currency	Lev (BGL)

People

Population	7.2m	Life expectancy: men	70.5 yrs
Pop. per sq km	71.3	women	77.7 yrs
Average annual growth		Adult literacy	98.4
in pop. 2015–20	-0.8%	Fertility rate (per woman)	1.5
Pop. under 15	13.7%	Urban population	73.9%
Pop. over 60	26.4%		per 1,000 pop.
No. of men per 100 women	94.9	Crude birth rate	9
Human Development Index	77.7	Crude death rate	16.1

The economy

GDP	BGL80.3bn	GDP per head	$7,500
GDP	$54.5bn	GDP per head in purchasing	
Av. ann. growth in real		power parity (USA=100)	29.7
GDP 2008–13	-0.2%	Economic freedom index	66.8

Origins of GDP		**Components of GDP**	
	% of total		% of total
Agriculture	5	Private consumption	63
Industry, of which:	28	Public consumption	17
manufacturing	15	Investment	22
Services	67	Exports	68
		Imports	-69

Structure of employment

	% of total		% of labour force
Agriculture	6.4	Unemployed 2013	12.9
Industry	31.3	Av. ann. rate 2000–13	11.8
Services	62.2		

Energy

	m TOE		
Total output	11.1	Net energy imports as %	
Total consumption	18.9	of energy use	36
Consumption per person			
kg oil equivalent	2,593		

Inflation and finance

Consumer price		av. ann. change 2009–14	
inflation 2014	-1.6%	Narrow money (M1)	11.4%
Av. ann. inflation 2009–14	1.5%	Broad money	7.3%
Money market rate, Dec. 2014	0.01%		

Exchange rates

	end 2014		December 2014
BGL per $	1.61	Effective rates	2010 = 100
BGL per SDR	2.33	– nominal	105.66
BGL per €	1.95	– real	100.92

Trade

Principal exports	$bn fob	Principal imports	$bn cif
Other metals	3.2	Crude oil & natural gas	5.8
Clothing & footwear	2.1	Chemicals, plastics & rubber	2.7
Chemicals, plastics & rubber	1.3	Machinery & equipment	2.4
Iron & steel	0.8	Textiles	1.5
Total incl. others	29.6	Total incl. others	32.8

Main export destinations	% of total	Main origins of imports	% of total
Germany	12.3	Russia	19.3
Italy	8.6	Germany	11.3
Turkey	8.5	Italy	7.8
Romania	7.7	Romania	7.0
EU28	59.9	EU28	59.7

Balance of payments, reserves and debt, $bn

Visible exports fob	29.5	Change in reserves	-0.6
Visible imports fob	-32.6	Level of reserves	
Trade balance	-3.1	end Dec.	19.9
Invisibles inflows	8.8	No. months of import cover	5.9
Invisibles outflows	-7.8	Official gold holdings, m oz	1.3
Net transfers	3.1	Foreign debt	53.0
Current account balance	1.0	– as % of GDP	97.3
– as % of GDP	1.8	– as % of total exports	132.5
Capital balance	-1.3	Debt service ratio	12.5
Overall balance	-0.8	Aid given[a]	0.04
		– as % of GDP[a]	0.08

Health and education

Health spending, % of GDP	7.6	Education spending, % of GDP	3.8
Doctors per 1,000 pop.	3.9	Enrolment, %: primary	100
Hospital beds per 1,000 pop.	6.4	secondary	93
Improved-water source access,		tertiary	63
% of pop.	99.5		

Society

No. of households, m	3.0	Cost of living, Dec. 2014	
Av. no. per household	2.4	New York = 100	67
Marriages per 1,000 pop.	2.9	Cars per 1,000 pop.	397
Divorces per 1,000 pop.	1.6	Colour TV households, % with:	
Religion, % of pop.		cable	48.2
Christian	82.1	satellite	28.8
Muslim	13.7	Telephone lines per 100 pop.	26.9
Non-religious	4.2	Mobile telephone subscribers	
Hindu	<0.1	per 100 pop.	145.2
Jewish	<0.1	Broadband subs per 100 pop.	19.3
Other	<0.1	Internet users, % of pop.	53.1

a 2012

CAMEROON

Area	475,442 sq km	Capital	Yaoundé
Arable as % of total land	13.1	Currency	CFA franc (CFAfr)

People

Population	22.3m	Life expectancy: men	55.9 yrs
Pop. per sq km	46.9	women	58.2 yrs
Average annual growth		Adult literacy	71.3
in pop. 2015–20	2.4%	Fertility rate (per woman)	5.1
Pop. under 15	43.0%	Urban population	54.4%
Pop. over 60	4.9%		per 1,000 pop.
No. of men per 100 women	99.9	Crude birth rate	39
Human Development Index	50.4	Crude death rate	10.6

The economy

GDP	CFAfr14,608bn	GDP per head	$1,330
GDP	$29.6bn	GDP per head in purchasing	
Av. ann. growth in real		power parity (USA=100)	5.3
GDP 2008–13	3.9%	Economic freedom index	51.9

Origins of GDP		Components of GDP	
	% of total		% of total
Agriculture	23	Private consumption	77
Industry, of which:	30	Public consumption	12
manufacturing	14	Investment	20
Services	47	Exports	21
		Imports	-29

Structure of employment

	% of total		% of labour force
Agriculture	53.3	Unemployed 2012	3.8
Industry	12.6	Av. ann. rate 2000–12	4.8
Services	34.1		

Energy

	m TOE		
Total output	4.7	Net energy imports as %	
Total consumption	2.7	of energy use	-22
Consumption per person			
kg oil equivalent	127		

Inflation and finance

Consumer price		av. ann. change 2009–14	
inflation 2014	1.9%	Narrow money (M1)	9.0%
Av. ann. inflation 2009–14	2.1%	Broad money	8.9%
Deposit rate, Oct. 2014	2.45%		

Exchange rates

	end 2014		December 2014
CFAfr per $	540.28	Effective rates	2010 = 100
CFAfr per SDR	782.77	– nominal	102.20
CFAfr per €	655.95	– real	101.20

Trade

Principal exports	$bn fob	Principal imports	$bn cif
Fuels	2.1	Minerals & raw materials	3.2
Timber	0.6	Intermediate goods	1.7
Cocoa beans and products	0.4	Semi-finished goods	1.1
Cotton	0.1		
Total incl. others	**6.1**	Total incl. others	**6.2**

Main export destinations	% of total	Main origins of imports	% of total
Spain	18.5	China	23.2
China	10.0	France	14.1
Netherlands	8.4	Belgium	10.8
Italy	6.4	Italy	5.6

Balance of payments, reserves and debt, $bn

Visible exports fob	6.1	Change in reserves	0.0
Visible imports fob	-6.2	Level of reserves	
Trade balance	-0.1	end Dec.	3.4
Invisibles inflows	2.1	No. months of import cover	4.2
Invisibles outflows	-3.5	Official gold holdings, m oz	0.0
Net transfers	0.3	Foreign debt	4.9
Current account balance	-1.1	– as % of GDP	16.6
– as % of GDP	-3.8	– as % of total exports	58.5
Capital balance	1.2	Debt service ratio	4.0
Overall balance	-0.1		

Health and education

Health spending, % of GDP	5.1	Education spending, % of GDP	3.0
Doctors per 1,000 pop.	0.1	Enrolment, %: primary	111
Hospital beds per 1,000 pop.	1.3	secondary	50
Improved-water source access,		tertiary	12
% of pop.	74.1		

Society

No. of households, m	4.4	Cost of living, Dec. 2014	
Av. no. per household	4.8	New York = 100	66
Marriages per 1,000 pop.	...	Cars per 1,000 pop.	13
Divorces per 1,000 pop.	...	Colour TV households, % with:	
Religion, % of pop.		cable	...
Christian	70.3	satellite	2.4
Muslim	18.3	Telephone lines per 100 pop.	2.8
Other	6.0	Mobile telephone subscribers	
Non-religious	5.3	per 100 pop.	70.4
Hindu	<0.1	Broadband subs per 100 pop.	0.1
Jewish	<0.1	Internet users, % of pop.	6.4

CANADA

Area[a]	9,970,610 sq km	Capital	Ottawa
Arable as % of total land	5.0	Currency	Canadian dollar (C$)

People

Population	35.2m	Life expectancy: men	80.0 yrs
Pop. per sq km	3.5	women	84.2 yrs
Average annual growth		Adult literacy	...
in pop. 2015–20	1.0%	Fertility rate (per woman)	1.6
Pop. under 15	16.4%	Urban population	81.8%
Pop. over 60	21.2%		per 1,000 pop.
No. of men per 100 women	98.4	Crude birth rate	11
Human Development Index	90.2	Crude death rate	7.8

The economy

GDP	C$1,881bn	GDP per head	$51,960
GDP	$1,827bn	GDP per head in purchasing	
Av. ann. growth in real		power parity (USA=100)	80.6
GDP 2008–13	1.5%	Economic freedom index	79.1

Origins of GDP		**Components of GDP**	
	% of total		% of total
Agriculture	2	Private consumption	56
Industry, of which:	28	Public consumption	22
manufacturing	...	Investment	24
Services	70	Exports	30
		Imports	-32

Structure of employment

	% of total		% of labour force
Agriculture	2.0	Unemployed 2013	7.1
Industry	22.0	Av. ann. rate 2000–13	7.1
Services	77.0		

Energy

	m TOE		
Total output	478.5	Net energy imports as %	
Total consumption	333.8	of energy use	-66
Consumption per person			
kg oil equivalent	9,606		

Inflation and finance

Consumer price		av. ann. increase 2009–14	
inflation 2014	1.9%	Narrow money (M1)	6.3%
Av. ann. inflation 2009–14	1.8%	Broad money	4.5%
Money market rate, Dec. 2014	1.01%	H'hold saving rate, 2014	5.0%

Exchange rates

	end 2014		December 2014
C$ per $	1.16	Effective rates	2010 = 100
C$ per SDR	1.68	– nominal	91.60
C$ per €	1.41	– real	90.40

Trade

Principal exports		Principal imports	
	$bn fob		*$bn cif*
Energy products	110.1	Consumer goods	94.7
Motor vehicles & parts	66.2	Motor vehicles & parts	82.5
Metal & mineral products	52.1	Electronic & electrical equip.	54.9
Consumer goods	50.6	Energy products	42.5
Total incl. others	**465.3**	Total incl. others	**472.3**

Main export destinations		Main origins of imports	
	% of total		*% of total*
United States	75.9	United States	52.1
China	4.3	China	11.1
United Kingdom	3.0	Mexico	5.6
Japan	2.3	Germany	3.2
EU28	7.0	EU28	11.2

Balance of payments, reserves and aid, $bn

Visible exports fob	465.4	Overall balance	4.8
Visible imports fob	-472.4	Change in reserves	3.4
Trade balance	-7.0	Level of reserves	
Invisibles inflows	162.9	end Dec.	71.9
Invisibles outflows	-208.7	No. months of import cover	1.3
Net transfers	-1.8	Official gold holdings, m oz	0.1
Current account balance	-54.7	Aid given	4.9
– as % of GDP	-3.0	– as % of GDP	0.3
Capital balance	58.7		

Health and education

Health spending, % of GDP	10.9	Education spending, % of GDP	5.3
Doctors per 1,000 pop.	2.1	Enrolment, %: primary	98
Hospital beds per 1,000 pop.	2.7	secondary	103
Improved-water source access,		tertiary	...
% of pop.	99.8		

Society

No. of households, m	13.6	Cost of living, Dec. 2014	
Av. no. per household	2.6	New York = 100	92
Marriages per 1,000 pop.	4.4	Cars per 1,000 pop.	354
Divorces per 1,000 pop.	2.1	Colour TV households, % with:	
Religion, % of pop.		cable	66.4
Christian	69.0	satellite	22.2
Non-religious	23.7	Telephone lines per 100 pop.	48.1
Other	2.8	Mobile telephone subscribers	
Muslim	2.1	per 100 pop.	80.6
Hindu	1.4	Broadband subs per 100 pop.	33.2
Jewish	1.0	Internet users, % of pop.	85.8

a Including freshwater.

CHILE

Area	756,945 sq km	Capital	Santiago
Arable as % of total land	1.8	Currency	Chilean peso (Ps)

People

Population	17.6m	Life expectancy: men	78.3 yrs
Pop. per sq km	23.3	women	83.6 yrs
Average annual growth		Adult literacy	...
in pop. 2015–20	0.8%	Fertility rate (per woman)	1.9
Pop. under 15	21.1%	Urban population	89.5%
Pop. over 60	14.2%		per 1,000 pop.
No. of men per 100 women	97.9	Crude birth rate	14
Human Development Index	82.2	Crude death rate	5.8

The economy

GDP	137.2trn pesos	GDP per head	$15,730
GDP	$277bn	GDP per head in purchasing	
Av. ann. growth in real		power parity (USA=100)	41.4
GDP 2008–13	4.0%	Economic freedom index	78.5

Origins of GDP		Components of GDP	
	% of total		% of total
Agriculture	3	Private consumption	64
Industry, of which:	35	Public consumption	12
manufacturing	11	Investment	24
Services	61	Exports	33
		Imports	-33

Structure of employment

	% of total		% of labour force
Agriculture	10.2	Unemployed 2013	6.0
Industry	23.4	Av. ann. rate 2000–13	8.0
Services	66.4		

Energy

	m TOE		
Total output	8.2	Net energy imports as %	
Total consumption	35.5	of energy use	70
Consumption per person			
kg oil equivalent	2,031		

Inflation and finance

Consumer price		av. ann. increase 2009–14	
inflation 2014	4.4%	Narrow money (M1)	13.9%
Av. ann. inflation 2009–14	2.8%	Broad money	11.8%
Money market rate, Dec. 2014	3.00%	H'hold saving rate, 2014	...

Exchange rates

	end 2014		December 2014
Ps per $	607.38	Effective rates	2010 = 100
Ps per SDR	879.98	– nominal	93.90
Ps per €	737.42	– real	93.80

Trade

Principal exports		Principal imports	
	$bn fob		*$bn cif*
Copper	40.2	Intermediate goods	42.4
Fresh fruit	4.7	Consumer goods	21.6
Paper products	3.6	Capital goods	15.2
Total incl. others	**76.9**	Total	**79.2**

Main export destinations		Main origins of imports	
	% of total		*% of total*
China	24.8	United States	21.5
United States	12.7	China	20.9
Japan	9.9	Brazil	6.8
Brazil	5.8	Argentina	5.3
South Korea	5.5	Germany	4.3

Balance of payments, reserves and debt, $bn

Visible exports fob	76.5	Change in reserves	-0.6
Visible imports fob	-74.7	Level of reserves	
Trade balance	1.8	end Dec.	41.1
Invisibles inflows	20.7	No. months of import cover	4.5
Invisibles outflows	-34.9	Official gold holdings, m oz	0.0
Net transfers	2.2	Foreign debt	130.7
Current account balance	-10.1	– as % of GDP	47.2
– as % of GDP	-3.7	– as % of total exports	137.2
Capital balance	11.6	Debt service ratio	21.1
Overall balance	0.3		

Health and education

Health spending, % of GDP	7.7	Education spending, % of GDP	4.6
Doctors per 1,000 pop.	1.0	Enrolment, %: primary	101
Hospital beds per 1,000 pop.	2.1	secondary	89
Improved-water source access,		tertiary	74
% of pop.	98.8		

Society

No. of households, m	5.8	Cost of living, Dec. 2014	
Av. no. per household	3.0	New York = 100	68
Marriages per 1,000 pop.	3.8	Cars per 1,000 pop.	153
Divorces per 1,000 pop.	0.1	Colour TV households, % with:	
Religion, % of pop.		cable	34.2
Christian	89.4	satellite	5.2
Non-religious	8.6	Telephone lines per 100 pop.	18.2
Other	1.9	Mobile telephone subscribers	
Jewish	0.1	per 100 pop.	134.3
Hindu	<0.1	Broadband subs per 100 pop.	13.0
Muslim	<0.1	Internet users, % of pop.	66.5

CHINA

Area	9,560,900 sq km	Capital	Beijing
Arable as % of total land	11.3	Currency	Yuan

People

Population	1,385.6m	Life expectancy: men	74.8 yrs
Pop. per sq km	144.9	women	77.4 yrs
Average annual growth		Adult literacy	95.1
in pop. 2015–20	0.4%	Fertility rate (per woman)	1.6
Pop. under 15	18.0%	Urban population	55.6%
Pop. over 60	13.9%		per 1,000 pop.
No. of men per 100 women	107.4	Crude birth rate	12
Human Development Index	71.9	Crude death rate	7.5

The economy

GDP	Yuan56.9trn	GDP per head	$6,810
GDP	$9,240bn	GDP per head in purchasing	
Av. ann. growth in real		power parity (USA=100)	22.4
GDP 2008–13	8.9%	Economic freedom index	52.7

Origins of GDP		Components of GDP	
	% of total		% of total
Agriculture	10	Private consumption	34
Industry, of which:	44	Public consumption	14
manufacturing	32	Investment	49
Services	46	Exports	26
		Imports	-24

Structure of employment

	% of total		% of labour force
Agriculture	34.8	Unemployed 2013	4.0
Industry	29.5	Av. ann. rate 2000–13	4.3
Services	35.7		

Energy

	m TOE		
Total output	2,544.5	Net energy imports as %	
Total consumption	2,647.1	of energy use	11
Consumption per person			
kg oil equivalent	1,960		

Inflation and finance

Consumer price		av. ann. increase 2009–14	
inflation 2014	2.0%	Narrow money (M1)	9.6%
Av. ann. inflation 2009–14	3.2%	Broad money	15.2%
Deposit rate, Dec. 2014	0.05%		

Exchange rates

	end 2014		December 2014
Yuan per $	6.12	Effective rates	2010 = 100
Yuan per SDR	8.87	– nominal	121.57
Yuan per €	7.43	– real	127.37

Trade

Principal exports		Principal imports	
	$bn fob		*$bn cif*
Electrical goods	292.6	Electrical machnery	356.8
Telecoms equipment	257.8	Petroleum & products	260.8
Office machinery	218.9	Metal ores & scrap	171.3
Clothing & apparel	177.5	Professional instruments	88.0
Total incl. others	**2,209.2**	Total incl. others	**1,951.7**

Main export destinations		Main origins of imports	
	% of total		*% of total*
Hong Kong	17.4	South Korea	9.4
United States	16.7	Japan	8.3
Japan	6.8	Taiwan	8.0
South Korea	4.1	United States	7.5
EU28	15.3	EU28	11.3

Balance of payments, reserves and debt, $bn

Visible exports fob	2,147	Change in reserves	493
Visible imports fob	-1,796	Level of reserves	
Trade balance	352	end Dec.	3,880
Invisibles inflows	401	No. months of import cover	19.8
Invisibles outflows	-561	Official gold holdings, m oz	34
Net transfers	-9	Foreign debt	874.5
Current account balance	183	– as % of GDP	9.2
– as % of GDP	2.0	– as % of total exports	33.8
Capital balance	326	Debt service ratio	1.5
Overall balance	431		

Health and education

Health spending, % of GDP	5.6	Education spending, % of GDP	...
Doctors per 1,000 pop.	1.9	Enrolment, %: primary	128
Hospital beds per 1,000 pop.	3.8	secondary	89
Improved-water source access,		tertiary	27
% of pop.	91.9		

Society

No. of households, m	438.9	Cost of living, Dec. 2014	
Av. no. per household	3.1	New York = 100	86
Marriages per 1,000 pop.	9.6	Cars per 1,000 pop.	75
Divorces per 1,000 pop.	1.8	Colour TV households, % with:	
Religion, % of pop.		cable	50.0
Non-religious	52.2	satellite	...
Other	22.7	Telephone lines per 100 pop.	19.3
Buddhist	18.2	Mobile telephone subscribers	
Christian	5.1	per 100 pop.	88.7
Muslim	1.8	Broadband subs per 100 pop.	13.6
Jewish	<0.1	Internet users, % of pop.	45.8

Note: Data excludes Special Administrative Regions ie, Hong Kong and Macau.

COLOMBIA

Area	1,141,748 sq km	Capital	Bogota
Arable as % of total land	1.4	Currency	Colombian peso (peso)

People

Population	48.3m	Life expectancy: men	71.4 yrs
Pop. per sq km	42.3	women	78.6 yrs
Average annual growth		Adult literacy	93.6
in pop. 2015–20	1.1%	Fertility rate (per woman)	2.3
Pop. under 15	27.7%	Urban population	76.4%
Pop. over 60	9.5%		per 1,000 pop.
No. of men per 100 women	96.9	Crude birth rate	19
Human Development Index	71.1	Crude death rate	5.7

The economy

GDP	707trn pesos	GDP per head	$7,830
GDP	$378bn	GDP per head in purchasing	
Av. ann. growth in real		power parity (USA=100)	23.4
GDP 2008–13	4.2%	Economic freedom index	71.7

Origins of GDP

	% of total
Agriculture	6
Industry, of which:	37
manufacturing	12
Services	57

Components of GDP

	% of total
Private consumption	61
Public consumption	17
Investment	25
Exports	18
Imports	-20

Structure of employment

	% of total		% of labour force
Agriculture	16.9	Unemployed 2013	8.9
Industry	20.9	Av. ann. rate 2000–13	12.1
Services	62.2		

Energy

	m TOE		
Total output	133.8	Net energy imports as %	
Total consumption	38.6	of energy use	-281
Consumption per person			
kg oil equivalent	810		

Inflation and finance

		av. ann. increase 2009–14	
Consumer price			
inflation 2014	2.9%	Narrow money (M1)	12.3%
Av. ann. inflation 2009–14	2.8%	Broad money	12.8%
Money market rate, Dec. 2014	4.59%		

Exchange rates

	end 2014		December 2014
Peso per $	2,393.00	Effective rates	2010 = 100
Peso per SDR	3,466.00	– nominal	94.00
Peso per €	2,905.34	– real	84.80

Trade

Principal exports	$bn fob	Principal imports	$bn cif
Petroleum & products	32.8	Intermediate goods & raw materials	24.2
Coal	6.7	Capital goods	18.8
Coffee	1.9	Consumer goods	12.1
Nickel	0.7		
Total incl. others	**58.8**	Total incl. others	**59.4**

Main export destinations	% of total	Main origins of imports	% of total
United States	31.8	United States	27.7
China	8.7	China	17.5
Panama	5.6	Mexico	9.3
India	5.1	Brazil	4.4

Balance of payments, reserves and debt, $bn

Visible exports fob	60.3	Change in reserves	6.2
Visible imports fob	-57.1	Level of reserves	
Trade balance	3.2	end Dec.	43.2
Invisibles inflows	10.5	No. months of import cover	5.9
Invisibles outflows	-30.6	Official gold holdings, m oz	0.3
Net transfers	4.6	Foreign debt	92
Current account balance	-12.3	– as % of GDP	24.2
– as % of GDP	-3.3	– as % of total exports	122.8
Capital balance	18.8	Debt service ratio	13.4
Overall balance	6.9		

Health and education

Health spending, % of GDP	6.8	Education spending, % of GDP	4.9
Doctors per 1,000 pop.	1.5	Enrolment, %: primary	115
Hospital beds per 1,000 pop.	1.5	secondary	93
Improved-water source access, % of pop.	91.2	tertiary	48

Society

No. of households, m	12.8	Cost of living, Dec. 2014	
Av. no. per household	3.8	New York = 100	81
Marriages per 1,000 pop.	...	Cars per 1,000 pop.	59
Divorces per 1,000 pop.	...	Colour TV households, % with:	
Religion, % of pop.		cable	57.0
Christian	92.5	satellite	7.4
Non-religious	6.6	Telephone lines per 100 pop.	14.8
Other	0.8	Mobile telephone subscribers	
Hindu	<0.1	per 100 pop.	104.1
Jewish	<0.1	Broadband subs per 100 pop.	9.3
Muslim	<0.1	Internet users, % of pop.	51.7

CZECH REPUBLIC

Area	78,864 sq km	Capital	Prague
Arable as % of total land	40.9	Currency	Koruna (Kc)

People

Population	10.7m	Life expectancy: men	75.4 yrs
Pop. per sq km	135.7	women	81.3 yrs
Average annual growth		Adult literacy	...
in pop. 2015–20	0.3%	Fertility rate (per woman)	1.5
Pop. under 15	14.9%	Urban population	73.0%
Pop. over 60	23.7%		per 1,000 pop.
No. of men per 100 women	96.5	Crude birth rate	10
Human Development Index	86.1	Crude death rate	10.7

The economy

GDP	Kc4,086bn	GDP per head	$19,860
GDP	$209bn	GDP per head in purchasing	
Av. ann. growth in real		power parity (USA=100)	54.7
GDP 2008–13	-0.5%	Economic freedom index	72.5

Origins of GDP		Components of GDP	
	% of total		% of total
Agriculture	3	Private consumption	50
Industry, of which:	37	Public consumption	20
manufacturing	25	Investment	25
Services	61	Exports	77
		Imports	-71

Structure of employment

	% of total		% of labour force
Agriculture	3.1	Unemployed 2013	7.0
Industry	38.1	Av. ann. rate 2000–13	7.1
Services	58.8		

Energy

	m TOE		
Total output	26.6	Net energy imports as %	
Total consumption	39.3	of energy use	25
Consumption per person			
kg oil equivalent	3,739		

Inflation and finance

Consumer price		av. ann. increase 2009–14	
inflation 2014	0.4%	Narrow money (M1)	9.6%
Av. ann. inflation 2009–14	1.7%	Broad money	4.0%
Money market rate, Dec. 2014	0.34%	H'hold saving rate, 2014	5.2%

Exchange rates

	end 2014		December 2014
Kc per $	22.83	Effective rates	2010 = 100
Kc per SDR	33.08	– nominal	92.02
Kc per €	27.72	– real	91.13

Trade

Principal exports		Principal imports	
	$bn fob		*$bn cif*
Machinery & transport equip.	87.3	Machinery & transport equip.	58.8
Semi-manufactures	28.2	Semi-manufactures	25.8
Chemicals	10.4	Chemicals	16.5
Raw materials & fuels	9.5	Raw materials & fuels	15.4
Total incl. others	**162.3**	Total incl. others	**144.3**

Main export destinations		Main origins of imports	
	% of total		*% of total*
Germany	31.2	Germany	25.5
Slovakia	8.9	Poland	17.4
Poland	5.9	Slovakia	6.4
United Kingdom	4.9	China	5.8
EU28	81.1	EU28	76.8

Balance of payments, reserves and debt, $bn

Visible exports fob	137.0	Change in reserves	11.3
Visible imports fob	-128.5	Level of reserves	
Trade balance	8.5	end Dec.	56.2
Invisibles inflows	30.9	No. months of import cover	4.0
Invisibles outflows	-40.0	Official gold holdings, m oz	0.3
Net transfers	-0.5	Foreign debt	114.4
Current account balance	-1.1	– as % of GDP	54.8
– as % of GDP	-0.5	– as % of total exports	4.7
Capital balance	10.3	Debt service ratio	0.8
Overall balance	9.6	Aid given	0.2
		– as % of GDP	0.1

Health and education

Health spending, % of GDP	7.2	Education spending, % of GDP	4.5
Doctors per 1,000 pop.	3.6	Enrolment, %: primary	100
Hospital beds per 1,000 pop.	6.8	secondary	97
Improved-water source access,		tertiary	64
% of pop.	99.8		

Society

No. of households, m	4.4	Cost of living, Dec. 2014	
Av. no. per household	2.4	New York = 100	71
Marriages per 1,000 pop.	4.3	Cars per 1,000 pop.	450
Divorces per 1,000 pop.	2.5	Colour TV households, % with:	
Religion, % of pop.		cable	24.5
Non-religious	76.4	satellite	27.0
Christian	23.3	Telephone lines per 100 pop.	18.7
Other	0.2	Mobile telephone subscribers	
Hindu	<0.1	per 100 pop.	127.7
Jewish	<0.1	Broadband subs per 100 pop.	17.0
Muslim	<0.1	Internet users, % of pop.	74.1

DENMARK

Area	43,075 sq km	Capital	Copenhagen
Arable as % of total land	57.0	Currency	Danish krone (DKr)

People

Population	5.6m	Life expectancy: men	78.0 yrs
Pop. per sq km	130.0	women	82.1 yrs
Average annual growth		Adult literacy	...
in pop. 2015–20	0.4%	Fertility rate (per woman)	1.7
Pop. under 15	17.6%	Urban population	87.7%
Pop. over 60	24.1%		per 1,000 pop.
No. of men per 100 women	98.4	Crude birth rate	10
Human Development Index	90	Crude death rate	10.1

The economy

GDP	DKr1,886bn	GDP per head	$59,820
GDP	$336bn	GDP per head in purchasing	
Av. ann. growth in real		power parity (USA=100)	82.5
GDP 2008–13	-0.7%	Economic freedom index	76.3

Origins of GDP		**Components of GDP**	
	% of total		% of total
Agriculture	1	Private consumption	49
Industry, of which:	23	Public consumption	27
manufacturing	14	Investment	19
Services	76	Exports	54
		Imports	-49

Structure of employment

	% of total		% of labour force
Agriculture	2.6	Unemployed 2013	7.0
Industry	19.7	Av. ann. rate 2000–13	5.4
Services	77.5		

Energy

	m TOE		
Total output	19.7	Net energy imports as %	
Total consumption	18.5	of energy use	-17
Consumption per person			
kg oil equivalent	3,302		

Inflation and finance

Consumer price		av. ann. increase 2009–14	
inflation 2014	0.6%	Narrow money (M1)	2.9%
Av. ann. inflation 2009–14	1.8%	Broad money	-1.6%
Money market rate, Sep. 2014	0.09%	H'hold saving rate, 2014	-0.2%

Exchange rates

	end 2014		December 2014
DKr per $	6.12	Effective rates	2010 = 100
DKr per SDR	8.87	– nominal	100.00
DKr per €	7.43	– real	98.60

Trade

Principal exports		**Principal imports**	
	$bn fob		*$bn cif*
Machinery & transport equip.	26.6	Machinery & transport equip.	28.7
Food, drink & tobacco	20.1	Food, drink & tobacco	13.0
Chemicals & related products	19.4	Chemicals & related products	11.9
Mineral fuels & lubricants	10.2	Mineral fuels & lubricants	9.8
Total incl. others	**110.4**	Total incl. others	**96.6**

Main export destinations		**Main origins of imports**	
	% of total		*% of total*
Germany	16.8	Germany	20.8
Sweden	12.1	Sweden	12.5
United Kingdom	8.7	Netherlands	7.5
United States	6.1	Norway	6.7
EU28	63.4	EU28	70.0

Balance of payments, reserves and aid, $bn

Visible exports fob	111.7	Overall balance	-0.6
Visible imports fob	-99.8	Change in reserves	-1.0
Trade balance	11.9	Level of reserves	
Invisibles inflows	103.1	end Dec.	88.7
Invisibles outflows	-83.9	No. months of import cover	5.8
Net transfers	-7.1	Official gold holdings, m oz	2.1
Current account balance	24.0	Aid given	2.9
– as % of GDP	7.2	– as % of GDP	0.9
Capital balance	-29.8		

Health and education

Health spending, % of GDP	10.6	Education spending, % of GDP	8.7
Doctors per 1,000 pop.	3.5	Enrolment, %: primary	101
Hospital beds per 1,000 pop.	3.5	secondary	120
Improved-water source access,		tertiary	80
% of pop.	100		

Society

No. of households, m	2.6	Cost of living, Dec. 2014	
Av. no. per household	2.1	New York = 100	115
Marriages per 1,000 pop.	5.1	Cars per 1,000 pop.	407
Divorces per 1,000 pop.	2.8	Colour TV households, % with:	
Religion, % of pop.		cable	65.3
Christian	83.5	satellite	11.8
Non-religious	11.8	Telephone lines per 100 pop.	37.3
Muslim	4.1	Mobile telephone subscribers	
Hindu	0.4	per 100 pop.	127.1
Other	0.2	Broadband subs per 100 pop.	40.2
Jewish	<0.1	Internet users, % of pop.	94.6

EGYPT

Area	1,000,250 sq km	Capital	Cairo
Arable as % of total land	2.8	Currency	Egyptian pound (£E)

People

Population	82.1m	Life expectancy: men	69.7 yrs
Pop. per sq km	82.1	women	74.6 yrs
Average annual growth		Adult literacy	73.9
in pop. 2015–20	1.5%	Fertility rate (per woman)	3.5
Pop. under 15	31.1%	Urban population	43.1%
Pop. over 60	8.7%		per 1,000 pop.
No. of men per 100 women	100.9	Crude birth rate	32
Human Development Index	68.2	Crude death rate	6.3

The economy

GDP	£E1,753bn	GDP per head	$3,310
GDP	$272bn	GDP per head in purchasing	
Av. ann. growth in real		power parity (USA=100)	20.9
GDP 2008–13	3.2%	Economic freedom index	55.2

Origins of GDP		Components of GDP	
	% of total		% of total
Agriculture	15	Private consumption	81
Industry, of which:	39	Public consumption	12
manufacturing	16	Investment	14
Services	46	Exports	18
		Imports	-25

Structure of employment

	% of total		% of labour force
Agriculture	29.2	Unemployed 2013	13.2
Industry	23.5	Av. ann. rate 2000–13	10.3
Services	47.1		

Energy

	m TOE		
Total output	95.2	Net energy imports as %	
Total consumption	88.5	of energy use	-14
Consumption per person			
kg oil equivalent	1,096		

Inflation and finance

Consumer price		av. ann. increase 2009–14	
inflation 2014	10.1%	Narrow money (M1)	17.7%
Av. ann. inflation 2009–14	9.7%	Broad money	13.1%
Treasury bill rate, Dec. 2014	11.65%		

Exchange rates

	end 2014		December 2014
£E per $	7.14	Effective rates	2010 = 100
£E per SDR	10.35	– nominal	...
£E per €	8.67	– real	...

Trade

Principal exports[a]		Principal imports[a]	
	$bn fob		*$bn cif*
Petroleum & products	11.7	Intermediate goods	16.5
Finished goods incl. textiles	9.9	Consumer goods	12.5
Semi-finished products	2.1	Fuels	11.8
Iron & steel	0.5	Capital goods	9.0
Total incl. others	**26.5**	Total incl. others	**55.8**

Main export destinations		Main origins of imports	
	% of total		*% of total*
Italy	9.3	China	10.5
India	7.4	Germany	7.8
Saudi Arabia	7.0	United States	7.8
Libya	4.4	Kuwait	4.0

Balance of payments[b], reserves and debt, $bn

Visible exports fob	26.8	Change in reserves	-3.0
Visible imports fob	-52.4	Level of reserves	
Trade balance	-25.5	end Dec.	15.7
Invisibles inflows	22.0	No. months of import cover	2.5
Invisibles outflows	-23.2	Official gold holdings, m oz	2.4
Net transfers	19.8	Foreign debt	44.4
Current account balance	-7.0	– as % of GDP	16.5
– as % of GDP	-2.7	– as % of total exports	68.9
Capital balance	3.3	Debt service ratio	5.3
Overall balance	-5.8		

Health and education

Health spending, % of GDP	5.1	Education spending, % of GDP	...
Doctors per 1,000 pop.	2.8	Enrolment, %: primary	113
Hospital beds per 1,000 pop.	0.5	secondary	86
Improved-water source access,		tertiary	30
% of pop.	99.3		

Society

No. of households, m	21.9	Cost of living, Dec. 2014	
Av. no. per household	3.8	New York = 100	63
Marriages per 1,000 pop.	11.2	Cars per 1,000 pop.	46
Divorces per 1,000 pop.	1.9	Colour TV households, % with:	
Religion, % of pop.		cable	...
Muslim	94.9	satellite	71.6
Christian	5.1	Telephone lines per 100 pop.	8.3
Hindu	<0.1	Mobile telephone subscribers	
Jewish	<0.1	per 100 pop.	121.5
Non-religious	<0.1	Broadband subs per 100 pop.	3.3
Other	<0.1	Internet users, % of pop.	49.6

a Year ending June 30 2013.   b 2012

ESTONIA

Area	45,200 sq km	Capital	Tallinn
Arable as % of total land	14.9	Currency	Euro (€)

People

Population	1.3m	Life expectancy: men	69.8 yrs
Pop. per sq km	28.8	women	80.1 yrs
Average annual growth		Adult literacy	99.9
in pop. 2015–20	-0.3%	Fertility rate (per woman)	1.5
Pop. under 15	15.8%	Urban population	67.5%
Pop. over 60	24.1%		per 1,000 pop.
No. of men per 100 women	86.4	Crude birth rate	11
Human Development Index	84	Crude death rate	6.7

The economy

GDP	€18.7bn	GDP per head	$18,880
GDP	$24.9bn	GDP per head in purchasing	
Av. ann. growth in real		power parity (USA=100)	48.7
GDP 2008–13	0.1%	Economic freedom index	76.8

Origins of GDP		Components of GDP	
	% of total		% of total
Agriculture	4	Private consumption	53
Industry, of which:	29	Public consumption	19
manufacturing	16	Investment	27
Services	67	Exports	86
		Imports	-85

Structure of employment

	% of total		% of labour force
Agriculture	4.7	Unemployed 2013	8.6
Industry	31.1	Av. ann. rate 2000–13	10.1
Services	64.1		

Energy

	m TOE		
Total output	0.4	Net energy imports as %	
Total consumption	2.3	of energy use	12
Consumption per person			
kg oil equivalent	1,750		

Inflation and finance

Consumer price		av. ann. increase 2009–14	
inflation 2014	0.5%	Euro area:	
Av. ann. inflation 2009–14	3.1%	Narrow money (M1)	5.6%
Deposit rate, h'holds, Dec. 2014	0.47%	Broad money	2.0%
		H'hold saving rate, 2014	0.3%

Exchange rates

	end 2014		December 2014
€ per $	0.82	Effective rates	2010 = 100
€ per SDR	1.19	– nominal	...
		– real	...

Trade

Principal exports		**Principal imports**	
	$bn fob		*$bn cif*
Machinery & transport equip.	4.6	Machinery & equipment	5.1
Timber products	1.8	Chemicals	2.4
Mineral products	1.7	Mineral products	2.3
Foodstuffs	1.7	Foodstuffs	2.0
Total incl. others	**16.3**	Total incl. others	**18.4**

Main export destinations		**Main origins of imports**	
	% of total		*% of total*
Sweden	16.8	Finland	15.0
Finland	16.1	Germany	10.5
Russia	11.5	Latvia	9.4
Latvia	10.4	Sweden	8.4
EU28	70.9	EU28	82.6

Balance of payments, reserves and debt, $bn

Visible exports fob	15.2	Change in reserves	0.0
Visible imports fob	-16.6	Level of reserves	
Trade balance	-1.3	end Dec.	0.3
Invisibles inflows	7.4	No. months of import cover	0.2
Invisibles outflows	-6.6	Official gold holdings, m oz	0.0
Net transfers	0.2	Foreign debt	21.3
Current account balance	-0.3	– as % of GDP	85.7
– as % of GDP	-1.2	– as % of total exports	94.0
Capital balance	0.2	Debt service ratio	10.3
Overall balance	0.0	Aid given	0.03
		– as % of GDP	0.1

Health and education

Health spending, % of GDP	5.7	Education spending, % of GDP	5.2
Doctors per 1,000 pop.	3.2	Enrolment, %: primary	98
Hospital beds per 1,000 pop.	5.3	secondary	107
Improved-water source access,		tertiary	77
% of pop.	99.1		

Society

No. of households, m	0.6	Cost of living, Dec. 2014	
Av. no. per household	2.2	New York = 100	...
Marriages per 1,000 pop.	4.5	Cars per 1,000 pop.	489
Divorces per 1,000 pop.	2.4	Colour TV households, % with:	
Religion, % of pop.		cable	47.1
Non-religious	59.6	satellite	16.6
Christian	39.9	Telephone lines per 100 pop.	33.1
Muslim	0.2	Mobile telephone subscribers	
Hindu	<0.1	per 100 pop.	159.7
Jewish	<0.1	Broadband subs per 100 pop.	26.5
Other	<0.1	Internet users, % of pop.	80.0

FINLAND

Area	338,145 sq km	Capital	Helsinki
Arable as % of total land	7.4	Currency	Euro (€)

People

Population	5.4m	Life expectancy: men	78.1 yrs
Pop. per sq km	16.0	women	84.4 yrs
Average annual growth		Adult literacy	...
in pop. 2015–20	0.3%	Fertility rate (per woman)	1.8
Pop. under 15	16.4%	Urban population	84.2%
Pop. over 60	26.3%		per 1,000 pop.
No. of men per 100 women	96.3	Crude birth rate	11
Human Development Index	87.9	Crude death rate	10.0

The economy

GDP	€201bn	GDP per head	$49,150
GDP	$267bn	GDP per head in purchasing	
Av. ann. growth in real		power parity (USA=100)	74.9
GDP 2008–13	-1.2%	Economic freedom index	73.4

Origins of GDP		Components of GDP	
	% of total		% of total
Agriculture	3	Private consumption	55
Industry, of which:	27	Public consumption	25
manufacturing	17	Investment	21
Services	70	Exports	38
		Imports	-39

Structure of employment

	% of total		% of labour force
Agriculture	4.1	Unemployed 2013	8.2
Industry	22.7	Av. ann. rate 2000–13	8.2
Services	72.7		

Energy

	m TOE		
Total output	12.3	Net energy imports as %	
Total consumption	30.5	of energy use	49
Consumption per person			
kg oil equivalent	5,640		

Inflation and finance

Consumer price		av. ann. increase 2009–14	
inflation 2014	1.2%	Euro area:	
Av. ann. inflation 2009–14	2.3%	Narrow money (M1)	5.6%
Money market rate, Dec. 2014	0.08%	Broad money	2.0%
		H'hold saving rate, 2014	2.1%

Exchange rates

	end 2014		December 2014
€ per $	0.82	Effective rates	2010 = 100
€ per SDR	1.19	– nominal	101.10
		– real	100.50

Trade

Principal exports		Principal imports	
	$bn fob		*$bn cif*
Machinery & transport equip.	20.0	Machinery & transport equip.	21.5
Mineral fuels & lubricants	9.4	Mineral fuels & lubricants	16.2
Chemicals & related products	6.2	Chemicals & related products	8.5
Raw materials	6.0	Raw materials	5.5
Total incl. others	**74.1**	Total incl. others	**74.0**

Main export destinations		Main origins of imports	
	% of total		*% of total*
Sweden	11.5	Russia	18.7
Germany	9.7	Sweden	16.8
Russia	9.4	Germany	14.6
Netherlands	6.2	Netherlands	8.6
EU28	55.3	EU28	66.3

Balance of payments, reserves and aid, $bn

Visible exports fob	78.6	Overall balance	1.1
Visible imports fob	-73.8	Change in reserves	0.2
Trade balance	4.8	Level of reserves	
Invisibles inflows	44.4	end Dec.	11.3
Invisibles outflows	-48.9	No. months of import cover	1.1
Net transfers	-2.8	Official gold holdings, m oz	1.6
Current account balance	-2.5	Aid given	1.4
– as % of GDP	-0.9	– as % of GDP	0.5
Capital balance	0.2		

Health and education

Health spending, % of GDP	9.4	Education spending, % of GDP	6.8
Doctors per 1,000 pop.	2.9	Enrolment, %: primary	100
Hospital beds per 1,000 pop.	5.5	secondary	108
Improved-water source access,		tertiary	94
% of pop.	100		

Society

No. of households, m	2.6	Cost of living, Dec. 2014	
Av. no. per household	2.1	New York = 100	109
Marriages per 1,000 pop.	5.3	Cars per 1,000 pop.	576
Divorces per 1,000 pop.	2.4	Colour TV households, % with:	
Religion, % of pop.		cable	68.5
Christian	81.6	satellite	11.1
Non-religious	17.6	Telephone lines per 100 pop.	13.9
Muslim	0.8	Mobile telephone subscribers	
Hindu	<0.1	per 100 pop.	171.6
Jewish	<0.1	Broadband subs per 100 pop.	30.8
Other	<0.1	Internet users, % of pop.	91.5

FRANCE

Area	543,965 sq km	Capital	Paris
Arable as % of total land	33.4	Currency	Euro (€)

People

Population	64.3m	Life expectancy: men	79.0 yrs
Pop. per sq km	118.2	women	85.9 yrs
Average annual growth		Adult literacy	...
in pop. 2015–20	0.5%	Fertility rate (per woman)	2
Pop. under 15	18.2%	Urban population	79.5%
Pop. over 60	24.1%		per 1,000 pop.
No. of men per 100 women	93.6	Crude birth rate	12
Human Development Index	88.4	Crude death rate	9.1

The economy

GDP	€2,114bn	GDP per head	$42,560
GDP	$2,806bn	GDP per head in purchasing	
Av. ann. growth in real		power parity (USA=100)	70.8
GDP 2008–13	0.3%	Economic freedom index	62.5

Origins of GDP		Components of GDP	
	% of total		% of total
Agriculture	2	Private consumption	55
Industry, of which:	20	Public consumption	24
manufacturing	11	Investment	22
Services	78	Exports	28
		Imports	-30

Structure of employment

	% of total		% of labour force
Agriculture	2.9	Unemployed 2013	9.9
Industry	21.7	Av. ann. rate 2000–13	9.0
Services	74.9		

Energy

	m TOE		
Total output	126.9	Net energy imports as %	
Total consumption	267.4	of energy use	47
Consumption per person			
kg oil equivalent	4,072		

Inflation and finance

Consumer price		av. ann. increase 2009–14	
inflation 2014	0.6%	Euro area:	
Av. ann. inflation 2009–14	1.6%	Narrow money (M1)	5.6%
Deposit rate, h'holds, Dec. 2014	2.68%	Broad money	2.0%
		H'hold saving rate[a], 2014	15.7%

Exchange rates

	end 2014		December 2014
€ per $	0.82	Effective rates	2010 = 100
€ per SDR	1.19	– nominal	98.40
		– real	95.60

Trade

Principal exports		Principal imports	
	$bn fob		*$bn cif*
Machinery & transport equip.	213.9	Machinery & transport equip.	217.0
Chemicals & related products	108.2	Mineral fuels & lubricants	108.6
Food, drink & tobacco	72.2	Chemicals & related products	93.0
Mineral fuels & lubricants	24.3	Food, drink & tobacco	56.5
Total incl. others	**579.6**	**Total incl. others**	**660.8**

Main export destinations		Main origins of imports	
	% of total		*% of total*
Germany	16.3	Germany	19.8
Belgium	7.7	Belgium	11.5
Italy	7.1	Italy	7.7
United Kingdom	6.9	Netherlands	7.6
EU28	59.4	EU28	67.8

Balance of payments, reserves and aid, $bn

Visible exports fob	580.8	Overall balance	-2.0
Visible imports fob	-637.3	Change in reserves	-39.4
Trade balance	-56.5	Level of reserves	
Invisibles inflows	460.3	end Dec.	145.2
Invisibles outflows	-384.0	No. months of import cover	1.7
Net transfers	-60.0	Official gold holdings, m oz	78.3
Current account balance	-40.2	Aid given	11.3
– as % of GDP	-1.4	– as % of GDP	0.4
Capital balance	19.6		

Health and education

Health spending, % of GDP	11.7	Education spending, % of GDP	5.7
Doctors per 1,000 pop.	3.2	Enrolment, %: primary	107
Hospital beds per 1,000 pop.	6.4	secondary	110
Improved-water source access,		tertiary	58
% of pop.	100		

Society

No. of households, m	28.8	Cost of living, Dec. 2014	
Av. no. per household	2.2	New York = 100	126
Marriages per 1,000 pop.	3.8	Cars per 1,000 pop.	497
Divorces per 1,000 pop.	2.0	Colour TV households, % with:	
Religion, % of pop.		cable	13.1
Christian	63.0	satellite	34.1
Non-religious	28.0	Telephone lines per 100 pop.	60.8
Muslim	7.5	Mobile telephone subscribers	
Other	1.0	per 100 pop.	98.5
Jewish	0.5	Broadband subs per 100 pop.	38.8
Hindu	<0.1	Internet users, % of pop.	81.9

a Gross.

GERMANY

Area	357,868 sq km	Capital	Berlin
Arable as % of total land	34.0	Currency	Euro (€)

People

Population	82.7m	Life expectancy: men	79.1 yrs
Pop. per sq km	231.1	women	83.8 yrs
Average annual growth		Adult literacy	...
in pop. 2015–20	-0.2%	Fertility rate (per woman)	1.4
Pop. under 15	13.1%	Urban population	75.3%
Pop. over 60	27.1%		per 1,000 pop.
No. of men per 100 women	96.1	Crude birth rate	8
Human Development Index	91.1	Crude death rate	11.5

The economy

GDP	€2,810bn	GDP per head	$46,250
GDP	$3,730bn	GDP per head in purchasing	
Av. ann. growth in real		power parity (USA=100)	82.7
GDP 2008–13	0.5%	Economic freedom index	73.8

Origins of GDP		Components of GDP	
	% of total		% of total
Agriculture	1	Private consumption	56
Industry, of which:	31	Public consumption	19
manufacturing	22	Investment	19
Services	68	Exports	46
		Imports	-40

Structure of employment

	% of total		% of labour force
Agriculture	1.5	Unemployed 2013	5.3
Industry	28.2	Av. ann. rate 2000–13	8.0
Services	70.2		

Energy

	m TOE		
Total output	120.1	Net energy imports as %	
Total consumption	336.6	of energy use	60
Consumption per person			
kg oil equivalent	4,186		

Inflation and finance

Consumer price			av. ann. increase 2009–14
inflation 2014	0.8%	Euro area:	
Av. ann. inflation 2009–14	1.6%	Narrow money (M1)	5.6%
Deposit rate, h'holds, Dec. 2014	0.70%	Broad money	2.0%
		H'hold saving rate, 2014	9.9%

Exchange rates

	end 2014		December 2014
€ per $	0.82	Effective rates	2010 = 100
€ per SDR	1.19	– nominal	99.80
		– real	97.30

Trade

Principal exports		Principal imports	
	$bn fob		*$bn cif*
Machinery & transport equip.	685.2	Machinery & transport equip.	392.5
Chemicals & related products	225.8	Mineral fuels & lubricants	176.1
Food, drink & tobacco	80.0	Chemicals & related products	152.0
Mineral fuels & lubricants	46.8	Food, drink & tobacco	85.4
Total incl. others	**1,457.8**	Total incl. others	**1,196.1**

Main export destinations		Main origins of imports	
	% of total		*% of total*
France	9.1	Netherlands	13.9
United Kingdom	6.9	France	7.6
Netherlands	6.5	China	6.3
United States	6.1	Belgium	6.3
EU28	57.1	EU28	64.5

Balance of payments, reserves and aid, $bn

Visible exports fob	1,439	Overall balance	1
Visible imports fob	-1,163	Change in reserves	-50
Trade balance	276	Level of reserves	
Invisibles inflows	521	end Dec.	199
Invisibles outflows	-500	No. months of import cover	1.4
Net transfers	-55	Official gold holdings, m oz	109
Current account balance	242	Aid given	14.3
– as % of GDP	6.5	– as % of GDP	0.4
Capital balance	-274		

Health and education

Health spending, % of GDP	11.3	Education spending, % of GDP	5.0
Doctors per 1,000 pop.	3.9	Enrolment, %: primary	100
Hospital beds per 1,000 pop.	8.2	secondary	101
Improved-water source access,		tertiary	62
% of pop.	100		

Society

No. of households, m	41.0	Cost of living, Dec. 2014	
Av. no. per household	2.0	New York = 100	91
Marriages per 1,000 pop.	4.7	Cars per 1,000 pop.	539
Divorces per 1,000 pop.	2.2	Colour TV households, % with:	
Religion, % of pop.		cable	46.0
Christian	68.7	satellite	45.1
Non-religious	24.7	Telephone lines per 100 pop.	58.9
Muslim	5.8	Mobile telephone subscribers	
Other	0.5	per 100 pop.	120.9
Jewish	0.3	Broadband subs per 100 pop.	34.6
Hindu	<0.1	Internet users, % of pop.	84.0

GREECE

Area	131,957 sq km	Capital	Athens
Arable as % of total land	19.7	Currency	Euro (€)

People

Population	11.1m	Life expectancy: men	79.2 yrs
Pop. per sq km	84.1	women	83.7 yrs
Average annual growth		Adult literacy	97.4
in pop. 2015-20	-0.1%	Fertility rate (per woman)	1.3
Pop. under 15	14.7%	Urban population	78.0%
Pop. over 60	25.7%		per 1,000 pop.
No. of men per 100 women	97.3	Crude birth rate	9
Human Development Index	85.3	Crude death rate	10.9

The economy

GDP	€182bn	GDP per head	$21,970
GDP	$242bn	GDP per head in purchasing	
Av. ann. growth in real		power parity (USA=100)	48.4
GDP 2008-13	-5.9%	Economic freedom index	54

Origins of GDP		**Components of GDP**	
	% of total		% of total
Agriculture	4	Private consumption	71
Industry, of which:	14	Public consumption	20
manufacturing	8	Investment	12
Services	82	Exports	30
		Imports	-33

Structure of employment

	% of total		% of labour force
Agriculture	13	Unemployed 2013	27.3
Industry	16.7	Av. ann. rate 2000-13	12.7
Services	70.3		

Energy

	m TOE		
Total output	10.2	Net energy imports as %	
Total consumption	30.6	of energy use	61
Consumption per person			
kg oil equivalent	2,761		

Inflation and finance

Consumer price		av. ann. increase 2009-14	
inflation 2014	-1.4%	Euro area:	
Av. ann. inflation 2009-14	1.4%	Narrow money (M1)	5.6%
Treasury bill rate, Dec. 2014	0.33%	Broad money	2.0%

Exchange rates

	end 2014		December 2014
€ per $	0.82	Effective rates	2010 = 100
€ per SDR	1.19	– nominal	99.30
		– real	91.90

Trade

Principal exports		**Principal imports**	
	$bn fob		*$bn cif*
Mineral fuels & lubricants	14.2	Mineral fuels & lubricants	22.4
Food, drink & tobacco	5.5	Machinery & transport equip.	9.3
Chemicals & related products	3.4	Chemicals & related products	8.5
Machinery & transport equip.	2.7	Food, drink & tobacco	7.4
Total incl. others	**36.6**	Total incl. others	**62.3**

Main export destinations		**Main origins of imports**	
	% of total		*% of total*
Turkey	11.8	Russia	14.0
Italy	9.1	Germany	9.8
Germany	6.7	Italy	8.1
Bulgaria	5.4	Iraq	7.8
EU28	46.6	EU28	47.3

Balance of payments, reserves and debt, $bn

Visible exports fob	29.6	Overall balance	-6.5
Visible imports fob	-52.5	Change in reserves	-1.5
Trade balance	-22.9	Level of reserves	
Invisibles inflows	45.9	end Dec.	5.8
Invisibles outflows	-23.9	No. months of import cover	0.9
Net transfers	2.4	Official gold holdings, m oz	3.6
Current account balance	1.4	Aid given	0.2
– as % of GDP	0.6	– as % of GDP	0.1
Capital balance	-6.8		

Health and education

Health spending, % of GDP	9.8	Education spending, % of GDP	...
Doctors per 1,000 pop.	6.2	Enrolment, %: primary	102
Hospital beds per 1,000 pop.	4.8	secondary	109
Improved-water source access,		tertiary	117
% of pop.	100		

Society

No. of households, m	4.2	Cost of living, Dec. 2014	
Av. no. per household	2.6	New York = 100	74
Marriages per 1,000 pop.	4.5	Cars per 1,000 pop.	463
Divorces per 1,000 pop.	1.2	Colour TV households, % with:	
Religion, % of pop.		cable	0.9
Christian	88.1	satellite	13.5
Non-religious	6.1	Telephone lines per 100 pop.	47.9
Muslim	5.3	Mobile telephone subscribers	
Other	0.3	per 100 pop.	116.8
Hindu	0.1	Broadband subs per 100 pop.	26.2
Jewish	<0.1	Internet users, % of pop.	59.9

Note: At the time of going to press, uncertainty remained over Greece's future as part of the euro zone.

HONG KONG

Area	1,075 sq km	Capital	Victoria
Arable as % of total land	...	Currency	Hong Kong dollar (HK$)

People

Population	7.2m	Life expectancy: men	81.2 yrs
Pop. per sq km	6,697.7	women	87.2 yrs
Average annual growth		Adult literacy	...
in pop. 2015-20	0.6%	Fertility rate (per woman)	1.1
Pop. under 15	11.7%	Urban population	100.0%
Pop. over 60	20.1%		per 1,000 pop.
No. of men per 100 women	88.1	Crude birth rate	8
Human Development Index	89.1	Crude death rate	6.7

The economy

GDP	HK$2,125bn	GDP per head	$38,120
GDP	$274bn	GDP per head in purchasing	
Av. ann. growth in real		power parity (USA=100)	100.3
GDP 2008-13	2.7%	Economic freedom index	89.6

Origins of GDP		Components of GDP	
	% of total		% of total
Agriculture	0	Private consumption	66
Industry, of which:	7	Public consumption	9
manufacturing	1	Investment	24
Services	93	Exports	230
		Imports	-229

Structure of employment

	% of total		% of labour force
Agriculture	0	Unemployed 2013	3.4
Industry	11.6	Av. ann. rate 2000-13	5.0
Services	88.4		

Energy

	m TOE		
Total output	0.0	Net energy imports as %	
Total consumption	30.3	of energy use	100
Consumption per person			
kg oil equivalent	4,239		

Inflation and finance

			av. ann. increase 2009-14
Consumer price			
inflation 2014	4.4%	Narrow money (M1)	13.6%
Av. ann. inflation 2009-14	4.1%	Broad money	10.7%
Money market rate, Dec. 2014	0.13%		

Exchange rates

	end 2014		December 2014
HK$ per $	7.76	Effective rates	2010 = 100
HK$ per SDR	11.24	– nominal	...
HK$ per €	9.42	– real	...

Trade

Principal exports[a]		Principal imports[a]	
	$bn fob		*$bn cif*
Capital goods	186.3	Capital goods	187.7
Raw materials &		Raw materials &	
semi-manufactures	150.3	semi-manufactures	175.2
Consumer goods	108.5	Consumer goods	120.5
Foodstuffs	5.5	Foodstuffs	21.8
Total incl. others	**459.3**	Total incl. others	**524.1**

Main export destinations		Main origins of imports	
	% of total		*% of total*
China	54.0	China	47.8
United States	9.3	Japan	7.0
Japan	3.8	Singapore	6.4
Taiwan	2.3	Taiwan	5.4

Balance of payments, reserves and debt, $bn

Visible exports fob	506.2	Change in reserves	-6.2
Visible imports fob	-534.1	Level of reserves	
Trade balance	-27.9	end Dec.	311.2
Invisibles inflows	257.3	No. months of import cover	4.9
Invisibles outflows	-222.6	Official gold holdings, m oz	0.1
Net transfers	-2.7	Foreign debt	172.0
Current account balance	4.2	– as % of GDP	62.6
– as % of GDP	1.5	– as % of total exports	22.5
Capital balance	-3.7	Debt service ratio	2.3
Overall balance	7.5		

Health and education

Health spending, % of GDP	...	Education spending, % of GDP	3.8
Doctors per 1,000 pop.	...	Enrolment, %: primary	105
Hospital beds per 1,000 pop.	...	secondary	99
Improved-water source access,		tertiary	67
% of pop.	...		

Society

No. of households, m	2.4	Cost of living, Dec. 2014	
Av. no. per household	3.0	New York = 100	113
Marriages per 1,000 pop.	7.7	Cars per 1,000 pop.	68
Divorces per 1,000 pop.	...	Colour TV households, % with:	
Religion, % of pop.		cable	94.4
Non-religious	56.1	satellite	0.1
Christian	14.3	Telephone lines per 100 pop.	63.1
Other	14.2	Mobile telephone subscribers	
Buddhist	13.2	per 100 pop.	237.4
Muslim	1.8	Broadband subs per 100 pop.	30.8
Hindu	0.4	Internet users, % of pop.	74.2

a Including re-exports.
Note: Hong Kong became a Special Administrative Region of China on July 1 1997.

HUNGARY

Area	93,030 sq km	Capital	Budapest
Arable as % of total land	48.6	Currency	Forint (Ft)

People

Population	10.0m	Life expectancy: men	71.2 yrs
Pop. per sq km	107.5	women	79.2 yrs
Average annual growth		Adult literacy	99.4
in pop. 2015-20	-0.2%	Fertility rate (per woman)	1.3
Pop. under 15	14.7%	Urban population	71.2%
Pop. over 60	23.9%		per 1,000 pop.
No. of men per 100 women	90.5	Crude birth rate	9
Human Development Index	81.8	Crude death rate	13.6

The economy

GDP	Ft29,846bn	GDP per head	$13,490
GDP	$133bn	GDP per head in purchasing	
Av. ann. growth in real		power parity (USA=100)	44.0
GDP 2008–13	-0.8%	Economic freedom index	66.8

Origins of GDP		**Components of GDP**	
	% of total		% of total
Agriculture	4	Private consumption	53
Industry, of which:	30	Public consumption	20
manufacturing	23	Investment	20
Services	65	Exports	89
		Imports	-81

Structure of employment

	% of total		% of labour force
Agriculture	5.2	Unemployed 2013	10.2
Industry	29.8	Av. ann. rate 2000–13	8.1
Services	64.9		

Energy

	m TOE		
Total output	9.3	Net energy imports as %	
Total consumption	23.8	of energy use	55
Consumption per person			
kg oil equivalent	2,395		

Inflation and finance

Consumer price		av. ann. increase 2009–14	
inflation 2014	-0.3%	Narrow money (M1)	11.9%
Av. ann. inflation 2009–14	3.2%	Broad money	1.7%
Treasury bill rate, Dec. 2014	1.59%	H'hold saving rate, 2014	5.4%

Exchange rates

	end 2014		December 2014
Ft per $	259.13	Effective rates	2010 = 100
Ft per SDR	375.43	– nominal	89.40
Ft per €	314.61	– real	90.90

Trade

Principal exports		Principal imports	
	$bn fob		*$bn cif*
Machinery & equipment	57.8	Machinery & equipment	45.3
Manufactured goods	34.6	Manufactured goods	33.9
Food, drink & tobacco	8.8	Fuels & energy	5.1
Raw materials	3.3	Food, drink & tobacco	2.3
Total incl. others	**107.8**	Total incl. others	**99.1**

Main export destinations		Main origins of imports	
	% of total		*% of total*
Germany	26.0	Germany	25.3
Romania	5.7	Russia	8.5
Slovakia	5.6	Austria	6.8
Austria	5.4	China	6.7
EU28	77.8	EU28	71.7

Balance of payments, reserves and debt, $bn

Visible exports fob	96.1	Change in reserves	1.8
Visible imports fob	-91.4	Level of reserves	
Trade balance	4.7	end Dec.	46.5
Invisibles inflows	39.1	No. months of import cover	4.3
Invisibles outflows	-37.6	Official gold holdings, m oz	0.1
Net transfers	-0.8	Foreign debt	149.1
Current account balance	5.3	– as % of GDP	111.7
– as % of GDP	4.0	– as % of total exports	110.6
Capital balance	4.7	Debt service ratio	30.3
Overall balance	8.3	Aid given	0.1
		– as % of GDP	0.1

Health and education

Health spending, % of GDP	8	Education spending, % of GDP	4.7
Doctors per 1,000 pop.	3.1	Enrolment, %: primary	100
Hospital beds per 1,000 pop.	7.2	secondary	102
Improved-water source access,		tertiary	60
% of pop.	100		

Society

No. of households, m	4.1	Cost of living, Dec. 2014	
Av. no. per household	2.4	New York = 100	63
Marriages per 1,000 pop.	3.6	Cars per 1,000 pop.	307
Divorces per 1,000 pop.	2.2	Colour TV households, % with:	
Religion, % of pop.		cable	56.4
Christian	81.0	satellite	28.5
Non-religious	18.6	Telephone lines per 100 pop.	29.9
Other	0.2	Mobile telephone subscribers	
Jewish	0.1	per 100 pop.	116.4
Hindu	<0.1	Broadband subs per 100 pop.	24.9
Muslim	<0.1	Internet users, % of pop.	72.6

INDIA

Area	3,287,263 sq km	Capital	New Delhi
Arable as % of total land	52.5	Currency	Indian rupee (Rs)

People

Population	1,252.1m	Life expectancy: men	65.8 yrs
Pop. per sq km	380.9	women	69.3 yrs
Average annual growth		Adult literacy	...
in pop. 2015-20	1.1%	Fertility rate (per woman)	2.4
Pop. under 15	29.1%	Urban population	32.7%
Pop. over 60	8.3%		per 1,000 pop.
No. of men per 100 women	107.2	Crude birth rate	22
Human Development Index	58.6	Crude death rate	6.3

The economy

GDP	Rs113.5trn	GDP per head	$1,500
GDP	$1,875bn	GDP per head in purchasing	
Av. ann. growth in real		power parity (USA=100)	10.2
GDP 2008–13	7.5%	Economic freedom index	54.6

Origins of GDP		**Components of GDP**	
	% of total		% of total
Agriculture	18	Private consumption	59
Industry, of which:	31	Public consumption	11
manufacturing	17	Investment	33
Services	51	Exports	25
		Imports	-28

Structure of employment

	% of total		% of labour force
Agriculture	47.2	Unemployed 2013	4.5
Industry	24.7	Av. ann. rate 2000–13	4.0
Services	28.1		

Energy

	m TOE		
Total output	396.9	Net energy imports as %	
Total consumption	597.9	of energy use	28
Consumption per person			
kg oil equivalent	483		

Inflation and finance

		av. ann. increase 2009–14	
Consumer price			
inflation 2014	6.0%	Narrow money (M1)	10.6%
Av. ann. inflation 2009–14	9.0%	Broad money	14.3%
Lending rate, Dec. 2014	10.25%		

Exchange rates

	end 2014		December 2014
Rs per $	63.33	Effective rates	2010 = 100
Rs per SDR	91.76	– nominal	...
Rs per €	76.89	– real	...

Trade

Principal exports[a]		Principal imports[a]	
	$bn fob		$bn cif
Engineering products	67.9	Petroleum & products	164.7
Petroleum & products	64.0	Gold & silver	43.9
Agricultural products	42.9	Electronic goods	31.7
Gems & jewellery	42.5	Machinery	24.5
Total incl. others	**318.4**	**Total incl. others**	**470.8**

Main export destinations		Main origins of imports	
	% of total		% of total
United Arab Emirates	10.0	China	10.9
United States	12.2	Saudi Arabia	7.7
China	4.6	United Arab Emirates	7.1
Hong Kong	4.1	United States	5.0

Balance of payments, reserves and debt, $bn

Visible exports fob	319.1	Change in reserves	-2.3
Visible imports fob	-433.8	Level of reserves	
Trade balance	-114.7	end Dec.	298.1
Invisibles inflows	159.9	No. months of import cover	6.0
Invisibles outflows	-159.3	Official gold holdings, m oz	17.9
Net transfers	64.8	Foreign debt	427.6
Current account balance	-49.2	– as % of GDP	22.8
– as % of GDP	-2.6	– as % of total exports	77.8
Capital balance	60.1	Debt service ratio	7.5
Overall balance	10.9		

Health and education

Health spending, % of GDP	4.0	Education spending, % of GDP	3.8
Doctors per 1,000 pop.	0.7	Enrolment, %: primary	113
Hospital beds per 1,000 pop.	0.7	secondary	69
Improved-water source access,		tertiary	25
% of pop.	92.6		

Society

No. of households, m	257.8	Cost of living, Dec. 2014	
Av. no. per household	4.8	New York = 100	48
Marriages per 1,000 pop.	...	Cars per 1,000 pop.	22
Divorces per 1,000 pop.	...	Colour TV households, % with:	
Religion, % of pop.		cable	62.5
Hindu	79.5	satellite	17.1
Muslim	14.4	Telephone lines per 100 pop.	2.3
Other	3.6	Mobile telephone subscribers	
Christian	2.5	per 100 pop.	70.8
Jewish	<0.1	Broadband subs per 100 pop.	1.2
Non-religious	<0.1	Internet users, % of pop.	15.1

a Year ending March 31 2013.

INDONESIA

Area	1,904,443 sq km	Capital	Jakarta
Arable as % of total land	13.0	Currency	Rupiah (Rp)

People

Population	249.9m	Life expectancy: men	69.7
Pop. per sq km	131.2	women	73.9
Average annual growth		Adult literacy	92.8
in pop. 2015-20	1.0%	Fertility rate (per woman)	2.6
Pop. under 15	28.9%	Urban population	53.7%
Pop. over 60	8.1%		per 1,000 pop.
No. of men per 100 women	101.3	Crude birth rate	20
Human Development Index	68.4	Crude death rate	6.3

The economy

GDP	Rp9,084trn	GDP per head	$3,480
GDP	$868bn	GDP per head in purchasing	
Av. ann. growth in real		power parity (USA=100)	18.0
GDP 2008-13	5.8%	Economic freedom index	58.1

Origins of GDP		Components of GDP	
	% of total		% of total
Agriculture	14	Private consumption	59
Industry, of which:	46	Public consumption	9
manufacturing	24	Investment	34
Services	40	Exports	24
		Imports	-26

Structure of employment

	% of total		% of labour force
Agriculture	35.1	Unemployed 2013	6.2
Industry	21.7	Av. ann. rate 2000-13	8.3
Services	43.2		

Energy

	m TOE		
Total output	407.1	Net energy imports as %	
Total consumption	160.6	of energy use	-89
Consumption per person			
kg oil equivalent	651		

Inflation and finance

Consumer price		av. ann. increase 2009-14	
inflation 2014	6.4%	Narrow money (M1)	12.8%
Av. ann. inflation 2009-14	5.5%	Broad money	14.3%
Money market rate, Dec. 2014	5.84%		

Exchange rates

	end 2014		December 2014
Rp per $	12,440.00	Effective rates	2010 = 100
Rp per SDR	18,023.00	– nominal	...
Rp per €	15,103.40	– real	...

Trade

Principal exports		Principal imports	
	$bn fob		$bn cif
Mineral fuels	58.0	Machinery & transport equip.	59.7
Machinery & transport equip.	32.0	Mineral fuels	44.8
Crude materials, excl. fuels	27.0	Manufactured goods	27.1
Animal & vegetable oils	23.0	Chemicals & related products	23.1
Total incl. others	**182.6**	**Total incl. others**	**186.6**

Main export destinations		Main origins of imports	
	% of total		% of total
Japan	14.8	China	16.0
China	12.4	Singapore	13.7
Singapore	9.1	Japan	10.3
United States	8.6	Malaysia	7.1

Balance of payments, reserves and debt, $bn

Visible exports fob	182.1	Change in reserves	-13.4
Visible imports fob	-176.3	Level of reserves	
Trade balance	5.8	end Dec.	99.4
Invisibles inflows	25.5	No. months of import cover	5.0
Invisibles outflows	-64.7	Official gold holdings, m oz	2.5
Net transfers	4.2	Foreign debt	259.1
Current account balance	-29.1	– as % of GDP	28.5
– as % of GDP	-3.4	– as % of total exports	120.4
Capital balance	22.0	Debt service ratio	18.7
Overall balance	-7.3		

Health and education

Health spending, % of GDP	3.1	Education spending, % of GDP	3.6
Doctors per 1,000 pop.	0.2	Enrolment, %: primary	109
Hospital beds per 1,000 pop.	0.9	secondary	83
Improved-water source access,		tertiary	32
% of pop.	84.9		

Society

No. of households, m	63.3	Cost of living, Dec. 2014	
Av. no. per household	3.9	New York = 100	70
Marriages per 1,000 pop.	...	Cars per 1,000 pop.	47
Divorces per 1,000 pop.	...	Colour TV households, % with:	
Religion, % of pop.		cable	6.0
Muslim	87.2	satellite	25.5
Christian	9.9	Telephone lines per 100 pop.	12.3
Hindu	1.7	Mobile telephone subscribers	
Other	1.1	per 100 pop.	125.4
Jewish	<0.1	Broadband subs per 100 pop.	1.3
Non-religious	<0.1	Internet users, % of pop.	15.8

IRAN

Area	1,648,000 sq km	Capital	Tehran
Arable as % of total land	10.9	Currency	Rial (IR)

People

Population	77.4m	Life expectancy: men	73.5 yrs
Pop. per sq km	47.0	women	77.3 yrs
Average annual growth		Adult literacy	84.3
in pop. 2015-20	1.1%	Fertility rate (per woman)	1.8
Pop. under 15	23.8%	Urban population	73.4%
Pop. over 60	8.1%		per 1,000 pop.
No. of men per 100 women	102.3	Crude birth rate	19
Human Development Index	74.9	Crude death rate	5.1

The economy

GDP	IR6,793trn	GDP per head	$4,760
GDP	$369bn	GDP per head in purchasing	
Av. ann. growth in real		power parity (USA=100)	29.4
GDP 2008-13	0.7%	Economic freedom index	41.8

Origins of GDP		Components of GDP	
	% of total		% of total
Agriculture	9	Private consumption	50
Industry, of which:	40	Public consumption	10
manufacturing	12	Investment	32
Services	53	Exports	28
		Imports	-20

Structure of employment

	% of total		% of labour force
Agriculture	21.2	Unemployed 2013	10.4
Industry	32.2	Av. ann. rate 2000-13	12.0
Services	46.5		

Energy

	m TOE		
Total output	341.1	Net energy imports as %	
Total consumption	241.1	of energy use	-67
Consumption per person			
kg oil equivalent	3,155		

Inflation and finance

Consumer price		av. ann. increase 2009-14	
inflation 2014	15.5%	Narrow money (M1)	8.1%
Av. ann. inflation 2009-14	22.6%	Broad money	4.3%
Deposit rate, 1yr, 2014	...		

Exchange rates

	end 2014		December 2014
IR per $	27,138.00	Effective rates	2010 = 100
IR per SDR	39,318.00	– nominal	41.71
IR per €	32,948.25	– real	101.28

Trade

Principal exports[a]		Principal imports[a]	
	$bn fob		*$bn cif*
Oil & gas	64.8	Machinery & transport equip.	15.5
Industrial goods excl. oil &		Foodstuffs & live animals	10.6
gas products	19.6	Chemicals	7.3
Agricultural & traditional goods	4.5	Iron & steel	3.6
Metallic minerals & ores	1.7	Mineral products & fuels	1.6
Total incl. others	**93.0**	Total incl. others	**49.4**

Main export destinations		Main origins of imports	
	% of total		*% of total*
China	27.3	United Arab Emirates	36.3
Turkey	11.1	China	18.9
India	10.8	India	6.5
Japan	7.4	South Korea	5.9

Balance of payments[a], reserves and debt, $bn

Visible exports fob	93.0	Change in reserves	...
Visible imports fob	-60.0	Level of reserves	
Trade balance	33.0	end Dec.	...
Invisibles inflows	7.7	No. months of import cover	...
Invisibles outflows	-14.5	Official gold holdings, m oz	...
Net transfers	0.6	Foreign debt	7.6
Current account balance	28.0	– as % of GDP	1.5
– as % of GDP	7.6	– as % of total exports	7.4
Capital balance	25.8	Debt service ratio	0.4
Overall balance	52.4		

Health and education

Health spending, % of GDP	6.7	Education spending, % of GDP	3.7
Doctors per 1,000 pop.	0.9	Enrolment, %: primary	119
Hospital beds per 1,000 pop.	0.1	secondary	86
Improved-water source access,		tertiary	55
% of pop.	95.9		

Society

No. of households, m	22.6	Cost of living, Dec. 2014	
Av. no. per household	3.4	New York = 100	49
Marriages per 1,000 pop.	10.9	Cars per 1,000 pop.	149
Divorces per 1,000 pop.	2.0	Colour TV households, % with:	
Religion, % of pop.		cable	...
Muslim	99.5	satellite	37.0
Christian	0.2	Telephone lines per 100 pop.	38.3
Other	0.2	Mobile telephone subscribers	
Non-religious	0.1	per 100 pop.	84.3
Hindu	<0.1	Broadband subs per 100 pop.	5.6
Jewish	<0.1	Internet users, % of pop.	31.4

a Iranian year ending March 20 2014.

IRELAND

Area	70,282 sq km	Capital	Dublin
Arable as % of total land	17.0	Currency	Euro (€)

People

Population	4.6m	Life expectancy: men	79.5 yrs
Pop. per sq km	65.5	women	83.5 yrs
Average annual growth		Adult literacy	...
in pop. 2015-20	0.1%	Fertility rate (per woman)	2
Pop. under 15	21.6%	Urban population	63.2%
Pop. over 60	16.9%		per 1,000 pop.
No. of men per 100 women	98.4	Crude birth rate	15
Human Development Index	89.9	Crude death rate	6.4

The economy

GDP	€175bn	GDP per head	$50,480
GDP	$232bn	GDP per head in purchasing	
Av. ann. growth in real		power parity (USA=100)	86.1
GDP 2008-13	-0.8%	Economic freedom index	76.6

Origins of GDP		**Components of GDP**	
	% of total		% of total
Agriculture	2	Private consumption	46
Industry, of which:	24	Public consumption	17
manufacturing	19	Investment	16
Services	74	Exports	105
		Imports	-84

Structure of employment

	% of total		% of labour force
Agriculture	4.7	Unemployed 2013	13.0
Industry	18.3	Av. ann. rate 2000-13	7.8
Services	76.9		

Energy

	m TOE		
Total output	1.5	Net energy imports as %	
Total consumption	14.5	of energy use	90
Consumption per person			
kg oil equivalent	3,170		

Inflation and finance

Consumer price		av. ann. increase 2009-14	
inflation 2014	0.3%	Euro area:	
Av. ann. inflation 2009-14	0.5%	Narrow money (M1)	5.6%
Deposit rate, h'holds, Dec. 2014	1.70%	Broad money	2.0%
		H'hold saving rate, 2014	5.0%

Exchange rates

	end 2014		December 2014
€ per $	0.82	Effective rates	2010 = 100
€ per SDR	1.19	– nominal	93.54
		– real	87.76

Trade

Principal exports		Principal imports	
	$bn fob		*$bn cif*
Chemicals & related products	65.7	Machinery & transport equip.	15.8
Food, drink & tobacco	12.9	Chemicals & related products	14.1
Machinery & transport equip.	12.9	Mineral fuels & lubricants	9.0
Raw materials	2.3	Food, drink & tobacco	8.9
Total incl. others	**115.5**	Total incl. others	**66.5**

Main export destinations		Main origins of imports	
	% of total		*% of total*
United States	18.3	United Kingdom	39.0
United Kingdom	15.9	United States	9.7
Belgium	12.9	Germany	8.5
Germany	7.2	Netherlands	6.2
EU28	56.9	EU28	70.6

Balance of payments, reserves and aid, $bn

Visible exports fob	116.1	Overall balance	-4.4
Visible imports fob	-66.1	Change in reserves	-0.1
Trade balance	50.0	Level of reserves	
Invisibles inflows	191.9	end Dec.	1.6
Invisibles outflows	-225.6	No. months of import cover	0.1
Net transfers	-1.8	Official gold holdings, m oz	0.2
Current account balance	14.4	Aid given	0.8
– as % of GDP	6.2	– as % of GDP	0.5
Capital balance	-17.7		

Health and education

Health spending, % of GDP	8.9	Education spending, % of GDP	6.2
Doctors per 1,000 pop.	2.7	Enrolment, %: primary	104
Hospital beds per 1,000 pop.	2.9	secondary	119
Improved-water source access,		tertiary	71
% of pop.	99.9		

Society

No. of households, m	1.7	Cost of living, Dec. 2014	
Av. no. per household	2.7	New York = 100	100
Marriages per 1,000 pop.	4.5	Cars per 1,000 pop.	415
Divorces per 1,000 pop.	0.6	Colour TV households, % with:	
Religion, % of pop.		cable	31.7
Christian	92.0	satellite	47.6
Non-religious	6.2	Telephone lines per 100 pop.	44.0
Muslim	1.1	Mobile telephone subscribers	
Other	0.4	per 100 pop.	102.8
Hindu	0.2	Broadband subs per 100 pop.	24.2
Jewish	<0.1	Internet users, % of pop.	78.3

ISRAEL

Area	20,770 sq km	Capital	Jerusalem[a]
Arable as % of total land	13.6	Currency	New Shekel (NIS)

People

Population	7.7m	Life expectancy: men	80.6 yrs
Pop. per sq km	370.7	women	84.2 yrs
Average annual growth		Adult literacy	97.8
in pop. 2015-20	1.4%	Fertility rate (per woman)	3
Pop. under 15	27.7%	Urban population	92.1%
Pop. over 60	15.3%		per 1,000 pop.
No. of men per 100 women	97.6	Crude birth rate	21
Human Development Index	88.8	Crude death rate	5.4

The economy

GDP	NIS1,049bn	GDP per head	$36,050
GDP	$291bn	GDP per head in purchasing	
Av. ann. growth in real		power parity (USA=100)	61.3
GDP 2008–13	3.6%	Economic freedom index	70.5

Origins of GDP		**Components of GDP**	
	% of total		% of total
Agriculture	2	Private consumption	57
Industry, of which:	27	Public consumption	22
manufacturing	20	Investment	20
Services	69	Exports	33
		Imports	-32

Structure of employment

	% of total		% of labour force
Agriculture	1.7	Unemployed 2013	6.2
Industry	20.4	Av. ann. rate 2000–13	8.1
Services	77.1		

Energy

	m TOE		
Total output	2.4	Net energy imports as %	
Total consumption	26.1	of energy use	86
Consumption per person			
kg oil equivalent	3,299		

Inflation and finance

Consumer price		av. ann. increase 2009–14	
inflation 2014	0.5%	Narrow money (M1)	11.1%
Av. ann. inflation 2009–14	2.0%	Broad money	7.2%
Treasury bill rate, Dec. 2014	0.25%		

Exchange rates

	end 2014		December 2014
NIS per $	3.89	Effective rates	2010 = 100
NIS per SDR	5.63	– nominal	101.38
NIS per €	4.72	– real	98.18

Trade

Principal exports		**Principal imports**	
	$bn fob		*$bn cif*
Chemicals & chemical products	16.7	Fuel	14.6
Polished diamonds	9.2	Diamonds	8.3
Communications, medical &		Machinery & equipment	5.7
scientific equipment	7.9	Chemicals	4.6
Electronics	4.8		
Total incl. others	**56.9**	Total incl. others	**71.1**

Main export destinations		**Main origins of imports**	
	% of total		*% of total*
United States	31.0	United States	11.5
Hong Kong	9.5	China	7.9
United Kingdom	6.9	Germany	6.6
Belgium	5.5	Switzerland	6.2

Balance of payments, reserves and debt, $bn

Visible exports fob	62.0	Change in reserves	5.9
Visible imports fob	-71.3	Level of reserves	
Trade balance	-9.3	end Dec.	81.8
Invisibles inflows	41.8	No. months of import cover	9.3
Invisibles outflows	-34.7	Official gold holdings, m oz	0.0
Net transfers	9.1	Foreign debt	95.4
Current account balance	6.9	– as % of GDP	32.8
– as % of GDP	2.4	– as % of total exports	91.2
Capital balance	-3.9	Debt service ratio	12.6
Overall balance	4.7	Aid given	0.2
		– as % of GDP	0.07

Health and education

Health spending, % of GDP	7.2	Education spending, % of GDP	5.6
Doctors per 1,000 pop.	3.3	Enrolment, %: primary	106
Hospital beds per 1,000 pop.	3.3	secondary	101
Improved-water source access,		tertiary	68
% of pop.	100		

Society

No. of households, m	2.3	Cost of living, Dec. 2014	
Av. no. per household	3.5	New York = 100	103
Marriages per 1,000 pop.	6.6	Cars per 1,000 pop.	293
Divorces per 1,000 pop.	1.7	Colour TV households, % with:	
Religion, % of pop.		cable	77.8
Jewish	75.6	satellite	19.2
Muslim	18.6	Telephone lines per 100 pop.	37.5
Non-religious	3.1	Mobile telephone subscribers	
Christian	2.0	per 100 pop.	122.9
Other	0.6	Broadband subs per 100 pop.	25.9
Hindu	<0.1	Internet users, % of pop.	70.8

a Sovereignty over the city is disputed.

ITALY

Area	301,245 sq km	Capital	Rome
Arable as % of total land	24.2	Currency	Euro (€)

People

Population	61.0m	Life expectancy: men	80.3 yrs
Pop. per sq km	202.5	women	85.7 yrs
Average annual growth		Adult literacy	99.0
in pop. 2015-20	0.1%	Fertility rate (per woman)	1.4
Pop. under 15	14.1%	Urban population	69.0%
Pop. over 60	27.2%		per 1,000 pop.
No. of men per 100 women	94.3	Crude birth rate	9
Human Development Index	87.2	Crude death rate	10.5

The economy

GDP	€1,619bn	GDP per head	$35,690
GDP	$2,150bn	GDP per head in purchasing	
Av. ann. growth in real		power parity (USA=100)	66.5
GDP 2008-13	-1.6%	Economic freedom index	61.7

Origins of GDP		**Components of GDP**	
	% of total		% of total
Agriculture	2	Private consumption	60
Industry, of which:	23	Public consumption	19
manufacturing	15	Investment	18
Services	74	Exports	29
		Imports	-26

Structure of employment

	% of total		% of labour force
Agriculture	3.7	Unemployed 2013	12.2
Industry	27.8	Av. ann. rate 2000-13	8.7
Services	68.5		

Energy

	m TOE		
Total output	35.4	Net energy imports as %	
Total consumption	179.3	of energy use	79
Consumption per person			
kg oil equivalent	3,012		

Inflation and finance

Consumer price		*av. ann. increase 2009-14*	
inflation 2014	0.2%	Euro area:	
Av. ann. inflation 2009-14	1.9%	Narrow money (M1)	5.6%
Treasury bill rate, Dec. 2014	0.35%	Broad money	2.0%
		H'hold saving rate, 2014	5.2%

Exchange rates

	end 2014		December 2014
€ per $	0.82	Effective rates	2010 = 100
€ per SDR	1.19	– nominal	100.00
		– real	98.60

Trade

Principal exports

	$bn fob
Machinery & transport equip.	176.8
Chemicals & related products	62.4
Food, drink & tobacco	39.0
Mineral fuels & lubricants	24.5
Total incl. others	**518.1**

Principal imports

	$bn cif
Machinery & transport equip.	107.7
Mineral fuels & lubricants	93.9
Chemicals & related products	73.4
Food, drink & tobacco	44.0
Total incl. others	**479.3**

Main export destinations

	% of total
Germany	12.4
France	10.8
United States	6.6
Switzerland	5.1
EU28	53.8

Main origins of imports

	% of total
Germany	14.8
France	8.5
China	6.3
Netherlands	5.7
EU28	55.4

Balance of payments, reserves and aid, $bn

Visible exports fob	503.5	Overall balance	2.0
Visible imports fob	-455.4	Change in reserves	-35.9
Trade balance	48.0	Level of reserves	
Invisibles inflows	187.5	end Dec.	145.7
Invisibles outflows	-191.4	No. months of import cover	2.7
Net transfers	-23.9	Official gold holdings, m oz	78.8
Current account balance	20.1	Aid given	3.4
– as % of GDP	0.9	– as % of GDP	0.2
Capital balance	-12.4		

Health and education

Health spending, % of GDP	9.1	Education spending, % of GDP	4.3
Doctors per 1,000 pop.	3.8	Enrolment, %: primary	99
Hospital beds per 1,000 pop.	3.4	secondary	99
Improved-water source access,		tertiary	62
% of pop.	100		

Society

No. of households, m	26.2	Cost of living, Dec. 2014	
Av. no. per household	2.3	New York = 100	94
Marriages per 1,000 pop.	3.5	Cars per 1,000 pop.	619
Divorces per 1,000 pop.	0.9	Colour TV households, % with:	
Religion, % of pop.		cable	1.1
Christian	83.3	satellite	29.0
Non-religious	12.4	Telephone lines per 100 pop.	34.6
Muslim	3.7	Mobile telephone subscribers	
Other	0.4	per 100 pop.	158.8
Hindu	0.1	Broadband subs per 100 pop.	22.3
Jewish	<0.1	Internet users, % of pop.	58.5

IVORY COAST

Area	322,463 sq km	Capital	Abidjan/Yamoussoukro
Arable as % of total land	9.1	Currency	CFA franc (CFAfr)

People

Population	20.3m	Life expectancy: men	51.6 yrs
Pop. per sq km	63.0	women	53.4 yrs
Average annual growth		Adult literacy	41.0
in pop. 2015-20	2.2%	Fertility rate (per woman)	4.9
Pop. under 15	41.3%	Urban population	54.2%
Pop. over 60	5.1%		per 1,000 pop.
No. of men per 100 women	104.5	Crude birth rate	37
Human Development Index	45.2	Crude death rate	13.1

The economy

GDP	CFAfr15,346bn	GDP per head	$1,530
GDP	$31.1bn	GDP per head in purchasing	
Av. ann. growth in real		power parity (USA=100)	6.1
GDP 2008-13	3.9%	Economic freedom index	58.5

Origins of GDP		**Components of GDP**	
	% of total		% of total
Agriculture	22	Private consumption	75
Industry, of which:	22	Public consumption	8
manufacturing	13	Investment	17
Services	55	Exports	45
		Imports	-46

Structure of employment

	% of total		% of labour force
Agriculture	...	Unemployed 2012	4.0
Industry	...	Av. ann. rate 2000-12	4.1
Services	...		

Energy

	m TOE		
Total output	3.9	Net energy imports as %	
Total consumption	3.0	of energy use	-6
Consumption per person			
kg oil equivalent	153		

Inflation and finance

		av. ann. increase 2009-14	
Consumer price			
inflation 2014	3.2%	Narrow money (M1)	12.4%
Av. ann. inflation 2009-14	4.7%	Broad money	12.6%
Repurchase rate, Dec. 2014	3.50%		

Exchange rates

	end 2014		December 2014
CFAfr per $	540.28	Effective rates	2010 = 100
CFAfr per SDR	782.77	– nominal	103.80
CFAfr per €	655.95	– real	102.10

Trade

Principal exports		Principal imports	
	$bn fob		*$bn cif*
Cocoa beans & butter	3.9	Capital equip. & raw materials	4.4
Petroleum products	3.7	Foodstuffs	2.9
Timber	0.3	Fuels & lubricants	2.2
Coffee	0.2		
Total incl. others	**13.2**	**Total incl. others**	**12.7**

Main export destinations		Main origins of imports	
	% of total		*% of total*
Netherlands	8.8	Nigeria	25.0
United States	8.1	France	11.0
Nigeria	8.0	China	7.2
Germany	7.5	India	3.9
France	4.5	Colombia	3.6

Balance of payments, reserves and debt, $bn

Visible exports fob	12.0	Change in reserves	0.3
Visible imports fob	-9.1	Level of reserves	
Trade balance	3.0	end Dec.	4.2
Invisibles inflows	1.1	No. months of import cover	3.9
Invisibles outflows	-4.1	Official gold holdings, m oz	0.0
Net transfers	-0.4	Foreign debt	11.3
Current account balance	-0.4	– as % of GDP	36.3
– as % of GDP	-1.4	– as % of total exports	75.2
Capital balance	0.4	Debt service ratio	8.4
Overall balance	0.0		

Health and education

Health spending, % of GDP	5.7	Education spending, % of GDP	...
Doctors per 1,000 pop.	0.1	Enrolment, %: primary	96
Hospital beds per 1,000 pop.	-	secondary	39
Improved-water source access,		tertiary	9
% of pop.	80.2		

Society

No. of households, m	3.7	Cost of living, Dec. 2014	
Av. no. per household	5.3	New York = 100	67
Marriages per 1,000 pop.	...	Cars per 1,000 pop.	17
Divorces per 1,000 pop.	...	Colour TV households, % with:	
Religion, % of pop.	...	cable	...
		satellite	...
		Telephone lines per 100 pop.	1.3
		Mobile telephone subscribers	
		per 100 pop.	95.5
		Broadband subs per 100 pop.	0.3
		Internet users, % of pop.	2.6

JAPAN

Area	377,727 sq km	Capital	Tokyo
Arable as % of total land	11.6	Currency	Yen (¥)

People

Population	127.1m	Life expectancy: men	80.8 yrs
Pop. per sq km	336.5	women	87.7 yrs
Average annual growth		Adult literacy	...
in pop. 2015-20	-0.2%	Fertility rate (per woman)	1.4
Pop. under 15	13.1%	Urban population	93.5%
Pop. over 60	32.3%		per 1,000 pop.
No. of men per 100 women	95	Crude birth rate	8
Human Development Index	89	Crude death rate	10.7

The economy

GDP	¥480trn	GDP per head	$38,630
GDP	$4,920bn	GDP per head in purchasing	
Av. ann. growth in real		power parity (USA=100)	68.3
GDP 2008–13	0.3%	Economic freedom index	73.3

Origins of GDP		**Components of GDP**	
	% of total		% of total
Agriculture	1	Private consumption	61
Industry, of which:	26	Public consumption	21
manufacturing	18	Investment	21
Services	73	Exports	16
		Imports	-19

Structure of employment

	% of total		% of labour force
Agriculture	3.7	Unemployed 2013	4.0
Industry	25.3	Av. ann. rate 2000–13	4.6
Services	69.7		

Energy

	m TOE		
Total output	39.2	Net energy imports as %	
Total consumption	507.7	of energy use	94
Consumption per person			
kg oil equivalent	3,980		

Inflation and finance

			av. ann. increase 2009–14
Consumer price			
inflation 2014	2.7%	Narrow money (M1)	3.5%
Av. ann. inflation 2009–14	0.4%	Broad money	-3.9%
Money market rate, Dec. 2013	0.07%	H'hold saving rate, 2014	0.6%

Exchange rates

	end 2014		December 2014
¥ per $	120.64	Effective rates	2010 = 100
¥ per SDR	174.78	– nominal	73.40
¥ per €	146.47	– real	68.70

Trade

Principal exports	
	$bn fob
Capital equipment	363.4
Industrial supplies	187.9
Consumer durable goods	112.3
Consumer non-durable goods	4.4
Total incl. others	**714.9**

Principal imports	
	$bn cif
Industrial supplies	451.1
Capital equipment	189.0
Food & direct consumer goods	66.2
Consumer durable goods	54.5
Total incl. others	**832.6**

Main export destinations	
	% of total
United States	18.8
China	18.1
South Korea	7.9
Hong Kong	5.2
Thailand	5.0

Main origins of imports	
	% of total
China	21.7
United States	8.6
Australia	6.1
Saudi Arabia	6.0
United Arab Emirates	5.1

Balance of payments, reserves and aid, $bn

Visible exports fob	694.9	Overall balance	38.8
Visible imports fob	-784.6	Change in reserves	-1.2
Trade balance	-89.6	Level of reserves	
Invisibles inflows	357.7	end Dec.	1,266.9
Invisibles outflows	-223.9	No. months of import cover	15.1
Net transfers	-10.1	Official gold holdings, m oz	24.6
Current account balance	34.1	Aid given	11.6
– as % of GDP	0.7	– as % of GDP	0.2
Capital balance	47.6		

Health and education

Health spending, % of GDP	10.3	Education spending, % of GDP	3.8
Doctors per 1,000 pop.	2.3	Enrolment, %: primary	102
Hospital beds per 1,000 pop.	13.7	secondary	102
Improved-water source access,		tertiary	61
% of pop.	100		

Society

No. of households, m	52.7	Cost of living, Dec. 2014	
Av. no. per household	2.4	New York = 100	109
Marriages per 1,000 pop.	5.2	Cars per 1,000 pop.	472
Divorces per 1,000 pop.	1.8	Colour TV households, % with:	
Religion, % of pop.		cable	52.7
Non-religious	57.0	satellite	42.3
Buddhist	36.2	Telephone lines per 100 pop.	48.0
Other	5.0	Mobile telephone subscribers	
Christian	1.6	per 100 pop.	117.6
Muslim	0.2	Broadband subs per 100 pop.	28.9
Jewish	<0.1	Internet users, % of pop.	86.3

KENYA

Area	582,646 sq km	Capital	Nairobi
Arable as % of total land	9.8	Currency	Kenyan shilling (KSh)

People

Population	44.4m	Life expectancy: men	61.1 yrs
Pop. per sq km	76.2	women	65.2 yrs
Average annual growth		Adult literacy	...
in pop. 2015-20	2.5%	Fertility rate (per woman)	4.3
Pop. under 15	42.2%	Urban population	25.6%
Pop. over 60	4.3%		per 1,000 pop.
No. of men per 100 women	99.6	Crude birth rate	34
Human Development Index	53.5	Crude death rate	7.5

The economy

GDP	KSh4,758bn	GDP per head	$1,250
GDP	$55.2bn	GDP per head in purchasing	
Av. ann. growth in real		power parity (USA=100)	5.3
GDP 2008-13	5.6%	Economic freedom index	55.6

Origins of GDP		**Components of GDP**	
	% of total		% of total
Agriculture	30	Private consumption	81
Industry, of which:	20	Public consumption	14
manufacturing	12	Investment	20
Services	51	Exports	18
		Imports	-33

Structure of employment

	% of total		% of labour force
Agriculture	...	Unemployed 2012	9.2
Industry	...	Av. ann. rate 2000-12	9.5
Services	...		

Energy

	m TOE		
Total output	1.5	Net energy imports as %	
Total consumption	6.0	of energy use	20
Consumption per person			
kg oil equivalent	138		

Inflation and finance

Consumer price		av. ann. increase 2009-14	
inflation 2014	6.9%	Narrow money (M1)	17.0%
Av. ann. inflation 2009-14	8.0%	Broad money	17.1%
Treasury bill rate, Dec. 2014	8.58%		

Exchange rates

	end 2014		December 2014
KSh per $	90.50	Effective rates	2010 = 100
KSh per SDR	131.12	– nominal	...
KSh per €	109.88	– real	...

Trade

Principal exports		Principal imports	
	$bn fob		*$bn cif*
Tea	1.2	Industrial supplies	4.7
Horticultural products	1.2	Machinery & other capital equip.	2.8
Coffee	0.3	Transport equipment	1.8
Fish products	0.1		
Total incl. others	**5.9**	Total incl. others	**15.5**

Main export destinations		Main origins of imports	
	% of total		*% of total*
Uganda	13.0	India	19.8
Tanzania	8.9	China	17.7
Netherlands	7.1	United Arab Emirates	8.8
United Kingdom	6.6	South Africa	5.0

Balance of payments[a], reserves and debt, $bn

Visible exports fob	6.2	Change in reserves	1.4
Visible imports fob	-15.5	Level of reserves	
Trade balance	-9.3	end Dec.	5.7
Invisibles inflows	5.0	No. months of import cover	3.8
Invisibles outflows	-2.8	Official gold holdings, m oz	0.0
Net transfers	2.8	Foreign debt	13.5
Current account balance	-4.3	– as % of GDP	24.4
– as % of GDP	-10.4	– as % of total exports	109.1
Capital balance	5.0	Debt service ratio	5.2
Overall balance	1.2		

Health and education

Health spending, % of GDP	4.5	Education spending, % of GDP	6.6
Doctors per 1,000 pop.	0.2	Enrolment, %: primary	114
Hospital beds per 1,000 pop.	1.4	secondary	67
Improved-water source access,		tertiary	...
% of pop.	61.7		

Society

No. of households, m	10.2	Cost of living, Dec. 2014	
Av. no. per household	4.3	New York = 100	76
Marriages per 1,000 pop.	...	Cars per 1,000 pop.	16
Divorces per 1,000 pop.	...	Colour TV households, % with:	
Religion, % of pop.		cable	2.4
Christian	84.8	satellite	3.4
Muslim	9.7	Telephone lines per 100 pop.	0.5
Other	3.0	Mobile telephone subscribers	
Non-religious	2.5	per 100 pop.	71.8
Hindu	0.1	Broadband subs per 100 pop.	0.1
Jewish	<0.1	Internet users, % of pop.	39.0

a 2012

LATVIA

Area	63,700 sq km	Capital	Riga
Arable as % of total land	18.9	Currency	Lats (LVL)/Euro (€)[a]

People

Population	2.1m	Life expectancy: men	67.2 yrs
Pop. per sq km	33.0	women	77.9 yrs
Average annual growth		Adult literacy	...
in pop. 2015-20	-0.6%	Fertility rate (per woman)	1.5
Pop. under 15	14.8%	Urban population	67.4%
Pop. over 60	24.3%		per 1,000 pop.
No. of men per 100 women	84.1	Crude birth rate	10
Human Development Index	81	Crude death rate	16.0

The economy

GDP	LVL16.4bn	GDP per head	$15,380
GDP	$31.0bn	GDP per head in purchasing	
Av. ann. growth in real		power parity (USA=100)	42.5
GDP 2008–13	-0.9%	Economic freedom index	69.7

Origins of GDP		**Components of GDP**	
	% of total		% of total
Agriculture	4	Private consumption	62
Industry, of which:	23	Public consumption	15
manufacturing	...	Investment	26
Services	73	Exports	59
		Imports	-63

Structure of employment

	% of total		% of labour force
Agriculture	6.6	Unemployed 2013	11.9
Industry	17.0	Av. ann. rate 2000–13	12.1
Services	76.4		

Energy

	m TOE		
Total output	1.0	Net energy imports as %	
Total consumption	4.2	of energy use	53
Consumption per person			
kg oil equivalent	2,072		

Inflation and finance

Consumer price		av. ann. increase 2009–14	
inflation 2014	0.7%	Euro area:	
Av. ann. inflation 2009–14	1.2%	Narrow money (M1)	5.6%
Deposit rate, h'holds, Dec. 2014	0.84%	Broad money	2.0%

Exchange rates

	end 2014		December 2014
€ per $	0.82	Effective rates	2010 = 100
€ per SDR	1.19	– nominal	106.60
		– real	101.40

Trade

Principal exports	$bn fob	Principal imports	$bn cif
Wood & wood products	2.6	Machinery & equipment	2.9
Metals	2.0	Mineral products	2.9
Mineral products	1.8	Metals	2.5
Chemical products	1.7	Chemicals	1.7
Total incl. others	**13.4**	**Total incl. others**	**17.1**

Main export destinations	% of total	Main origins of imports	% of total
United Kingdom	17.2	Germany	20.2
Germany	17.2	Lithuania	12.0
Lithuania	12.7	Russia	9.7
Sweden	7.5	Estonia	8.3
EU28	66.4	EU28	80.0

Balance of payments, reserves and debt, $bn

Visible exports fob	13.0	Change in reserves	0.4
Visible imports fob	-16.4	Level of reserves	
Trade balance	-3.4	end Dec.	7.9
Invisibles inflows	6.8	No. months of import cover	4.5
Invisibles outflows	-4.6	Official gold holdings, m oz	0.2
Net transfers	0.4	Foreign debt	41.0
Current account balance	-0.7	– as % of GDP	133.0
– as % of GDP	-2.3	– as % of total exports	205.8
Capital balance	1.0	Debt service ratio	33.4
Overall balance	0.5	Aid given	0.02
		– as % of GDP	0.08

Health and education

Health spending, % of GDP	7.2	Education spending, % of GDP	4.9
Doctors per 1,000 pop.	2.1	Enrolment, %: primary	103
Hospital beds per 1,000 pop.	5.9	secondary	97
Improved-water source access, % of pop.	97.8	tertiary	98

Society

No. of households, m	0.9	Cost of living, Dec. 2014	
Av. no. per household	2.3	New York = 100	...
Marriages per 1,000 pop.	5.7	Cars per 1,000 pop.	314
Divorces per 1,000 pop.	3.5	Colour TV households, % with:	
Religion, % of pop.		cable	42.1
Christian	55.8	satellite	12.7
Non-religious	43.8	Telephone lines per 100 pop.	20.6
Other	0.2	Mobile telephone subscribers	
Muslim	0.1	per 100 pop.	228.4
Hindu	<0.1	Broadband subs per 100 pop.	23.5
Jewish	<0.1	Internet users, % of pop.	75.2

a Latvia joined the euro area on January 1 2014.

LITHUANIA

Area	65,200 sq km	Capital	Vilnius
Arable as % of total land	36.1	Currency	Litas (LTL)/Euro (€)[a]

People

Population	3.0m	Life expectancy: men	66.8 yrs
Pop. per sq km	46.0	women	78.6 yrs
Average annual growth		Adult literacy	99.9
in pop. 2015-20	-0.4%	Fertility rate (per woman)	1.6
Pop. under 15	15.2%	Urban population	66.5%
Pop. over 60	20.8%		per 1,000 pop.
No. of men per 100 women	85.7	Crude birth rate	10
Human Development Index	83.4	Crude death rate	14.1

The economy

GDP	LTL120bn	GDP per head	$15,530
GDP	$45.9bn	GDP per head in purchasing	
Av. ann. growth in real		power parity (USA=100)	48.0
GDP 2008–13	-0.3%	Economic freedom index	74.7

Origins of GDP

Components of GDP

	% of total		% of total
Agriculture	4	Private consumption	64
Industry, of which:	31	Public consumption	19
manufacturing	...	Investment	19
Services	66	Exports	77
		Imports	-79

Structure of employment

	% of total		% of labour force
Agriculture	8.4	Unemployed 2013	11.9
Industry	23.5	Av. ann. rate 2000–13	11.8
Services	68.1		

Energy

	m TOE		
Total output	0.4	Net energy imports as %	
Total consumption	7.7	of energy use	79
Consumption per person			
kg oil equivalent	2,580		

Inflation and finance

Consumer price		av. ann. increase 2009–14	
inflation 2014	0.2%	Euro area:	
Av. ann. inflation 2009–14	2.0%	Narrow money (M1)	5.6%
Money market rate, Sep. 2014	0.05%	Broad money	2.0%

Exchange rates

	end 2014		December 2014
LTL per $	2.84	Effective rates	2010 = 100
LTL per SDR	4.11	– nominal	...
LTL per €	3.45	– real	...

Trade

Principal exports		**Principal imports**	
	$bn fob		*$bn cif*
Mineral products	7.6	Transport equipment	10.8
Machinery & equipment	3.9	Machinery & equipment	4.7
Chemicals	2.6	Chemicals	3.4
Transport equipment	2.0	Mineral products	3.0
Total incl. others	**32.6**	Total incl. others	**34.8**

Main export destinations		**Main origins of imports**	
	% of total		*% of total*
Russia	68.5	Russia	28.1
Latvia	34.4	Germany	10.5
Poland	25.6	Poland	9.5
Germany	24.8	Latvia	6.2
EU28	55.5	EU28	60.3

Balance of payments, reserves and debt, $bn

Visible exports fob	31.8	Change in reserves	-0.5
Visible imports fob	-33.4	Level of reserves	
Trade balance	-1.6	end Dec.	8.1
Invisibles inflows	8.0	No. months of import cover	2.4
Invisibles outflows	-7.6	Official gold holdings, m oz	0.2
Net transfers	1.9	Foreign debt	31.0
Current account balance	0.7	– as % of GDP	66.7
– as % of GDP	1.5	– as % of total exports	75.4
Capital balance	-1.3	Debt service ratio	18.6
Overall balance	-0.6	Aid given[b]	0.05
		– as % of GDP[b]	0.12

Health and education

Health spending, % of GDP	5.7	Education spending, % of GDP	4.9
Doctors per 1,000 pop.	3.6	Enrolment, %: primary	103
Hospital beds per 1,000 pop.	5.9	secondary	98
Improved-water source access,		tertiary	65
% of pop.	98.4		

Society

No. of households, m	1.2	Cost of living, Dec. 2014	
Av. no. per household	2.4	New York = 100	...
Marriages per 1,000 pop.	6.9	Cars per 1,000 pop.	609
Divorces per 1,000 pop.	3.5	Colour TV households, % with:	
Religion, % of pop.		cable	53.0
Christian	89.8	satellite	12.0
Non-religious	10.0	Telephone lines per 100 pop.	20.7
Hindu	<0.1	Mobile telephone subscribers	
Jewish	<0.1	per 100 pop.	151.3
Muslim	<0.1	Broadband subs per 100 pop.	22.0
Other	<0.1	Internet users, % of pop.	68.5

a Lithuania joined the euro area on January 1 2015.   b 2012

MALAYSIA

Area	332,665 sq km	Capital	Kuala Lumpur
Arable as % of total land	5.5	Currency	Malaysian dollar/ringgit (M$)

People

Population	29.7m	Life expectancy: men	73.5 yrs
Pop. per sq km	89.3	women	78.2 yrs
Average annual growth		Adult literacy	93.1
in pop. 2015–20	1.4%	Fertility rate (per woman)	2.1
Pop. under 15	26.1%	Urban population	74.7%
Pop. over 60	8.5%		per 1,000 pop.
No. of men per 100 women	94.5	Crude birth rate	17
Human Development Index	77.3	Crude death rate	4.9

The economy

GDP	M$987bn	GDP per head	$10,540
GDP	$313bn	GDP per head in purchasing	
Av. ann. growth in real		power parity (USA=100)	44.0
GDP 2008–13	4.3%	Economic freedom index	70.8

Origins of GDP		Components of GDP	
	% of total		% of total
Agriculture	9	Private consumption	51
Industry, of which:	41	Public consumption	14
manufacturing	24	Investment	26
Services	50	Exports	82
		Imports	-72

Structure of employment

	% of total		% of labour force
Agriculture	12.6	Unemployed 2013	3.1
Industry	28.4	Av. ann. rate 2000–13	3.3
Services	59.0		

Energy

	m TOE		
Total output	95.4	Net energy imports as %	
Total consumption	77.8	of energy use	-11
Consumption per person			
kg oil equivalent	2,660		

Inflation and finance

Consumer price			av. ann. increase 2009–14
inflation 2014	3.1%	Narrow money (M1)	11.5%
Av. ann. inflation 2009–14	2.4%	Broad money	8.3%
Money market rate, Nov. 2014	3.19%		

Exchange rates

	end 2014		December 2014
M$ per $	3.50	Effective rates	2010 = 100
M$ per SDR	5.06	– nominal	98.70
M$ per €	4.25	– real	98.60

Trade

Principal exports	$bn fob	Principal imports	$bn cif
Machinery & transport equip.	86.8	Machinery & transport equip.	87.8
Mineral fuels	50.8	Mineral fuels	33.3
Manufactured goods	21.5	Manufactured goods	27.1
Chemicals	16.0	Chemicals	18.8
Total incl. others	**228.3**	**Total incl. others**	**205.9**

Main export destinations	% of total	Main origins of imports	% of total
Singapore	14.0	China	16.4
China	13.5	Singapore	12.4
Japan	11.1	Japan	8.7
United States	8.1	United States	7.9

Balance of payments, reserves and debt, $bn

Visible exports fob	219.2	Change in reserves	-4.9
Visible imports fob	-186.7	Level of reserves	
Trade balance	32.5	end Dec.	134.9
Invisibles inflows	54.8	No. months of import cover	6.3
Invisibles outflows	-70.8	Official gold holdings, m oz	1.2
Net transfers	-4.8	Foreign debt	213.1
Current account balance	11.7	– as % of GDP	68.1
– as % of GDP	3.7	– as % of total exports	77.4
Capital balance	-4.6	Debt service ratio	3.5
Overall balance	4.3		

Health and education

Health spending, % of GDP	4	Education spending, % of GDP	5.9
Doctors per 1,000 pop.	1.2	Enrolment, %: primary	-
Hospital beds per 1,000 pop.	1.9	secondary	71
Improved-water source access,		tertiary	37
% of pop.	99.6		

Society

No. of households, m	6.9	Cost of living, Dec. 2014	
Av. no. per household	4.3	New York = 100	72
Marriages per 1,000 pop.	...	Cars per 1,000 pop.	358
Divorces per 1,000 pop.	...	Colour TV households, % with:	
Religion, % of pop.		cable	12.7
Muslim	63.7	satellite	56.2
Buddhist	17.7	Telephone lines per 100 pop.	15.3
Christian	9.4	Mobile telephone subscribers	
Hindu	6.0	per 100 pop.	144.7
Other	2.5	Broadband subs per 100 pop.	8.2
Non-religious	0.7	Internet users, % of pop.	67.0

MEXICO

Area	1,972,545 sq km	Capital	Mexico city
Arable as % of total land	11.9	Currency	Mexican peso (PS)

People

Population	122.3m	Life expectancy: men	76.1 yrs
Pop. per sq km	62.0	women	80.6 yrs
Average annual growth		Adult literacy	94.2
in pop. 2015-20	1.0%	Fertility rate (per woman)	2.2
Pop. under 15	28.5%	Urban population	79.2%
Pop. over 60	9.5%		per 1,000 pop.
No. of men per 100 women	93.8	Crude birth rate	19
Human Development Index	75.6	Crude death rate	4.7

The economy

GDP	PS16,104bn	GDP per head	$10,310
GDP	$1,261bn	GDP per head in purchasing	
Av. ann. growth in real		power parity (USA=100)	30.9
GDP 2008-13	1.9%	Economic freedom index	66.4

Origins of GDP		Components of GDP	
	% of total		% of total
Agriculture	3	Private consumption	67
Industry, of which:	35	Public consumption	12
manufacturing	18	Investment	22
Services	62	Exports	32
		Imports	-32

Structure of employment

	% of total		% of labour force
Agriculture	13.5	Unemployed 2013	4.9
Industry	24.2	Av. ann. rate 2000-13	3.8
Services	62.3		

Energy

	m TOE		
Total output	217.8	Net energy imports as %	
Total consumption	193.8	of energy use	-17
Consumption per person			
kg oil equivalent	1,604		

Inflation and finance

Consumer price		av. ann. increase 2009-14	
inflation 2014	4.0%	Narrow money (M1)	12.3%
Av. ann. inflation 2009-14	3.9%	Broad money	12.5%
Money market rate, Dec. 2014	3.30%		

Exchange rates

	end 2014		December 2014
PS per $	14.72	Effective rates	2010 = 100
PS per SDR	21.32	– nominal	90.11
PS per €	17.87	– real	97.99

Trade

Principal exports		Principal imports	
	$bn fob		*$bn cif*
Manufactured goods	314.6	Intermediate goods	284.8
Crude oil & products	49.6	Consumer goods	57.3
Agricultural products	11.3	Capital goods	39.1
Mining products	4.7		
Total incl. others	**397.5**	Total	**381.2**

Main export destinations		Main origins of imports	
	% of total		*% of total*
United States	78.8	United States	54.0
Canada	2.8	China	16.9
Spain	1.9	Japan	5.2
China	1.7	South Korea	4.0

Balance of payments, reserves and debt, $bn

Visible exports fob	380.7	Change in reserves	13.1
Visible imports fob	-381.6	Level of reserves	
Trade balance	-0.9	end Dec.	180.2
Invisibles inflows	31.4	No. months of import cover	4.7
Invisibles outflows	-82.3	Official gold holdings, m oz	4.0
Net transfers	22.1	Foreign debt	443.0
Current account balance	-29.7	– as % of GDP	35.1
– as % of GDP	-2.4	– as % of total exports	102.1
Capital balance	65.2	Debt service ratio	9.8
Overall balance	17.8		

Health and education

Health spending, % of GDP	6.2	Education spending, % of GDP	5.1
Doctors per 1,000 pop.	2.1	Enrolment, %: primary	105
Hospital beds per 1,000 pop.	1.5	secondary	86
Improved-water source access,		tertiary	29
% of pop.	94.9		

Society

No. of households, m	29.8	Cost of living, Dec. 2014	
Av. no. per household	3.9	New York = 100	84
Marriages per 1,000 pop.	5.0	Cars per 1,000 pop.	207
Divorces per 1,000 pop.	0.9	Colour TV households, % with:	
Religion, % of pop.		cable	21.4
Christian	95.1	satellite	23.5
Non-religious	4.7	Telephone lines per 100 pop.	16.8
Hindu	<0.1	Mobile telephone subscribers	
Jewish	<0.1	per 100 pop.	85.8
Muslim	<0.1	Broadband subs per 100 pop.	10.9
Other	<0.1	Internet users, % of pop.	43.5

MOROCCO

Area	446,550 sq km	Capital	Rabat
Arable as % of total land	18.0	Currency	Dirham (Dh)

People

Population	33.0m	Life expectancy: men	70.0 yrs
Pop. per sq km	73.9	women	73.7 yrs
Average annual growth		Adult literacy	67.1
in pop. 2015-20	1.1%	Fertility rate (per woman)	2.6
Pop. under 15	27.9%	Urban population	60.2%
Pop. over 60	7.8%		per 1,000 pop.
No. of men per 100 women	96.7	Crude birth rate	22
Human Development Index	61.7	Crude death rate	6.3

The economy

GDP	Dh873bn	GDP per head	$3,090
GDP	$104bn	GDP per head in purchasing	
Av. ann. growth in real		power parity (USA=100)	13.6
GDP 2008-13	4.1%	Economic freedom index	60.1

Origins of GDP		**Components of GDP**	
	% of total		% of total
Agriculture	17	Private consumption	60
Industry, of which:	29	Public consumption	19
manufacturing	15	Investment	34
Services	55	Exports	34
		Imports	-47

Structure of employment

	% of total		% of labour force
Agriculture	39.2	Unemployed 2013	9.2
Industry	21.4	Av. ann. rate 2000-13	10.5
Services	39.3		

Energy

	m TOE		
Total output	0.6	Net energy imports as %	
Total consumption	15.7	of energy use	96
Consumption per person			
kg oil equivalent	482		

Inflation and finance

Consumer price		av. ann. increase 2009-14	
inflation 2014	0.4%	Narrow money (M1)	4.6%
Av. ann. inflation 2009-14	1.1%	Broad money	-1.7%
Money market rate, Dec. 2014	2.64%		

Exchange rates

	end 2014		December 2014
Dh per $	9.04	Effective rates	2010 = 100
Dh per SDR	13.10	– nominal	103.10
Dh per €	10.98	– real	98.70

Trade

Principal exports	$bn fob	Principal imports	$bn cif
Clothing & textiles	2.3	Fuel & lubricants	12.2
Electric cables & wires	2.0	Semi-finished goods	9.6
Fertilizers & chemicals	1.9	Capital goods	9.6
Phosphoric acid	1.4	Consumer goods	7.6
Phosphate rock	1.1	Food, drink & tobacco	4.3
Total incl. others	**22.0**	Total incl. others	**45.0**

Main export destinations	% of total	Main origins of imports	% of total
France	21.5	Spain	13.5
Spain	18.9	France	12.9
Brazil	6.0	United States	7.5
United States	4.2	China	6.9

Balance of payments, reserves and debt, $bn

Visible exports fob	18.3	Change in reserves	1.7
Visible imports fob	-39.9	Level of reserves	
Trade balance	-21.6	end Dec.	19.3
Invisibles inflows	14.8	No. months of import cover	4.7
Invisibles outflows	-9.8	Official gold holdings, m oz	0.7
Net transfers	7.9	Foreign debt	39.3
Current account balance	-8.7	– as % of GDP	37.7
– as % of GDP	-8.4	– as % of total exports	98.2
Capital balance	3.1	Debt service ratio	12.7
Overall balance	-5.3		

Health and education

Health spending, % of GDP	6.0	Education spending, % of GDP	6.6
Doctors per 1,000 pop.	0.6	Enrolment, %: primary	118
Hospital beds per 1,000 pop.	0.9	secondary	69
Improved-water source access,		tertiary	16
% of pop.	83.6		

Society

No. of households, m	6.9	Cost of living, Dec. 2014	
Av. no. per household	4.7	New York = 100	68
Marriages per 1,000 pop.	...	Cars per 1,000 pop.	67
Divorces per 1,000 pop.	...	Colour TV households, % with:	
Religion, % of pop.		cable	...
Muslim	99.9	satellite	92.0
Christian	<0.1	Telephone lines per 100 pop.	8.9
Hindu	<0.1	Mobile telephone subscribers	
Jewish	<0.1	per 100 pop.	128.5
Non-religious	<0.1	Broadband subs per 100 pop.	2.5
Other	<0.1	Internet users, % of pop.	56.0

NETHERLANDS

Area[a]	41,526 sq km	Capital	Amsterdam
Arable as % of total land	30.0	Currency	Euro (€)

People

Population	16.8m	Life expectancy: men	79.8 yrs
Pop. per sq km	404.6	women	83.5 yrs
Average annual growth		Adult literacy	...
in pop. 2015–20	0.2%	Fertility rate (per woman)	1.7
Pop. under 15	17.1%	Urban population	90.5%
Pop. over 60	23.4%		per 1,000 pop.
No. of men per 100 women	98.1	Crude birth rate	10
Human Development Index	91.5	Crude death rate	9.0

The economy

GDP	€643bn	GDP per head	$50,790
GDP	$854bn	GDP per head in purchasing	
Av. ann. growth in real		power parity (USA=100)	87.0
GDP 2008–13	-0.6%	Economic freedom index	73.7

Origins of GDP		**Components of GDP**	
	% of total		% of total
Agriculture	2	Private consumption	45
Industry, of which:	22	Public consumption	26
manufacturing	12	Investment	18
Services	76	Exports	83
		Imports	-73

Structure of employment

	% of total		% of labour force
Agriculture	2.5	Unemployed 2013	6.7
Industry	18.4	Av. ann. rate 2000–13	3.9
Services	78.9		

Energy

	m TOE		
Total output	68.9	Net energy imports as %	
Total consumption	101.1	of energy use	17
Consumption per person			
kg oil equivalent	6,035		

Inflation and finance

Consumer price		av. ann. increase 2009–14	
inflation 2014	0.3%	Euro area:	
Av. ann. inflation 2009–14	1.8%	Narrow money (M1)	5.6%
Deposit rate, h'holds, Dec. 2014	2.00%	Broad money	2.0%
		H'hold saving rate, 2014	6.0%

Exchange rates

	end 2014		December 2014
€ per $	0.82	Effective rates	2010 = 100
€ per SDR	1.19	– nominal	99.10
		– real	99.10

Trade

Principal exports		Principal imports	
	$bn fob		*$bn cif*
Machinery & transport equip.	185.3	Machinery & transport equip.	162.2
Mineral fuels & lubricants	132.6	Mineral fuels & lubricants	144.3
Chemicals & related products	103.1	Chemicals & related products	70.2
Food, drink & tobacco	83.1	Food, drink & tobacco	53.9
Total incl. others	**575.3**	Total incl. others	**513.2**

Main export destinations		Main origins of imports	
	% of total		*% of total*
Germany	29.4	Germany	16.5
Belgium	15.0	China	13.8
France	10.0	Belgium	9.7
United Kingdom	9.8	United Kingdom	7.5
EU28	75.7	EU28	46.3

Balance of payments, reserves and aid, $bn

Visible exports fob	550.9	Overall balance	-0.1
Visible imports fob	-484.5	Change in reserves	-8.5
Trade balance	66.4	Level of reserves	
Invisibles inflows	225.8	end Dec.	46.3
Invisibles outflows	-186.5	No. months of import cover	0.8
Net transfers	-18.6	Official gold holdings, m oz	19.7
Current account balance	87.1	Aid given	5.4
– as % of GDP	10.2	– as % of GDP	0.7
Capital balance	-76.4		

Health and education

Health spending, % of GDP	12.9	Education spending, % of GDP	5.9
Doctors per 1,000 pop.	2.9	Enrolment, %: primary	106
Hospital beds per 1,000 pop.	4.7	secondary	130
Improved-water source access,		tertiary	77
% of pop.	100		

Society

No. of households, m	7.6	Cost of living, Dec. 2014	
Av. no. per household	2.2	New York = 100	87
Marriages per 1,000 pop.	4.2	Cars per 1,000 pop.	469
Divorces per 1,000 pop.	2.1	Colour TV households, % with:	
Religion, % of pop.		cable	69.3
Christian	50.6	satellite	7.2
Non-religious	42.1	Telephone lines per 100 pop.	42.5
Muslim	6.0	Mobile telephone subscribers	
Other	0.6	per 100 pop.	113.7
Hindu	0.5	Broadband subs per 100 pop.	40.1
Jewish	0.2	Internet users, % of pop.	94.0

a Includes water.

NEW ZEALAND

Area	270,534 sq km	Capital	Wellington
Arable as % of total land	2.2	Currency	New Zealand dollar (NZ$)

People

Population	4.5m	Life expectancy: men	80.0 yrs
Pop. per sq km	16.6	women	83.6 yrs
Average annual growth		Adult literacy	...
in pop. 2015-20	0.9%	Fertility rate (per woman)	2
Pop. under 15	20.2%	Urban population	86.3%
Pop. over 60	19.3%		per 1,000 pop.
No. of men per 100 women	96.5	Crude birth rate	13
Human Development Index	91	Crude death rate	7.2

The economy

GDP	NZ$227bn	GDP per head	$41,820
GDP	$186bn	GDP per head in purchasing	
Av. ann. growth in real		power parity (USA=100)	65.5
GDP 2008-13	1.3%	Economic freedom index	82.1

Origins of GDP		Components of GDP	
	% of total		% of total
Agriculture	4	Private consumption	58
Industry, of which:	26	Public consumption	19
manufacturing	...	Investment	22
Services	70	Exports	30
		Imports	-28

Structure of employment

	% of total		% of labour force
Agriculture	6.6	Unemployed 2013	6.2
Industry	20.9	Av. ann. rate 2000-13	5.3
Services	72.5		

Energy

	m TOE		
Total output	17.2	Net energy imports as %	
Total consumption	21.3	of energy use	14
Consumption per person			
kg oil equivalent	4,837		

Inflation and finance

		av. ann. increase 2009-14	
Consumer price			
inflation 2014	1.2%	Narrow money (M1)	11.5%
Av. ann. inflation 2009-14	1.9%	Broad money	6.1%
Money market rate, Dec. 2014	3.40%	H'hold saving rate, 2014	0.2%

Exchange rates

	end 2014		December 2014
NZ$ per $	1.28	Effective rates	2010 = 100
NZ$ per SDR	1.85	– nominal	115.90
NZ$ per €	1.55	– real	114.20

Trade

Principal exports	$bn fob	Principal imports	$bn cif
Dairy produce	11.0	Machinery & electrical equip.	7.8
Meat	4.3	Mineral fuels	6.7
Forestry products	4.1	Transport equipment	5.6
Wool	0.6		
Total incl. others	**39.4**	Total incl. others	**39.6**

Main export destinations	% of total	Main origins of imports	% of total
China	20.8	China	17.5
Australia	19.0	Australia	13.3
United States	8.5	United States	9.4
Japan	5.9	Japan	6.4

Balance of payments, reserves and aid, $bn

Visible exports fob	39.7	Overall balance	-0.8
Visible imports fob	-38.7	Change in reserves	-1.3
Trade balance	1.1	Level of reserves	
Invisibles inflows	19.2	end Dec.	16.3
Invisibles outflows	-25.9	No. months of import cover	3.0
Net transfers	-0.4	Official gold holdings, m oz	0.0
Current account balance	-5.9	Aid given	0.5
– as % of GDP	-3.2	– as % of GDP	0.3
Capital balance	-2.7		

Health and education

Health spending, % of GDP	9.7	Education spending, % of GDP	7.4
Doctors per 1,000 pop.	2.7	Enrolment, %: primary	99
Hospital beds per 1,000 pop.	2.3	secondary	120
Improved-water source access,		tertiary	80
% of pop.	100		

Society

No. of households, m	1.5	Cost of living, Dec. 2014	
Av. no. per household	2.9	New York = 100	105
Marriages per 1,000 pop.	4.6	Cars per 1,000 pop.	543
Divorces per 1,000 pop.	2.0	Colour TV households, % with:	
Religion, % of pop.		cable	5.9
Christian	57.0	satellite	40.7
Non-religious	36.6	Telephone lines per 100 pop.	41.1
Other	2.8	Mobile telephone subscribers	
Hindu	2.1	per 100 pop.	105.8
Muslim	1.2	Broadband subs per 100 pop.	29.2
Jewish	0.2	Internet users, % of pop.	82.8

NIGERIA

Area	923,768 sq km	Capital	Abuja
Arable as % of total land	38.4	Currency	Naira (N)

People

Population	173.6m	Life expectancy: men	53.9 yrs
Pop. per sq km	187.9	women	54.6 yrs
Average annual growth		Adult literacy	51.1
in pop. 2015-20	2.7%	Fertility rate (per woman)	5.6
Pop. under 15	44.4%	Urban population	47.8%
Pop. over 60	4.5%		per 1,000 pop.
No. of men per 100 women	103.4	Crude birth rate	39
Human Development Index	50.4	Crude death rate	12.0

The economy

GDP	N81,010bn	GDP per head	$3,010
GDP	$522bn	GDP per head in purchasing	
Av. ann. growth in real		power parity (USA=100)	10.6
GDP 2008-13	6.7%	Economic freedom index	55.6

Origins of GDP		**Components of GDP**	
	% of total		% of total
Agriculture	21	Private consumption	72
Industry, of which:	22	Public consumption	8
manufacturing	9	Investment	15
Services	57	Exports	18
		Imports	-13

Structure of employment

	% of total		% of labour force
Agriculture	...	Unemployed 2013	28.5
Industry	...	Av. ann. rate 2000-13	9.1
Services	...		

Energy

	m TOE		
Total output	167.3	Net energy imports as %	
Total consumption	22.6	of energy use	-117
Consumption per person			
kg oil equivalent	134		

Inflation and finance

Consumer price		*av. ann. increase 2009-14*	
inflation 2014	8.1%	Narrow money (M1)	4.6%
Av. ann. inflation 2009-14	10.6%	Broad money	10.5%
Treasury bill rate, Dec. 2014	10.80%		

Exchange rates

	end 2014		December 2014
N per $	168.68	Effective rates	2010 = 100
N per SDR	245.83	– nominal	98.10
N per €	204.79	– real	130.80

Trade

Principal exports		Principal imports	
	$bn fob		$bn cif
Crude oil	81.1	Machinery & transport equip.	14.1
Gas	9.4	Food & live animals	8.2
Cocoa & cocoa butter	0.1	Manufactured goods	7.4
Rubber	0.1	Chemicals	5.9
Total incl. others	**95.1**	Total incl. others	**58.2**

Main export destinations		Main origins of imports	
	% of total		% of total
India	12.3	China	21.0
United States	11.5	United States	11.3
Brazil	10.1	India	4.6
Spain	7.2	France	3.5

Balance of payments, reserves and debt, $bn

Visible exports fob	95.7	Change in reserves	11.3
Visible imports fob	-53.4	Level of reserves	
Trade balance	42.3	end Dec.	47.5
Invisibles inflows	3.4	No. months of import cover	5.7
Invisibles outflows	-47.2	Official gold holdings, m oz	0.7
Net transfers	21.9	Foreign debt	18.7
Current account balance	20.4	– as % of GDP	3.6
– as % of GDP	7.8	– as % of total exports	15.6
Capital balance	-1.3	Debt service ratio	0.4
Overall balance	11.1		

Health and education

Health spending, % of GDP	3.9	Education spending, % of GDP	...
Doctors per 1,000 pop.	0.4	Enrolment, %: primary	85
Hospital beds per 1,000 pop.	-	secondary	44
Improved-water source access,		tertiary	...
% of pop.	64		

Society

No. of households, m	35.7	Cost of living, Dec. 2014	
Av. no. per household	4.8	New York = 100	60
Marriages per 1,000 pop.	...	Cars per 1,000 pop.	16
Divorces per 1,000 pop.	...	Colour TV households, % with:	
Religion, % of pop.		cable	1.9
Christian	49.3	satellite	...
Muslim	48.8	Telephone lines per 100 pop.	5.3
Other	1.4	Mobile telephone subscribers	
Non-religious	0.4	per 100 pop.	73.3
Hindu	<0.1	Broadband subs per 100 pop.	0.0
Jewish	<0.1	Internet users, % of pop.	38.0

NORWAY

Area	323,878 sq km	Capital	Oslo
Arable as % of total land	2.2	Currency	Norwegian krone (Nkr)

People

Population	5.0m	Life expectancy: men	80.0 yrs
Pop. per sq km	15.4	women	84.2 yrs
Average annual growth		Adult literacy	...
in pop. 2015-20	1.0%	Fertility rate (per woman)	1.8
Pop. under 15	18.6%	Urban population	89.2%
Pop. over 60	21.6%		per 1,000 pop.
No. of men per 100 women	99.9	Crude birth rate	12
Human Development Index	94.4	Crude death rate	8.1

The economy

GDP	Nkr3,011bn	GDP per head	$100,900
GDP	$513bn	GDP per head in purchasing	
Av. ann. growth in real		power parity (USA=100)	121.4
GDP 2008-13	0.7%	Economic freedom index	71.8

Origins of GDP

	% of total
Agriculture	2
Industry, of which:	41
manufacturing	7
Services	58

Components of GDP

	% of total
Private consumption	41
Public consumption	22
Investment	26
Exports	39
Imports	-28

Structure of employment

	% of total		% of labour force
Agriculture	2.2	Unemployed 2013	3.5
Industry	20.3	Av. ann. rate 2000-13	3.5
Services	77.5		

Energy

	m TOE		
Total output	239.2	Net energy imports as %	
Total consumption	48.6	of energy use	-577
Consumption per person			
kg oil equivalent	9,681		

Inflation and finance

		av. ann. increase 2009-14	
Consumer price inflation 2014	2.0%	Narrow money (M1)	3.9%
Av. ann. inflation 2009-14	1.7%	Broad money	5.3%
Interbank rate, Oct. 2014	1.63%	H'hold saving rate, 2014	9.2%

Exchange rates

	end 2014		December 2014
Nkr per $	7.43	Effective rates	2010 = 100
Nkr per SDR	10.77	– nominal	88.50
Nkr per €	9.02	– real	87.90

Trade

Principal exports		Principal imports	
	$bn fob		*$bn cif*
Mineral fuels & lubricants	105.2	Machinery & transport equip.	34.8
Machinery & transport equip.	13.6	Miscellaneous manufactured	
Manufactured goods	11.4	articles	13.5
Food & beverages	10.9	Manufactured goods	13.0
		Chemicals & mineral products	8.6
Total incl. others	**155.3**	Total incl. others	**89.8**

Main export destinations		Main origins of imports	
	% of total		*% of total*
United Kingdom	24.1	Sweden	13.3
Netherlands	12.9	Germany	12.4
Germany	12.7	China	9.2
France	6.0	United Kingdom	6.4
EU28	81.4	EU28	64.5

Balance of payments, reserves and aid, $bn

Visible exports fob	153.5	Overall balance	3.1
Visible imports fob	-93.0	Change in reserves	6.4
Trade balance	60.5	Level of reserves	
Invisibles inflows	90.2	end Dec.	58.3
Invisibles outflows	-92.0	No. months of import cover	3.8
Net transfers	-7.8	Official gold holdings, m oz	0.0
Current account balance	51.0	Aid given	5.6
– as % of GDP	9.9	– as % of GDP	1.1
Capital balance	-42.2		

Health and education

Health spending, % of GDP	9.6	Education spending, % of GDP	6.6
Doctors per 1,000 pop.	4.3	Enrolment, %: primary	99
Hospital beds per 1,000 pop.	3.3	secondary	111
Improved-water source access,		tertiary	74
% of pop.	100		

Society

No. of households, m	2.3	Cost of living, Dec. 2014	
Av. no. per household	2.2	New York = 100	124
Marriages per 1,000 pop.	4.9	Cars per 1,000 pop.	495
Divorces per 1,000 pop.	2.0	Colour TV households, % with:	
Religion, % of pop.		cable	44.5
Christian	84.7	satellite	38.5
Non-religious	10.1	Telephone lines per 100 pop.	24.5
Muslim	3.7	Mobile telephone subscribers	
Other	0.9	per 100 pop.	116.3
Hindu	0.5	Broadband subs per 100 pop.	38.1
Jewish	<0.1	Internet users, % of pop.	95.1

PAKISTAN

Area	803,940 sq km	Capital	Islamabad
Arable as % of total land	27.5	Currency	Pakistan rupee (PRs)

People

Population	182.1m	Life expectancy: men	66.3 yrs
Pop. per sq km	226.5	women	68.3 yrs
Average annual growth		Adult literacy	54.7
in pop. 2015-20	1.6%	Fertility rate (per woman)	3.8
Pop. under 15	33.8%	Urban population	38.8%
Pop. over 60	6.5%		per 1,000 pop.
No. of men per 100 women	105.6	Crude birth rate	28
Human Development Index	53.7	Crude death rate	6.8

The economy

GDP	PRs22,489bn	GDP per head	$1,280
GDP	$232bn	GDP per head in purchasing	
Av. ann. growth in real		power parity (USA=100)	8.7
GDP 2008-13	2.8%	Economic freedom index	55.6

Origins of GDP		Components of GDP	
	% of total		% of total
Agriculture	25	Private consumption	81
Industry, of which:	21	Public consumption	11
manufacturing	14	Investment	15
Services	54	Exports	13
		Imports	-20

Structure of employment

	% of total		% of labour force
Agriculture	43.7	Unemployed 2013	6.2
Industry	21.5	Av. ann. rate 2000-13	6.2
Services	33.2		

Energy

	m TOE		
Total output	45.2	Net energy imports as %	
Total consumption	66.1	of energy use	23
Consumption per person			
kg oil equivalent	369		

Inflation and finance

Consumer price		av. ann. increase 2009-14	
inflation 2014	8.6%	Narrow money (M1)	15.7%
Av. ann. inflation 2009-14	10.1%	Broad money	13.8%
Money market rate, Dec. 2014	9.49%		

Exchange rates

	end 2014		December 2014
PRs per $	100.46	Effective rates	2010 = 100
PRs per SDR	145.55	– nominal	89.60
PRs per €	121.97	– real	116.00

Trade

Principal exports		**Principal imports**	
	$bn fob		*$bn cif*
Cotton fabrics	2.8	Petroleum products	9.9
Cotton yarn & thread	2.3	Crude oil	6.1
Knitwear	2.1	Palm oil	2.0
Rice	2.1	Telecoms equipment	1.3
Total incl. others	**25.1**	Total incl. others	**44.7**

Main export destinations		**Main origins of imports**	
	% of total		*% of total*
United States	14.1	China	27.1
China	11.6	Saudi Arabia	14.3
United Arab Emirates	9.7	United Arab Emirates	14.1
Afghanistan	8.5	Kuwait	14.1

Balance of payments, reserves and debt, $bn

Visible exports fob	25.1	Change in reserves	-6.0
Visible imports fob	-41.2	Level of reserves	
Trade balance	-16.1	end Dec.	7.7
Invisibles inflows	5.4	No. months of import cover	1.7
Invisibles outflows	-12.4	Official gold holdings, m oz	2.1
Net transfers	18.7	Foreign debt	56.5
Current account balance	-4.4	– as % of GDP	24.3
– as % of GDP	-1.9	– as % of total exports	124.9
Capital balance	2.4	Debt service ratio	17.4
Overall balance	-2.6		

Health and education

Health spending, % of GDP	2.8	Education spending, % of GDP	2.5
Doctors per 1,000 pop.	0.8	Enrolment, %: primary	92
Hospital beds per 1,000 pop.	0.6	secondary	38
Improved-water source access,		tertiary	10
% of pop.	91.4		

Society

No. of households, m	31.1	Cost of living, Dec. 2014	
Av. no. per household	6.8	New York = 100	44
Marriages per 1,000 pop.	...	Cars per 1,000 pop.	11
Divorces per 1,000 pop.	...	Colour TV households, % with:	
Religion, % of pop.		cable	1.3
Muslim	96.4	satellite	15.4
Hindu	1.9	Telephone lines per 100 pop.	3.5
Christian	1.6	Mobile telephone subscribers	
Jewish	<0.1	per 100 pop.	70.1
Non-religious	<0.1	Broadband subs per 100 pop.	0.6
Other	<0.1	Internet users, % of pop.	10.9

PERU

Area	1,285,216 sq km	Capital	Lima
Arable as % of total land	3.2	Currency	Nuevo Sol (New Sol)

People

Population	30.4m	Life expectancy: men	73.5 yrs
Pop. per sq km	23.6	women	78.8 yrs
Average annual growth		Adult literacy	93.8
in pop. 2015-20	1.2%	Fertility rate (per woman)	2.4
Pop. under 15	28.8%	Urban population	78.6%
Pop. over 60	9.3%		per 1,000 pop.
No. of men per 100 women	100.5	Crude birth rate	20
Human Development Index	73.7	Crude death rate	5.3

The economy

GDP	New Soles 547bn	GDP per head	$6,660
GDP	$202bn	GDP per head in purchasing	
Av. ann. growth in real		power parity (USA=100)	22.2
GDP 2008–13	5.5%	Economic freedom index	67.7

Origins of GDP		Components of GDP	
	% of total		% of total
Agriculture	7	Private consumption	61
Industry, of which:	37	Public consumption	11
manufacturing	...	Investment	28
Services	56	Exports	24
		Imports	-25

Structure of employment

	% of total		% of labour force
Agriculture	25.8	Unemployed 2013	4.0
Industry	17.4	Av. ann. rate 2000–13	4.7
Services	56.8		

Energy

	m TOE		
Total output	25.3	Net energy imports as %	
Total consumption	27.3	of energy use	-14
Consumption per person			
kg oil equivalent	911		

Inflation and finance

Consumer price		av. ann. increase 2009–14	
inflation 2014	3.2%	Narrow money (M1)	14.2%
Av. ann. inflation 2009–14	2.9%	Broad money	13.6%
Money market rate, Dec. 2014	3.80%		

Exchange rates

	end 2014		December 2014
New Soles per $	2.99	Effective rates	2010 = 100
New Soles per SDR	4.32	– nominal	...
New Soles per €	3.63	– real	...

Trade

Principal exports		Principal imports	
	$bn fob		*$bn cif*
Copper	9.8	Intermediate goods	19.6
Gold	8.1	Capital goods	13.7
Fishmeal	1.4	Consumer goods	8.8
Zinc	1.7	Other goods	0.2
Total incl. others	**42.5**	Total	**42.2**

Main export destinations		Main origins of imports	
	% of total		*% of total*
United States	17.5	United States	26.2
China	17.0	China	16.1
Canada	6.7	Brazil	5.6
Japan	5.0	Argentina	5.0

Balance of payments, reserves and debt, $bn

Visible exports fob	42.2	Change in reserves	1.6
Visible imports fob	-41.6	Level of reserves	
Trade balance	0.6	end Dec.	65.8
Invisibles inflows	6.4	No. months of import cover	12.9
Invisibles outflows	-19.5	Official gold holdings, m oz	1.1
Net transfers	3.3	Foreign debt	56.7
Current account balance	-9.1	– as % of GDP	28.0
– as % of GDP	-4.5	– as % of total exports	108.2
Capital balance	10.0	Debt service ratio	13.0
Overall balance	1.7		

Health and education

Health spending, % of GDP	5.3	Education spending, % of GDP	3.3
Doctors per 1,000 pop.	1.1	Enrolment, %: primary	102
Hospital beds per 1,000 pop.	1.5	secondary	94
Improved-water source access,		tertiary	41
% of pop.	86.8		

Society

No. of households, m	7.6	Cost of living, Dec. 2014	
Av. no. per household	4.0	New York = 100	70
Marriages per 1,000 pop.	2.8	Cars per 1,000 pop.	57
Divorces per 1,000 pop.	0.4	Colour TV households, % with:	
Religion, % of pop.		cable	32.5
Christian	95.5	satellite	0.2
Non-religious	3.0	Telephone lines per 100 pop.	11.3
Other	1.5	Mobile telephone subscribers	
Hindu	<0.1	per 100 pop.	98.1
Jewish	<0.1	Broadband subs per 100 pop.	5.2
Muslim	<0.1	Internet users, % of pop.	39.2

PHILIPPINES

Area	300,000 sq km	Capital	Manila
Arable as % of total land	18.6	Currency	Philippine peso (P)

People

Population	98.4m	Life expectancy: men	66.0 yrs
Pop. per sq km	328.0	women	73.0 yrs
Average annual growth		Adult literacy	...
in pop. 2015-20	1.6%	Fertility rate (per woman)	3
Pop. under 15	34.1%	Urban population	44.4%
Pop. over 60	6.4%		per 1,000 pop.
No. of men per 100 women	100.5	Crude birth rate	24
Human Development Index	66	Crude death rate	6.1

The economy

GDP	P11,548bn	GDP per head	$2,770
GDP	$272bn	GDP per head in purchasing	
Av. ann. growth in real		power parity (USA=100)	12.3
GDP 2008-13	5.3%	Economic freedom index	62.2

Origins of GDP		Components of GDP	
	% of total		% of total
Agriculture	11	Private consumption	73
Industry, of which:	31	Public consumption	11
manufacturing	20	Investment	20
Services	58	Exports	28
		Imports	-32

Structure of employment

	% of total		% of labour force
Agriculture	32.1	Unemployed 2013	7.1
Industry	15.4	Av. ann. rate 2000-13	8.8
Services	52.5		

Energy

	m TOE		
Total output	12.5	Net energy imports as %	
Total consumption	32.7	of energy use	41
Consumption per person			
kg oil equivalent	338		

Inflation and finance

			av. ann. increase 2009-14
Consumer price			
inflation 2014	4.2%	Narrow money (M1)	13.7%
Av. ann. inflation 2009-14	3.8%	Broad money	13.8%
Money market rate, Dec. 2014	2.56%		

Exchange rates

	end 2014		December 2014
P per $	44.62	Effective rates	2010 = 100
P per SDR	64.64	– nominal	106.90
P per €	54.17	– real	114.40

Trade

Principal exports		Principal imports	
	$bn fob		*$bn cif*
Electrical & electronic equip.	21.8	Capital goods	16.9
Clothing	1.6	Mineral fuels	13.1
Coconut oil	1.0	Chemicals	6.0
Petroleum products	0.8	Manufactured goods	5.5
Total incl. others	**56.7**	**Total incl. others**	**65.7**

Main export destinations		Main origins of imports	
	% of total		*% of total*
Japan	20.1	United States	11.2
United States	13.8	China	13.4
China	11.6	Japan	8.7
Hong Kong	7.8	South Korea	8.0

Balance of payments, reserves and debt, $bn

Visible exports fob	44.5	Change in reserves	-0.6
Visible imports fob	-62.2	Level of reserves	
Trade balance	-17.7	end Dec.	83.2
Invisibles inflows	31.7	No. months of import cover	11.6
Invisibles outflows	-23.7	Official gold holdings, m oz	6.2
Net transfers	21.1	Foreign debt	60.6
Current account balance	11.4	– as % of GDP	22.3
– as % of GDP	4.2	– as % of total exports	59.3
Capital balance	-2.1	Debt service ratio	5.7
Overall balance	5.1		

Health and education

Health spending, % of GDP	4.4	Education spending, % of GDP	3.4
Doctors per 1,000 pop.	...	Enrolment, %: primary	106
Hospital beds per 1,000 pop.	1.0	secondary	85
Improved-water source access,		tertiary	28
% of pop.	91.8		

Society

No. of households, m	21.8	Cost of living, Dec. 2014	
Av. no. per household	4.5	New York = 100	65
Marriages per 1,000 pop.	...	Cars per 1,000 pop.	31
Divorces per 1,000 pop.	...	Colour TV households, % with:	
Religion, % of pop.		cable	52.5
Christian	92.6	satellite	0.6
Muslim	5.5	Telephone lines per 100 pop.	3.2
Other	1.7	Mobile telephone subscribers	
Non-religious	0.1	per 100 pop.	104.5
Hindu	<0.1	Broadband subs per 100 pop.	9.1
Jewish	<0.1	Internet users, % of pop.	37.0

POLAND

Area	312,683 sq km	Capital	Warsaw
Arable as % of total land	35.7	Currency	Zloty (Zl)

People

Population	38.2m	Life expectancy: men	73.2 yrs
Pop. per sq km	122.2	women	81.1 yrs
Average annual growth		Adult literacy	99.7
in pop. 2015-20	0.0%	Fertility rate (per woman)	1.2
Pop. under 15	15.0%	Urban population	60.5%
Pop. over 60	21.1%		per 1,000 pop.
No. of men per 100 women	93.4	Crude birth rate	10
Human Development Index	83.4	Crude death rate	10.8

The economy

GDP	Zl1,662bn	GDP per head	$13,650
GDP	$526bn	GDP per head in purchasing	
Av. ann. growth in real		power parity (USA=100)	44.7
GDP 2008-13	2.9%	Economic freedom index	68.6

Origins of GDP		**Components of GDP**	
	% of total		% of total
Agriculture	3	Private consumption	61
Industry, of which:	33	Public consumption	18
manufacturing	19	Investment	19
Services	63	Exports	46
		Imports	-44

Structure of employment

	% of total		% of labour force
Agriculture	12.6	Unemployed 2013	10.3
Industry	30.4	Av. ann. rate 2000-13	13.5
Services	57.0		

Energy

	m TOE		
Total output	67.4	Net energy imports as %	
Total consumption	97.6	of energy use	26
Consumption per person			
kg oil equivalent	2,534		

Inflation and finance

Consumer price		av. ann. increase 2009-14	
inflation 2014	0.0%	Narrow money (M1)	8.3%
Av. ann. inflation 2009-14	2.3%	Broad money	7.2%
Money market rate, Dec. 2014	2.06%	H'hold saving rate, 2014	...

Exchange rates

	end 2014		December 2014
Zl per $	3.51	Effective rates	2010 = 100
Zl per SDR	5.08	– nominal	96.5
Zl per €	4.26	– real	95.8

Trade

Principal exports		Principal imports	
	$bn fob		*$bn cif*
Machinery & transport equip.	69.1	Machinery & transport equip.	63.7
Manufactured goods	39.0	Manufactured goods	34.4
Foodstuffs & live animals	19.3	Chemicals & chemical products	27.6
Total incl. others	**203.2**	Total incl. others	**206.3**

Main export destinations		Main origins of imports	
	% of total		*% of total*
Germany	25.3	Germany	26.5
United Kingdom	6.6	Russia	10.0
Czech Republic	6.2	Netherlands	5.8
France	5.7	China	5.4
EU28	75.0	EU28	69.0

Balance of payments, reserves and debt, $bn

Visible exports fob	197.8	Change in reserves	-2.7
Visible imports fob	-197.0	Level of reserves	
Trade balance	0.8	end Dec.	106.2
Invisibles inflows	60.4	No. months of import cover	4.8
Invisibles outflows	-67.7	Official gold holdings, m oz	3.3
Net transfers	-0.5	Foreign debt	361.2
Current account balance	-7.0	– as % of GDP	69.8
– as % of GDP	-1.3	– as % of total exports	137.0
Capital balance	19.7	Debt service ratio	17.4
Overall balance	0.9	Aid given	0.5
		– as % of GDP	0.1

Health and education

Health spending, % of GDP	6.7	Education spending, % of GDP	4.9
Doctors per 1,000 pop.	2.2	Enrolment, %: primary	101
Hospital beds per 1,000 pop.	6.5	secondary	98
Improved-water source access,		tertiary	73
% of pop.	...		

Society

No. of households, m	13.6	Cost of living, Dec. 2014	
Av. no. per household	2.8	New York = 100	69
Marriages per 1,000 pop.	5.3	Cars per 1,000 pop.	504
Divorces per 1,000 pop.	1.7	Colour TV households, % with:	
Religion, % of pop.		cable	33.8
Christian	94.3	satellite	62.8
Non-religious	5.6	Telephone lines per 100 pop.	14.3
Hindu	<0.1	Mobile telephone subscribers	
Jewish	<0.1	per 100 pop.	149.1
Muslim	<0.1	Broadband subs per 100 pop.	15.7
Other	<0.1	Internet users, % of pop.	62.9

PORTUGAL

Area	88,940 sq km	Capital	Lisbon
Arable as % of total land	11.9	Currency	Euro (€)

People

Population	10.6m	Life expectancy: men	78.0 yrs
Pop. per sq km	119.2	women	83.6 yrs
Average annual growth		Adult literacy	94.5
in pop. 2015-20	-0.1%	Fertility rate (per woman)	1.2
Pop. under 15	14.8%	Urban population	63.5%
Pop. over 60	24.7%		per 1,000 pop.
No. of men per 100 women	93.8	Crude birth rate	8
Human Development Index	82.2	Crude death rate	10.5

The economy

GDP	€171bn	GDP per head	$21,740
GDP	$227bn	GDP per head in purchasing	
Av. ann. growth in real		power parity (USA=100)	52.4
GDP 2008-13	-1.7%	Economic freedom index	65.3

Origins of GDP		**Components of GDP**	
	% of total		% of total
Agriculture	2	Private consumption	65
Industry, of which:	21	Public consumption	19
manufacturing	13	Investment	15
Services	77	Exports	39
		Imports	-38

Structure of employment

	% of total		% of labour force
Agriculture	10.5	Unemployed 2013	16.2
Industry	25.6	Av. ann. rate 2000-13	8.7
Services	63.9		

Energy

	m TOE		
Total output	4.6	Net energy imports as %	
Total consumption	24.5	of energy use	78
Consumption per person			
kg oil equivalent	2,326		

Inflation and finance

Consumer price		av. ann. increase 2009-14	
inflation 2014	-0.2%	Euro area:	
Av. ann. inflation 2009-14	1.6%	Narrow money (M1)	5.6%
Deposit rate, h'holds Dec. 2014	1.63%	Broad money	2.0%
		H'hold saving rate[a], 2014	11.3%

Exchange rates

	end 2014		December 2014
€ per $	0.82	Effective rates	2010 = 100
€ per SDR	1.19	– nominal	99.00
		– real	97.90

Trade

Principal exports		Principal imports	
	$bn fob		*$bn cif*
Machinery & transport equip.	15.5	Machinery & transport equip.	17.4
Food, drink & tobacco	6.4	Mineral fuels & lubricants	14.6
Chemicals & related products	6.4	Chemicals & related products	10.0
Mineral fuels & lubricants	5.5	Food, drink & tobacco	10.0
Total incl. others	**62.8**	Total incl. others	**75.6**

Main export destinations		Main origins of imports	
	% of total		*% of total*
Spain	23.7	Spain	32.2
Germany	11.6	Germany	11.4
France	11.6	France	6.7
Angola	6.4	Italy	5.1
EU28	70.3	EU28	72.0

Balance of payments, reserves and debt, $bn

Visible exports fob	63.0	Overall balance	-4.0
Visible imports fob	-72.6	Change in reserves	-5.1
Trade balance	-9.6	Level of reserves	
Invisibles inflows	36.4	end Dec.	17.6
Invisibles outflows	-30.8	No. months of import cover	2.0
Net transfers	5.3	Official gold holdings, m oz	12.3
Current account balance	1.2	Aid given	0.5
– as % of GDP	0.5	– as % of GDP	0.2
Capital balance	-5.4		

Health and education

Health spending, % of GDP	9.7	Education spending, % of GDP	5.3
Doctors per 1,000 pop.	4.1	Enrolment, %: primary	106
Hospital beds per 1,000 pop.	3.4	secondary	113
Improved-water source access,		tertiary	69
% of pop.	99.8		

Society

No. of households, m	4.0	Cost of living, Dec. 2014	
Av. no. per household	2.6	New York = 100	74
Marriages per 1,000 pop.	3.3	Cars per 1,000 pop.	427
Divorces per 1,000 pop.	2.4	Colour TV households, % with:	
Religion, % of pop.		cable	56.1
Christian	93.8	satellite	20.1
Non-religious	4.4	Telephone lines per 100 pop.	42.7
Other	1.0	Mobile telephone subscribers	
Muslim	0.6	per 100 pop.	113.0
Hindu	0.1	Broadband subs per 100 pop.	23.8
Jewish	<0.1	Internet users, % of pop.	62.1

a Gross.

ROMANIA

Area	237,500 sq km	Capital	Bucharest
Arable as % of total land	38.2	Currency	Leu (Lei)

People

Population	21.7m	Life expectancy: men	70.9 yrs
Pop. per sq km	91.4	women	78.0 yrs
Average annual growth		Adult literacy	98.6
in pop. 2015-20	-0.3%	Fertility rate (per woman)	1.3
Pop. under 15	15.1%	Urban population	54.6%
Pop. over 60	21.0%		per 1,000 pop.
No. of men per 100 women	95.1	Crude birth rate	10
Human Development Index	78.5	Crude death rate	12.8

The economy

GDP	RON631bn	GDP per head	$9,490
GDP	$190bn	GDP per head in purchasing	
Av. ann. growth in real		power parity (USA=100)	35.8
GDP 2008–13	-0.6%	Economic freedom index	66.6

Origins of GDP		**Components of GDP**	
	% of total		% of total
Agriculture	6	Private consumption	72
Industry, of which:	43	Public consumption	6
manufacturing	...	Investment	23
Services	50	Exports	42
		Imports	-43

Structure of employment

	% of total		% of labour force
Agriculture	29.0	Unemployed 2013	7.3
Industry	28.6	Av. ann. rate 2000–13	7.1
Services	42.4		

Energy

	m TOE		
Total output	27.3	Net energy imports as %	
Total consumption	36.5	of energy use	23
Consumption per person			
kg oil equivalent	1,821		

Inflation and finance

Consumer price		av. ann. increase 2009–14	
inflation 2014	1.1%	Narrow money (M1)	8.3%
Av. ann. inflation 2009–14	4.0%	Broad money	6.6%
Money market rate, Dec. 2014	0.55%		

Exchange rates

	end 2014		December 2014
Lei per $	3.69	Effective rates	2010 = 100
Lei per SDR	5.34	– nominal	95.80
Lei per €	4.48	– real	100.00

Trade

Principal exports		Principal imports	
	$bn fob		*$bn cif*
Machinery & equipment,		Machinery & equipment,	
incl. transport	23.1	incl. transport	23.1
Textiles & apparel	4.5	Chemical products	9.5
Basic metals & products	3.2	Minerals, fuels & lubricants	8.5
Minerals, fuels & lubricants	3.2	Textiles & products	4.4
Total incl. others	**65.9**	Total incl. others	**73.4**

Main export destinations		Main origins of imports	
	% of total		*% of total*
Germany	18.5	Germany	18.5
Italy	11.5	Italy	11.0
France	6.8	Hungary	8.3
Turkey	5.3	France	5.8
EU28	69.6	EU28	75.7

Balance of payments, reserves and debt, $bn

Visible exports fob	58.3	Change in reserves	2.1
Visible imports fob	-65.6	Level of reserves	
Trade balance	-7.3	end Dec.	48.8
Invisibles inflows	18.6	No. months of import cover	7.0
Invisibles outflows	-18.1	Official gold holdings, m oz	3.3
Net transfers	5.0	Foreign debt	134.0
Current account balance	-1.8	– as % of GDP	69.9
– as % of GDP	-0.9	– as % of total exports	159.7
Capital balance	11.4	Debt service ratio	36.9
Overall balance	9.0	Aid given[a]	0.1
		– as % of GDP[a]	0.1

Health and education

Health spending, % of GDP	5.3	Education spending, % of GDP	3.1
Doctors per 1,000 pop.	2.4	Enrolment, %: primary	94
Hospital beds per 1,000 pop.	6.1	secondary	95
Improved-water source access,		tertiary	52
% of pop.	...		

Society

No. of households, m	7.1	Cost of living, Dec. 2014	
Av. no. per household	2.8	New York = 100	54
Marriages per 1,000 pop.	5.1	Cars per 1,000 pop.	235
Divorces per 1,000 pop.	1.5	Colour TV households, % with:	
Religion, % of pop.		cable	45.9
Christian	99.5	satellite	37.4
Muslim	0.3	Telephone lines per 100 pop.	21.8
Non-religious	0.1	Mobile telephone subscribers	
Hindu	<0.1	per 100 pop.	105.6
Jewish	<0.1	Broadband subs per 100 pop.	17.3
Other	<0.1	Internet users, % of pop.	49.8

a 2012

RUSSIA

Area	17,075,400 sq km	Capital	Moscow
Arable as % of total land	7.3	Currency	Rouble (Rb)

People

Population	142.8m	Life expectancy: men	62.4 yrs
Pop. per sq km	8.4	women	75.0 yrs
Average annual growth		Adult literacy	99.7
in pop. 2015-20	-0.3%	Fertility rate (per woman)	1.7
Pop. under 15	15.8%	Urban population	74.0%
Pop. over 60	19.0%		per 1,000 pop.
No. of men per 100 women	85.9	Crude birth rate	13
Human Development Index	77.8	Crude death rate	15.6

The economy

GDP	Rb66,755bn	GDP per head	$14,610
GDP	$2,097bn	GDP per head in purchasing	
Av. ann. growth in real		power parity (USA=100)	47.6
GDP 2008-13	1.0%	Economic freedom index	52.1

Origins of GDP		Components of GDP	
	% of total		% of total
Agriculture	4	Private consumption	52
Industry, of which:	36	Public consumption	20
manufacturing	15	Investment	23
Services	60	Exports	28
		Imports	-22

Structure of employment

	% of total		% of labour force
Agriculture	9.7	Unemployed 2013	5.5
Industry	27.9	Av. ann. rate 2000-13	7.4
Services	62.3		

Energy

	m TOE		
Total output	1,382.4	Net energy imports as %	
Total consumption	788.1	of energy use	-80
Consumption per person			
kg oil equivalent	5,504		

Inflation and finance

		av. ann. increase 2009-14	
Consumer price			
inflation 2014	7.8%	Narrow money (M1)	22.9%
Av. ann. inflation 2009-14	7.0%	Broad money	11.0%
Money market rate, Dec. 2014	15.47%		

Exchange rates

	end 2014		December 2014
Rb per $	56.26	Effective rates	2010 = 100
Rb per SDR	81.51	– nominal	64.20
Rb per €	68.31	– real	75.80

Trade

Principal exports		**Principal imports**	
	$bn fob		*$bn cif*
Fuels	375.1	Machinery & equipment	157.6
Ores & metals	58.2	Chemicals	47.9
Machinery & equipment	32.0	Food & agricultural products	40.4
Chemicals	26.5	Metals	22.8
Total incl. others	**527.3**	Total incl. others	**315.0**

Main export destinations		**Main origins of imports**	
	% of total		*% of total*
Netherlands	13.3	China	16.9
Germany	7.5	Germany	12.0
Italy	7.0	United States	5.3
China	6.8	Ukraine	5.0

Balance of payments, reserves and debt, $bn

Visible exports fob	523.3	Change in reserves	-28.1
Visible imports fob	-341.3	Level of reserves	
Trade balance	181.9	end Dec.	509.7
Invisibles inflows	112.3	No. months of import cover	10.3
Invisibles outflows	-250.2	Official gold holdings, m oz	33.3
Net transfers	-9.3	Foreign debt	726.7
Current account balance	34.8	– as % of GDP	35.0
– as % of GDP	1.7	– as % of total exports	113.5
Capital balance	-46.6	Debt service ratio	11.5
Overall balance	-22.1	Aid given	0.6
		– as % of GDP	0.03

Health and education

Health spending, % of GDP	6.5	Education spending, % of GDP	...
Doctors per 1,000 pop.	4.3	Enrolment, %: primary	101
Hospital beds per 1,000 pop.	...	secondary	95
Improved-water source access,		tertiary	76
% of pop.	97		

Society

No. of households, m	55.7	Cost of living, Dec. 2014	
Av. no. per household	2.6	New York = 100	84
Marriages per 1,000 pop.	8.5	Cars per 1,000 pop.	282
Divorces per 1,000 pop.	4.5	Colour TV households, % with:	
Religion, % of pop.		cable	32.9
Christian	73.3	satellite	24.7
Non-religious	16.2	Telephone lines per 100 pop.	28.3
Muslim	10.0	Mobile telephone subscribers	
Jewish	0.2	per 100 pop.	152.8
Hindu	<0.1	Broadband subs per 100 pop.	16.6
Other	<0.1	Internet users, % of pop.	61.4

SAUDI ARABIA

Area	2,200,000 sq km	Capital	Riyadh
Arable as % of total land	1.5	Currency	Riyal (SR)

People

Population	28.8m	Life expectancy: men	74.8 yrs
Pop. per sq km	13.1	women	78.5 yrs
Average annual growth		Adult literacy	94.4
in pop. 2015–20	1.6%	Fertility rate (per woman)	2.9
Pop. under 15	29.0%	Urban population	83.1%
Pop. over 60	4.9%		per 1,000 pop.
No. of men per 100 women	129.7	Crude birth rate	22
Human Development Index	83.6	Crude death rate	3.3

The economy

GDP	SR2,795bn	GDP per head	$25,960
GDP	$748bn	GDP per head in purchasing	
Av. ann. growth in real		power parity (USA=100)	101.1
GDP 2008–13	4.9%	Economic freedom index	62.1

Origins of GDP		**Components of GDP**	
	% of total		% of total
Agriculture	2	Private consumption	30
Industry, of which:	61	Public consumption	22
manufacturing	10	Investment	27
Services	38	Exports	52
		Imports	-31

Structure of employment

	% of total		% of labour force
Agriculture	4.7	Unemployed 2013	5.6
Industry	24.6	Av. ann. rate 2000–13	5.3
Services	70.7		

Energy

	m TOE		
Total output	691.6	Net energy imports as %	
Total consumption	232.9	of energy use	-222
Consumption per person			
kg oil equivalent	8,232		

Inflation and finance

Consumer price		*av. ann. increase 2009–14*	
inflation 2014	2.7%	Narrow money (M1)	17.0%
Av. ann. inflation 2009–14	3.3%	Broad money	10.9%
Money market rate, Dec. 2014	0.86%		

Exchange rates

	end 2014		December 2014
SR per $	3.75	Effective rates	2010 = 100
SR per SDR	5.43	– nominal	109.10
SR per €	4.55	– real	112.00

Trade

Principal exports		Principal imports	
	$bn fob		*$bn cif*
Crude oil	278.1	Machinery & transport equip.	74.1
Refined petroleum products	42.1	Foodstuffs	23.3
		Chemical & metal products	14.0
Total incl. others	**376.0**	Total incl. others	**167.7**

Main export destinations		Main origins of imports	
	% of total		*% of total*
China	13.9	United States	12.9
United States	13.8	China	12.7
Japan	13.0	India	8.0
South Korea	9.8	Germany	7.3

Balance of payments, reserves and aid, $bn

Visible exports fob	376.0	Change in reserves	64.1
Visible imports fob	-153.4	Level of reserves	
Trade balance	222.6	end Dec.	737.8
Invisibles inflows	37.0	No. months of import cover	36.6
Invisibles outflows	-88.3	Official gold holdings, m oz	10.4
Net transfers	-35.9	Foreign debt	155.7
Current account balance	135.5	– as % of GDP	20.9
– as % of GDP	18.1	– as % of total exports	37.7
Capital balance	-57.7	Debt service ratio	2.7
Overall balance	69.1		

Health and education

Health spending, % of GDP	3.2	Education spending, % of GDP	...
Doctors per 1,000 pop.	2.5	Enrolment, %: primary	106
Hospital beds per 1,000 pop.	2.1	secondary	116
Improved-water source access,		tertiary	58
% of pop.	97		

Society

No. of households, m	5.0	Cost of living, Dec. 2014	
Av. no. per household	5.9	New York = 100	55
Marriages per 1,000 pop.	...	Cars per 1,000 pop.	403
Divorces per 1,000 pop.	...	Colour TV households, % with:	
Religion, % of pop.		cable	0.3
Muslim	93.0	satellite	99.5
Christian	4.4	Telephone lines per 100 pop.	17.1
Hindu	1.1	Mobile telephone subscribers	
Other	0.9	per 100 pop.	184.2
Non-religious	0.7	Broadband subs per 100 pop.	7.4
Jewish	<0.1	Internet users, % of pop.	60.5

SINGAPORE

Area	639 sq km	Capital	Singapore
Arable as % of total land	0.9	Currency	Singapore dollar (S$)

People

Population	5.4m	Life expectancy: men	80.6 yrs
Pop. per sq km	8,450.7	women	85.5 yrs
Average annual growth		Adult literacy	96.4
in pop. 2015-20	1.5%	Fertility rate (per woman)	1.2
Pop. under 15	16.1%	Urban population	100.0%
Pop. over 60	5.8%		per 1,000 pop.
No. of men per 100 women	97.4	Crude birth rate	9
Human Development Index	90.1	Crude death rate	5.1

The economy

GDP	S$373bn	GDP per head	$55,180
GDP	$298bn	GDP per head in purchasing	
Av. ann. growth in real		power parity (USA=100)	148.5
GDP 2008-13	5.6%	Economic freedom index	89.4

Origins of GDP		**Components of GDP**	
	% of total		% of total
Agriculture	0	Private consumption	38
Industry, of which:	25	Public consumption	10
manufacturing	19	Investment	29
Services	75	Exports	191
		Imports	-168

Structure of employment

	% of total		% of labour force
Agriculture	1.1	Unemployed 2013	2.8
Industry	21.8	Av. ann. rate 2000-13	3.7
Services	77.1		

Energy

	m TOE		
Total output	0.2	Net energy imports as %	
Total consumption	77.6	of energy use	97
Consumption per person			
kg oil equivalent	14,615		

Inflation and finance

Consumer price		*av. ann. increase 2009-14*	
inflation 2014	1.0%	Narrow money (M1)	11.4%
Av. ann. inflation 2009-14	3.2%	Broad money	6.3%
Money market rate, Dec. 2014	0.25%		

Exchange rates

	end 2014		December 2014
S$ per $	1.32	Effective rates	2010 = 100
S$ per SDR	1.91	– nominal	110.30
S$ per €	1.60	– real	112.10

Trade

Principal exports		Principal imports	
	$bn fob		*$bn cif*
Mineral fuels	99.9	Machinery & transport equip.	156.2
Electronic components & parts	98.9	Mineral fuels	116.9
Chemicals & chemical products	50.8	Manufactured products	28.8
Manufactured products	35.7	Misc. manufactured articles	23.4
Total incl. others	**410.3**	Total incl. others	**373.1**

Main export destinations		Main origins of imports	
	% of total		*% of total*
Malaysia	12.2	China	11.7
China	11.8	Malaysia	10.9
Hong Kong	11.2	United States	10.3
Indonesia	5.7	South Korea	6.4
United States	4.3	Japan	5.5

Balance of payments, reserves and debt, $bn

Visible exports fob	441.7	Change in reserves	11.9
Visible imports fob	-367.2	Level of reserves	
Trade balance	74.5	end Dec.	277.8
Invisibles inflows	203.8	No. months of import cover	5.7
Invisibles outflows	-217.4	Official gold holdings, m oz	4.1
Net transfers	-6.8	Foreign debt	28.3
Current account balance	54.1	– as % of GDP	9.4
– as % of GDP	18.2	– as % of total exports	4.4
Capital balance	-36.1	Debt service ratio	0.7
Overall balance	18.1		

Health and education

Health spending, % of GDP	4.6	Education spending, % of GDP	2.9
Doctors per 1,000 pop.	2.0	Enrolment, %: primary	...
Hospital beds per 1,000 pop.	2.0	secondary	...
Improved-water source access,		tertiary	...
% of pop.	100		

Society

No. of households, m	1.6	Cost of living, Dec. 2014	
Av. no. per household	3.5	New York = 100	129
Marriages per 1,000 pop.	6.8	Cars per 1,000 pop.	119
Divorces per 1,000 pop.	1.9	Colour TV households, % with:	
Religion, % of pop.		cable	55.8
Buddhist	33.9	satellite	...
Christian	18.2	Telephone lines per 100 pop.	36.4
Non-religious	16.4	Mobile telephone subscribers	
Muslim	14.3	per 100 pop.	155.9
Other	12.0	Broadband subs per 100 pop.	26.0
Hindu	5.2	Internet users, % of pop.	73.0

SLOVAKIA

Area	49,035 sq km	Capital	Bratislava
Arable as % of total land	29.0	Currency	Euro (€)

People

Population	5.5m	Life expectancy: men	72.2 yrs
Pop. per sq km	112.2	women	83.4 yrs
Average annual growth		Adult literacy	...
in pop. 2015-20	0.0%	Fertility rate (per woman)	1.3
Pop. under 15	15.1%	Urban population	53.6%
Pop. over 60	19.2%		per 1,000 pop.
No. of men per 100 women	94.6	Crude birth rate	10
Human Development Index	83	Crude death rate	10.6

The economy

GDP	€73.6bn	GDP per head	$18,050
GDP	$97.7bn	GDP per head in purchasing	
Av. ann. growth in real		power parity (USA=100)	50.0
GDP 2008–13	1.0%	Economic freedom index	67.2

Origins of GDP		Components of GDP	
	% of total		% of total
Agriculture	4	Private consumption	57
Industry, of which:	33	Public consumption	18
manufacturing	20	Investment	21
Services	63	Exports	93
		Imports	-88

Structure of employment

	% of total		% of labour force
Agriculture	3.2	Unemployed 2013	14.2
Industry	37.5	Av. ann. rate 2000–13	15.0
Services	59.3		

Energy

	m TOE		
Total output	6.4	Net energy imports as %	
Total consumption	17.4	of energy use	63
Consumption per person			
kg oil equivalent	3,225		

Inflation and finance

Consumer price		*av. ann. increase 2009–14*	
inflation 2014	-0.1%	Euro area:	
Av. ann. inflation 2009–14	2.0%	Narrow money (M1)	5.6%
Deposit rate, h'holds Dec. 2014	1.18%	Broad money	2.0%
		H'hold saving rate, 2014	3.0%

Exchange rates

	end 2014		December 2014
€ per $	0.82	Effective rates	2010 = 100
€ per SDR	1.19	– nominal	101.33
		– real	101.50

Trade

Principal exports		Principal imports	
	$bn fob		$bn cif
Machinery & transport equip.	37.4	Machinery & transport equip.	18.2
Intermediate & manuf. products	17.5	Intermediate & manuf. products	13.6
Miscellaneous manuf. products	2.4	Fuels	7.8
Chemicals	1.8	Chemicals	3.7
Total incl. others	**85.3**	Total incl. others	**83.6**

Main export destinations		Main origins of imports	
	% of total		% of total
Germany	20.9	Germany	17.8
Czech Republic	13.6	Czech Republic	16.1
Poland	8.5	Russia	9.6
Hungary	6.5	Hungary	9.1
EU28	82.9	EU28	74.3

Balance of payments, reserves and debt, $bn

Visible exports fob	85.5	Overall balance	0.1
Visible imports fob	-79.8	Change in reserves	-0.4
Trade balance	5.7	Level of reserves	
Invisibles inflows	10.9	end Dec.	2.2
Invisibles outflows	-13.1	No. months of import cover	0.3
Net transfers	-1.4	Official gold holdings, m oz	1.0
Current account balance	2.0	Aid given	0.09
– as % of GDP	2.1	– as % of GDP	0.09
Capital balance	3.3		

Health and education

Health spending, % of GDP	8.2	Education spending, % of GDP	4.1
Doctors per 1,000 pop.	3.3	Enrolment, %: primary	102
Hospital beds per 1,000 pop.	6.0	secondary	94
Improved-water source access,		tertiary	55
% of pop.	100		

Society

No. of households, m	2.3	Cost of living, Dec. 2014	
Av. no. per household	2.4	New York = 100	...
Marriages per 1,000 pop.	4.8	Cars per 1,000 pop.	348
Divorces per 1,000 pop.	2.0	Colour TV households, % with:	
Religion, % of pop.		cable	43.0
Christian	85.3	satellite	49.6
Non-religious	14.3	Telephone lines per 100 pop.	17.7
Muslim	0.2	Mobile telephone subscribers	
Other	0.1	per 100 pop.	113.9
Hindu	<0.1	Broadband subs per 100 pop.	15.5
Jewish	<0.1	Internet users, % of pop.	77.9

SLOVENIA

Area	20,253 sq km	Capital	Ljubljana
Arable as % of total land	8.5	Currency	Euro (€)

People

Population	2.1m	Life expectancy: men	77.2 yrs
Pop. per sq km	103.7	women	84.3 yrs
Average annual growth		Adult literacy	99.7
in pop. 2015-20	0.1%	Fertility rate (per woman)	1.5
Pop. under 15	14.3%	Urban population	49.7%
Pop. over 60	23.8%		per 1,000 pop.
No. of men per 100 women	98.4	Crude birth rate	10
Human Development Index	87.4	Crude death rate	10.3

The economy

GDP	€36.1bn	GDP per head	$23,300
GDP	$48.0bn	GDP per head in purchasing	
Av. ann. growth in real		power parity (USA=100)	54.4
GDP 2008-13	-2.0%	Economic freedom index	60.3

Origins of GDP		Components of GDP	
	% of total		% of total
Agriculture	2	Private consumption	54
Industry, of which:	32	Public consumption	20
manufacturing	22	Investment	20
Services	66	Exports	75
		Imports	-69

Structure of employment

	% of total		% of labour force
Agriculture	8.3	Unemployed 2013	10.1
Industry	30.8	Av. ann. rate 2000-13	6.7
Services	60.3		

Energy

	m TOE		
Total output	3.5	Net energy imports as %	
Total consumption	7.5	of energy use	50
Consumption per person			
kg oil equivalent	3,628		

Inflation and finance

Consumer price		av. ann. increase 2009-14	
inflation 2014	0.2%	Euro area:	
Av. ann. inflation 2009-14	1.6%	Narrow money (M1)	5.6%
Deposit rate, h'holds, Dec. 2014	1.50%	Broad money	2.0%
		H'hold saving rate, 2014	7.2%

Exchange rates

	end 2014		December 2014
€ per $	0.82	Effective rates	2010 = 100
€ per SDR	1.19	– nominal	...
		– real	...

Trade

Principal exports		Principal imports	
	$bn fob		*$bn cif*
Machinery & transport equip.	9.7	Machinery & transport equip.	7.7
Manufactures	5.9	Manufactures	5.2
Chemicals	4.8	Chemicals	4.1
Miscellaneous manufactures	2.8	Miscellaneous manufactures	2.5
Total incl. others	**28.9**	Total incl. others	**28.6**

Main export destinations		Main origins of imports	
	% of total		*% of total*
Germany	22.7	Italy	16.2
Italy	13.6	Germany	19.4
Austria	9.8	Austria	11.8
Croatia	7.2	Croatia	5.4
EU28	74.8	EU28	70.1

Balance of payments, reserves and debt, $bn

Visible exports fob	28.8	Overall balance	0.0
Visible imports fob	-27.8	Change in reserves	0.0
Trade balance	1.0	Level of reserves	
Invisibles inflows	8.4	end Dec.	0.9
Invisibles outflows	-6.4	No. months of import cover	0.3
Net transfers	-0.3	Official gold holdings, m oz	0.1
Current account balance	2.7	Aid given	0.06
– as % of GDP	5.6	– as % of GDP	0.13
Capital balance	-3.7		

Health and education

Health spending, % of GDP	9.2	Education spending, % of GDP	5.7
Doctors per 1,000 pop.	2.5	Enrolment, %: primary	99
Hospital beds per 1,000 pop.	4.6	secondary	98
Improved-water source access,		tertiary	86
% of pop.	99.6		

Society

No. of households, m	0.8	Cost of living, Dec. 2014	
Av. no. per household	2.4	New York = 100	...
Marriages per 1,000 pop.	3.4	Cars per 1,000 pop.	521
Divorces per 1,000 pop.	1.2	Colour TV households, % with:	
Religion, % of pop.		cable	70.7
Christian	78.4	satellite	9.1
Non-religious	18.0	Telephone lines per 100 pop.	47.7
Muslim	3.6	Mobile telephone subscribers	
Hindu	<0.1	per 100 pop.	110.2
Jewish	<0.1	Broadband subs per 100 pop.	25.0
Other	<0.1	Internet users, % of pop.	72.7

SOUTH AFRICA

Area	1,225,815 sq km	Capital	Pretoria
Arable as % of total land	9.9	Currency	Rand (R)

People

Population	52.8m	Life expectancy: men	55.7 yrs
Pop. per sq km	43.1	women	59.3 yrs
Average annual growth		Adult literacy	93.7
in pop. 2015-20	0.6%	Fertility rate (per woman)	2.3
Pop. under 15	29.5%	Urban population	64.8%
Pop. over 60	8.6%		per 1,000 pop.
No. of men per 100 women	94.2	Crude birth rate	20
Human Development Index	65.8	Crude death rate	13.2

The economy

GDP	R3,534bn	GDP per head	$6,890
GDP	$366bn	GDP per head in purchasing	
Av. ann. growth in real		power parity (USA=100)	24.3
GDP 2008-13	1.8%	Economic freedom index	62.6

Origins of GDP		**Components of GDP**	
	% of total		% of total
Agriculture	2	Private consumption	62
Industry, of which:	30	Public consumption	20
manufacturing	13	Investment	20
Services	68	Exports	31
		Imports	-33

Structure of employment

	% of total		% of labour force
Agriculture	4.6	Unemployed 2013	24.9
Industry	28.5	Av. ann. rate 2000-13	24.7
Services	66.9		

Energy

	m TOE		
Total output	157.4	Net energy imports as %	
Total consumption	142.0	of energy use	-15
Consumption per person			
kg oil equivalent	2,712		

Inflation and finance

		av. ann. increase 2009-14	
Consumer price			
inflation 2014	6.1%	Narrow money (M1)	9.1%
Av. ann. inflation 2009-14	5.3%	Broad money	2.7%
Money market rate, Dec. 2014	5.65%		

Exchange rates

	end 2014		December 2014
R per $	11.58	Effective rates	2010 = 100
R per SDR	16.78	– nominal	68.50
R per €	14.06	– real	78.00

Trade

Principal exports		Principal imports	
	$bn fob		*$bn cif*
Gold	9.6	Petrochemicals	15.5
Platinum	7.9	Equipment components for cars	5.7
Coal	6.7	Petroleum oils & other	5.0
Car & other components	3.4	Car & other components	3.6
Total incl. others	**95.7**	Total incl. others	**103.4**

Main export destinations		Main origins of imports	
	% of total		*% of total*
China	12.3	China	17.6
United States	7.6	Germany	11.9
Japan	5.9	Saudi Arabia	8.8
Germany	4.7	United States	7.3

Balance of payments, reserves and debt, $bn

Visible exports fob	96.5	Change in reserves	-1.0
Visible imports fob	-103.6	Level of reserves	
Trade balance	-7.1	end Dec.	49.7
Invisibles inflows	23.5	No. months of import cover	4.3
Invisibles outflows	-34.4	Official gold holdings, m oz	4.0
Net transfers	-3.2	Foreign debt	139.8
Current account balance	-21.2	– as % of GDP	38.2
– as % of GDP	-5.8	– as % of total exports	115.2
Capital balance	14.0	Debt service ratio	7.9
Overall balance	0.5		

Health and education

Health spending, % of GDP	8.9	Education spending, % of GDP	6.2
Doctors per 1,000 pop.	0.8	Enrolment, %: primary	101
Hospital beds per 1,000 pop.	10.3	secondary	111
Improved-water source access,		tertiary	20
% of pop.	95.1		

Society

No. of households, m	14.9	Cost of living, Dec. 2014	
Av. no. per household	3.5	New York = 100	61
Marriages per 1,000 pop.	...	Cars per 1,000 pop.	121
Divorces per 1,000 pop.	...	Colour TV households, % with:	
Religion, % of pop.		cable	...
Christian	81.2	satellite	8.9
Non-religious	14.9	Telephone lines per 100 pop.	7.3
Muslim	1.7	Mobile telephone subscribers	
Hindu	1.1	per 100 pop.	145.6
Other	0.9	Broadband subs per 100 pop.	3.1
Jewish	0.1	Internet users, % of pop.	48.9

SOUTH KOREA

Area	99,274 sq km	Capital	Seoul
Arable as % of total land	15.6	Currency	Won (W)

People

Population	49.3m	Life expectancy: men	79.2 yrs
Pop. per sq km	496.6	women	85.9 yrs
Average annual growth		Adult literacy	...
in pop. 2015-20	0.4%	Fertility rate (per woman)	1.2
Pop. under 15	14.9%	Urban population	82.5%
Pop. over 60	17.1%		per 1,000 pop.
No. of men per 100 women	99	Crude birth rate	9
Human Development Index	89.1	Crude death rate	6.2

The economy

GDP	W1,428trn	GDP per head	$25,980
GDP	$1,305bn	GDP per head in purchasing	
Av. ann. growth in real		power parity (USA=100)	62.3
GDP 2008-13	3.2%	Economic freedom index	71.5

Origins of GDP		**Components of GDP**	
	% of total		% of total
Agriculture	2	Private consumption	51
Industry, of which:	39	Public consumption	15
manufacturing	31	Investment	29
Services	59	Exports	54
		Imports	-49

Structure of employment

	% of total		% of labour force
Agriculture	6.6	Unemployed 2013	3.1
Industry	17.0	Av. ann. rate 2000-13	3.5
Services	76.4		

Energy

	m TOE		
Total output	39.0	Net energy imports as %	
Total consumption	288.0	of energy use	82
Consumption per person			
kg oil equivalent	5,759		

Inflation and finance

Consumer price		av. ann. increase 2009-14	
inflation 2014	0.4%	Narrow money (M1)	8.5%
Av. ann. inflation 2009-14	3.1%	Broad money	5.8%
Money market rate, Dec. 2014	1.99%	H'hold saving rate, 2014	...

Exchange rates

	end 2014		December 2014
W per $	1099.30	Effective rates	2010 = 100
W per SDR	1592.70	– nominal	...
W per €	1334.66	– real	...

Trade

Principal exports		**Principal imports**	
	$bn fob		*$bn cif*
Machinery & transport equip.	305.6	Mineral fuels & lubricants	180.4
Manufactured goods	71.7	Machinery & transport equip.	134.6
Chemicals & related products	66.2	Manufactured goods	55.1
Mineral fuels & lubricants	54.1	Chemicals & related products	46.9
Total incl. others	**559.6**	Total incl. others	**515.5**

Main export destinations		**Main origins of imports**	
	% of total		*% of total*
China	26.1	China	16.1
United States	11.1	Japan	11.6
Japan	6.2	United States	8.1
Hong Kong	5.0	Saudi Arabia	7.3

Balance of payments, reserves and debt, $bn

Visible exports fob	618.2	Change in reserves	18.0
Visible imports fob	-535.4	Level of reserves	
Trade balance	82.8	end Dec.	345.7
Invisibles inflows	133.8	No. months of import cover	6.2
Invisibles outflows	-131.3	Official gold holdings, m oz	3.4
Net transfers	-4.2	Foreign debt	422.6
Current account balance	81.1	– as % of GDP	32.4
– as % of GDP	6.2	– as % of total exports	56.2
Capital balance	-63.8	Debt service ratio	6.8
Overall balance	16.3	Aid given	1.7
		– as % of GDP	0.1

Health and education

Health spending, % of GDP	7.2	Education spending, % of GDP	4.9
Doctors per 1,000 pop.	2.1	Enrolment, %: primary	103
Hospital beds per 1,000 pop.	...	secondary	97
Improved-water source access,		tertiary	98
% of pop.	100		

Society

No. of households, m	18.2	Cost of living, Dec. 2014	
Av. no. per household	2.8	New York = 100	113
Marriages per 1,000 pop.	6.5	Cars per 1,000 pop.	300
Divorces per 1,000 pop.	2.3	Colour TV households, % with:	
Religion, % of pop.		cable	81.8
Non-religious	46.4	satellite	13.5
Christian	29.4	Telephone lines per 100 pop.	61.6
Buddhist	22.9	Mobile telephone subscribers	
Other	1.0	per 100 pop.	111.0
Muslim	0.2	Broadband subs per 100 pop.	38.0
Jewish	<0.1	Internet users, % of pop.	84.8

SPAIN

Area	504,782 sq km	Capital	Madrid
Arable as % of total land	24.9	Currency	Euro (€)

People

Population	46.9m	Life expectancy: men	79.5 yrs
Pop. per sq km	92.9	women	86.0 yrs
Average annual growth		Adult literacy	97.9
in pop. 2015-20	0.3%	Fertility rate (per woman)	1.3
Pop. under 15	15.4%	Urban population	79.6%
Pop. over 60	23.1%		per 1,000 pop.
No. of men per 100 women	97.5	Crude birth rate	9
Human Development Index	86.9	Crude death rate	9.0

The economy

GDP	€1,049bn	GDP per head	$29,880
GDP	$1,393bn	GDP per head in purchasing	
Av. ann. growth in real		power parity (USA=100)	62.4
GDP 2008-13	-1.5%	Economic freedom index	67.6

Origins of GDP		Components of GDP	
	% of total		% of total
Agriculture	3	Private consumption	58
Industry, of which:	23	Public consumption	19
manufacturing	...	Investment	19
Services	74	Exports	32
		Imports	-28

Structure of employment

	% of total		% of labour force
Agriculture	4.4	Unemployed 2013	26.1
Industry	20.7	Av. ann. rate 2000-13	14.9
Services	74.9		

Energy

	m TOE		
Total output	38.7	Net energy imports as %	
Total consumption	150.7	of energy use	74
Consumption per person			
kg oil equivalent	3,222		

Inflation and finance

Consumer price		av. ann. increase 2009-14	
inflation 2014	-0.2%	Euro area:	
Av. ann. inflation 2009-14	1.8%	Narrow money (M1)	5.6%
Money market rate, Dec. 2014	0.01%	Broad money	2.0%
		H'hold saving rate[a], 2014	10.7%

Exchange rates

	end 2014		December 2014
€ per $	0.82	Effective rates	2010 = 100
€ per SDR	1.19	– nominal	98.90
		– real	96.80

Trade

Principal exports		Principal imports	
	$bn fob		*$bn cif*
Machinery & transport equip.	99.8	Machinery & transport equip.	86.4
Food, drink & tobacco	43.8	Mineral fuels & lubricants	74.9
Chemicals & related products	41.8	Chemicals & related products	49.1
Mineral fuels & lubricants	29.8	Food, drink & tobacco	32.2
Total incl. others	**311.1**	Total incl. others	**332.4**

Main export destinations		Main origins of imports	
	% of total		*% of total*
France	16.5	Germany	12.5
Germany	10.4	France	11.9
Portugal	7.4	Italy	6.2
Italy	7.0	China	5.7
EU28	62.9	EU28	55.3

Balance of payments, reserves and aid, $bn

Visible exports fob	311.4	Overall balance	0.6
Visible imports fob	-326.5	Change in reserves	-4.3
Trade balance	-15.1	Level of reserves	
Invisibles inflows	194.5	end Dec.	46.3
Invisibles outflows	-161.0	No. months of import cover	1.1
Net transfers	-7.8	Official gold holdings, m oz	9.1
Current account balance	10.7	Aid given	2.4
– as % of GDP	0.8	– as % of GDP	0.1
Capital balance	-22.5		

Health and education

Health spending, % of GDP	8.9	Education spending, % of GDP	5.0
Doctors per 1,000 pop.	4.9	Enrolment, %: primary	103
Hospital beds per 1,000 pop.	3.1	secondary	131
Improved-water source access,		tertiary	85
% of pop.	100		

Society

No. of households, m	18.5	Cost of living, Dec. 2014	
Av. no. per household	2.5	New York = 100	95
Marriages per 1,000 pop.	3.5	Cars per 1,000 pop.	472
Divorces per 1,000 pop.	2.2	Colour TV households, % with:	
Religion, % of pop.		cable	13.9
Christian	78.6	satellite	12.7
Non-religious	19.0	Telephone lines per 100 pop.	41.3
Muslim	2.1	Mobile telephone subscribers	
Jewish	0.1	per 100 pop.	106.9
Other	0.1	Broadband subs per 100 pop.	25.8
Hindu	<0.1	Internet users, % of pop.	71.6

a Gross.

SWEDEN

Area	449,964 sq km	Capital	Stockholm
Arable as % of total land	6.4	Currency	Swedish krona (Skr)

People

Population	9.6m	Life expectancy: men	80.4 yrs
Pop. per sq km	21.3	women	84.5 yrs
Average annual growth		Adult literacy	...
in pop. 2015-20	0.7%	Fertility rate (per woman)	1.9
Pop. under 15	16.9%	Urban population	85.8%
Pop. over 60	25.5%		per 1,000 pop.
No. of men per 100 women	99.2	Crude birth rate	12
Human Development Index	89.8	Crude death rate	9.4

The economy

GDP	Skr3,776bn	GDP per head	$60,380
GDP	$580bn	GDP per head in purchasing	
Av. ann. growth in real		power parity (USA=100)	84.2
GDP 2008-13	0.8%	Economic freedom index	72.7

Origins of GDP		**Components of GDP**	
	% of total		% of total
Agriculture	1	Private consumption	47
Industry, of which:	26	Public consumption	26
manufacturing	16	Investment	22
Services	73	Exports	44
		Imports	-39

Structure of employment

	% of total		% of labour force
Agriculture	2.1	Unemployed 2013	8.0
Industry	19.5	Av. ann. rate 2000-13	6.9
Services	77.9		

Energy

	m TOE		
Total output	38.6	Net energy imports as %	
Total consumption	55.1	of energy use	29
Consumption per person			
kg oil equivalent	5,786		

Inflation and finance

		av. ann. increase 2009-14	
Consumer price			
inflation 2014	-0.2%	Narrow money (M1)	4.4%
Av. ann. inflation 2009-14	1.0%	Broad money	2.9%
Repurchase rate, Oct. 2014	1.00%	H'hold saving rate, 2014	13.1%

Exchange rates

	end 2014		December 2014
Skr per $	7.74	Effective rates	2010 = 100
Skr per SDR	11.21	– nominal	101.70
Skr per €	9.40	– real	96.70

Trade

Principal exports		Principal imports	
	$bn fob		*$bn cif*
Machinery & transport equip.	62.7	Machinery & transport equip.	56.3
Chemicals & related products	19.5	Mineral fuels & lubricants	22.6
Mineral fuels & lubricants	13.9	Chemicals & related products	18.1
Raw materials	11.1	Foods, drink & tobacco	15.9
Total incl. others	**167.5**	Total incl. others	**160.6**

Main export destinations		Main origins of imports	
	% of total		*% of total*
Norway	10.1	Germany	17.5
Germany	9.9	Denmark	8.1
Finland	7.1	Norway	8.1
Denmark	6.8	Netherlands	7.5
EU28	57.7	EU28	68.9

Balance of payments, reserves and aid, $bn

Visible exports fob	180.9	Overall balance	14.9
Visible imports fob	-160.7	Change in reserves	13.1
Trade balance	20.2	Level of reserves	
Invisibles inflows	136.3	end Dec.	65.4
Invisibles outflows	-104.5	No. months of import cover	3.0
Net transfers	-10.0	Official gold holdings, m oz	4.0
Current account balance	42.1	Aid given	5.8
– as % of GDP	7.3	– as % of GDP	1.0
Capital balance	-7.7		

Health and education

Health spending, % of GDP	9.7	Education spending, % of GDP	6.8
Doctors per 1,000 pop.	3.9	Enrolment, %: primary	102
Hospital beds per 1,000 pop.	2.7	secondary	98
Improved-water source access,		tertiary	70
% of pop.	100		

Society

No. of households, m	4.2	Cost of living, Dec. 2014	
Av. no. per household	2.3	New York = 100	93
Marriages per 1,000 pop.	5.3	Cars per 1,000 pop.	470
Divorces per 1,000 pop.	2.5	Colour TV households, % with:	
Religion, % of pop.		cable	57.5
Christian	67.2	satellite	20.1
Non-religious	27.0	Telephone lines per 100 pop.	40.6
Muslim	4.6	Mobile telephone subscribers	
Other	0.8	per 100 pop.	124.4
Hindu	0.2	Broadband subs per 100 pop.	32.6
Jewish	0.1	Internet users, % of pop.	94.8

SWITZERLAND

Area	41,293 sq km	Capital	Berne
Arable as % of total land	10.2	Currency	Swiss franc (SFr)

People

Population	8.1m	Life expectancy: men	80.8 yrs
Pop. per sq km	196.2	women	85.6 yrs
Average annual growth		Adult literacy	...
in pop. 2015-20	1.0%	Fertility rate (per woman)	1.5
Pop. under 15	14.8%	Urban population	73.9%
Pop. over 60	23.4%		per 1,000 pop.
No. of men per 100 women	97	Crude birth rate	10
Human Development Index	91.7	Crude death rate	8.3

The economy

GDP	SFr635bn	GDP per head	$84,750
GDP	$685bn	GDP per head in purchasing	
Av. ann. growth in real		power parity (USA=100)	107.4
GDP 2008-13	1.1%	Economic freedom index	80.5

Origins of GDP		**Components of GDP**	
	% of total		% of total
Agriculture	1	Private consumption	54
Industry, of which:	26	Public consumption	11
manufacturing	19	Investment	23
Services	74	Exports	72
		Imports	-60

Structure of employment

	% of total		% of labour force
Agriculture	3.5	Unemployed 2013	4.4
Industry	20.3	Av. ann. rate 2000-13	3.8
Services	72.5		

Energy

	m TOE		
Total output	15.8	Net energy imports as %	
Total consumption	31.9	of energy use	50
Consumption per person			
kg oil equivalent	3,984		

Inflation and finance

		av. ann. increase 2009-14	
Consumer price			
inflation 2014	0.0%	Narrow money (M1)	7.1%
Av. ann. inflation 2009-14	0.0%	Broad money	7.6%
Money market rate, Dec. 2014	-2.00%	H'hold saving rate, 2014	13.1%

Exchange rates

	end 2014		December 2014
SFr per $	0.99	Effective rates	2010 = 100
SFr per SDR	1.43	– nominal	113.90
SFr per €	1.20	– real	104.50

Trade

Principal exports		**Principal imports**	
	$bn fob		*$bn cif*
Chemicals	87.3	Chemicals	45.2
Precision instruments, watches & jewellery	48.9	Machinery, equipment & electronics	32.6
Machinery, equipment & electronics	35.9	Precision instruments, watches & jewellery	20.7
Metals & metal manufactures	13.0	Motor vehicles	17.1
Total incl. others	**217.1**	Total incl. others	**191.8**

Main export destinations		**Main origins of imports**	
	% of total		*% of total*
Germany	19.5	Germany	29.5
United States	12.4	Italy	10.6
Italy	7.5	France	8.7
France	7.5	United States	6.4
EU28	54.9	EU28	72.9

Balance of payments, reserves and aid, $bn

Visible exports fob	373.5	Overall balance	14.0
Visible imports fob	-319.8	Change in reserves	4.9
Trade balance	53.7	Level of reserves	
Invisibles inflows	235.9	end Dec.	536.2
Invisibles outflows	-197.2	No. months of import cover	12.4
Net transfers	-19.1	Official gold holdings, m oz	33.4
Current account balance	73.2	Aid given	3.2
– as % of GDP	10.7	– as % of GDP	0.5
Capital balance	-90.1		

Health and education

Health spending, % of GDP	11.5	Education spending, % of GDP	5.3
Doctors per 1,000 pop.	4.0	Enrolment, %: primary	103
Hospital beds per 1,000 pop.	5.0	secondary	96
Improved-water source access, % of pop.	100	tertiary	56

Society

No. of households, m	3.7	Cost of living, Dec. 2014	
Av. no. per household	2.2	New York = 100	116
Marriages per 1,000 pop.	5.3	Cars per 1,000 pop.	538
Divorces per 1,000 pop.	2.2	Colour TV households, % with:	
Religion, % of pop.		cable	82.4
Christian	81.3	satellite	16.0
Non-religious	11.9	Telephone lines per 100 pop.	56.9
Muslim	5.5	Mobile telephone subscribers	
Other	0.6	per 100 pop.	136.8
Hindu	0.4	Broadband subs per 100 pop.	42.5
Jewish	0.3	Internet users, % of pop.	86.7

TAIWAN

Area	36,179 sq km	Capital	Taipei
Arable as % of total land	...	Currency	Taiwan dollar (T$)

People

Population	23.3m	Life expectancy: men	76.7 yrs
Pop. per sq km	644.0	women	83.2 yrs
Average annual growth		Adult literacy	...
in pop. 2015-20	0.2%	Fertility rate (per woman)	1.1
Pop. under 15	14.3%	Urban population	73.0%
Pop. over 60	17.0%		per 1,000 pop.
No. of men per 100 women	101	Crude birth rate	8
Human Development Index	...	Crude death rate	7.0

The economy

GDP	T$15,221bn	GDP per head	$21,870
GDP	$511bn	GDP per head in purchasing	
Av. ann. growth in real		power parity (USA=100)	82.3
GDP 2008-13	3.4%	Economic freedom index	75.1

Origins of GDP		Components of GDP	
	% of total		% of total
Agriculture	2	Private consumption	58
Industry, of which:	30	Public consumption	12
manufacturing	25	Investment	19
Services	68	Exports	71
		Imports	-62

Structure of employment

	% of total		% of labour force
Agriculture	...	Unemployed 2013	4.2
Industry	...	Av. ann. rate 2000-13	4.6
Services	...		

Energy

	m TOE		
Total output	12.5	Net energy imports as %	
Total consumption	121.0	of energy use	...
Consumption per person			
kg oil equivalent	5,214		

Inflation and finance

		av. ann. increase 2009-14	
Consumer price			
inflation 2014	1.2%	Narrow money (M1)	6.4%
Av. ann. inflation 2009-14	1.3%	Broad money	5.1%
Money market rate, Dec. 2014	...		

Exchange rates

	end 2014		December 2014
T$ per $	3.67	Effective rates	2010 = 100
T$ per SDR	...	– nominal	...
T$ per €	4.46	– real	...

Trade

Principal exports		Principal imports	
	$bn fob		*$bn cif*
Machinery & electrical equip.	143.8	Machinery & electrical equip.	83.2
Basic metals & articles	27.6	Minerals	73.2
Plastic and rubber articles	24.8	Chemicals & related products	30.5
Chemicals	21.3	Basic metals & articles	21.7
Total incl. others	**288.0**	Total incl. others	**269.1**

Main export destinations		Main origins of imports	
	% of total		*% of total*
China	28.4	Japan	16.0
Hong Kong	13.7	China	15.8
United States	11.3	United States	9.4
Singapore	6.9	South Korea	5.9

Balance of payments, reserves and debt, $bn

Visible exports fob	304.6	Change in reserves	7.4
Visible imports fob	-267.6	Level of reserves	
Trade balance	37.0	end Dec.	434.0
Invisibles inflows	76.8	No. months of import cover	16.2
Invisibles outflows	-53.4	Official gold holdings, m oz	13.6
Net transfers	-3.0	Foreign debt	170.1
Current account balance	57.4	– as % of GDP	33.3
– as % of GDP	11.2	– as % of total exports	44.7
Capital balance	41.2	Debt service ratio	5.0
Overall balance	93.6	Aid given	0.3
		– as % of GDP	0.06

Health and education

Health spending, % of GDP	...	Education spending, % of GDP	...
Doctors per 1,000 pop.	...	Enrolment, %: primary	...
Hospital beds per 1,000 pop.	...	secondary	...
Improved-water source access,		tertiary	...
% of pop.	...		

Society

No. of households, m	7.6	Cost of living, Dec. 2014	
Av. no. per household	3.0	New York = 100	79
Marriages per 1,000 pop.	...	Cars per 1,000 pop.	268
Divorces per 1,000 pop.	...	Colour TV households, % with:	
Religion, % of pop.		cable	84.6
Other	60.5	satellite	0.4
Buddhist	21.3	Telephone lines per 100 pop.	71.2
Non-religious	12.7	Mobile telephone subscribers	
Christian	5.5	per 100 pop.	127.5
Hindu	<0.1	Broadband subs per 100 pop.	24.5
Jewish	<0.1	Internet users, % of pop.	80.0

THAILAND

Area	513,115 sq km	Capital	Bangkok
Arable as % of total land	32.4	Currency	Baht (Bt)

People

Population	67.0m	Life expectancy: men	72.0 yrs
Pop. per sq km	130.6	women	78.6 yrs
Average annual growth		Adult literacy	96.4
in pop. 2015-20	0.1%	Fertility rate (per woman)	1.8
Pop. under 15	18.2%	Urban population	50.4%
Pop. over 60	14.5%		per 1,000 pop.
No. of men per 100 women	96.2	Crude birth rate	12
Human Development Index	72.2	Crude death rate	8.3

The economy

GDP	Bt11,899bn	GDP per head	$5,780
GDP	$387bn	GDP per head in purchasing	
Av. ann. growth in real		power parity (USA=100)	27.1
GDP 2008–13	2.9%	Economic freedom index	62.4

Origins of GDP		Components of GDP	
	% of total		% of total
Agriculture	12	Private consumption	54
Industry, of which:	43	Public consumption	14
manufacturing	33	Investment	29
Services	45	Exports	74
		Imports	-70

Structure of employment

	% of total		% of labour force
Agriculture	39.6	Unemployed 2013	0.8
Industry	20.9	Av. ann. rate 2000–13	1.7
Services	39.4		

Energy

	m TOE		
Total output	65.6	Net energy imports as %	
Total consumption	128.8	of energy use	42
Consumption per person			
kg oil equivalent	1,928		

Inflation and finance

Consumer price		av. ann. increase 2009–14	
inflation 2014	1.9%	Narrow money (M1)	7.4%
Av. ann. inflation 2009–14	2.8%	Broad money	9.6%
Money market rate, Dec. 2014	1.96%		

Exchange rates

	end 2014		December 2014
Bt per $	32.96	Effective rates	2010 = 100
Bt per SDR	47.76	– nominal	...
Bt per €	40.02	– real	...

Trade

Principal exports		Principal imports	
	$bn fob		$bn cif
Machinery, equip. & supplies	93.7	Machinery, equip. & supplies	86.2
Manufactured goods	29.1	Fuel & lubricants	52.0
Food	26.8	Manufactured goods	40.6
Chemicals	24.0	Chemicals	23.6
Total incl. others	**224.9**	Total incl. others	**249.7**

Main export destinations		Main origins of imports	
	% of total		% of total
China	11.9	Japan	16.4
United States	10.1	China	15.1
Japan	9.7	United Arab Emirates	7.0
Hong Kong	5.8	United States	5.9

Balance of payments, reserves and debt, $bn

Visible exports fob	225.4	Change in reserves	-14.3
Visible imports fob	-218.7	Level of reserves	
Trade balance	6.7	end Dec.	167.2
Invisibles inflows	65.1	No. months of import cover	6.6
Invisibles outflows	-86.1	Official gold holdings, m oz	4.9
Net transfers	10.5	Foreign debt	135.4
Current account balance	-3.8	– as % of GDP	35.0
– as % of GDP	-1.0	– as % of total exports	150.7
Capital balance	-4.1	Debt service ratio	4.3
Overall balance	-5.1	Aid given[a]	0.2
		– as % of GDP[a]	0.0

Health and education

Health spending, % of GDP	4.6	Education spending, % of GDP	7.6
Doctors per 1,000 pop.	0.4	Enrolment, %: primary	93
Hospital beds per 1,000 pop.	2.1	secondary	87
Improved-water source access,		tertiary	51
% of pop.	95.8		

Society

No. of households, m	21.7	Cost of living, Dec. 2014	
Av. no. per household	3.1	New York = 100	81
Marriages per 1,000 pop.	...	Cars per 1,000 pop.	104
Divorces per 1,000 pop.	...	Colour TV households, % with:	
Religion, % of pop.		cable	9.9
Buddhist	93.2	satellite	4.9
Muslim	5.5	Telephone lines per 100 pop.	9.0
Christian	0.9	Mobile telephone subscribers	
Non-religious	0.3	per 100 pop.	140.1
Hindu	0.1	Broadband subs per 100 pop.	7.4
Jewish	<0.1	Internet users, % of pop.	28.9

a 2012

TURKEY

Area	779,452 sq km	Capital	Ankara
Arable as % of total land	26.7	Currency	Turkish Lira (YTL)

People

Population	74.9m	Life expectancy: men	73.3 yrs
Pop. per sq km	96.1	women	79.9 yrs
Average annual growth		Adult literacy	94.9
in pop. 2015-20	0.9%	Fertility rate (per woman)	2.1
Pop. under 15	25.7%	Urban population	73.4%
Pop. over 60	10.8%		per 1,000 pop.
No. of men per 100 women	96.6	Crude birth rate	16
Human Development Index	75.9	Crude death rate	5.7

The economy

GDP	YTL1,565bn	GDP per head	$10,970
GDP	$822bn	GDP per head in purchasing	
Av. ann. growth in real		power parity (USA=100)	35.4
GDP 2008-13	3.7%	Economic freedom index	63.2

Origins of GDP		**Components of GDP**	
	% of total		% of total
Agriculture	8	Private consumption	71
Industry, of which:	27	Public consumption	15
manufacturing	18	Investment	21
Services	64	Exports	26
		Imports	-32

Structure of employment

	% of total		% of labour force
Agriculture	23.6	Unemployed 2013	10.0
Industry	26	Av. ann. rate 2000-13	10.3
Services	50.4		

Energy

	m TOE		
Total output	34.5	Net energy imports as %	
Total consumption	126.3	of energy use	73
Consumption per person			
kg oil equivalent	1,707		

Inflation and finance

			av. ann. increase 2009-14
Consumer price			
inflation 2014	8.9%	Narrow money (M1)	19.2%
Av. ann. inflation 2009-14	8.1%	Broad money	14.4%
Money market rate, Dec. 2014	9.00%		

Exchange rates

	end 2014		December 2014
YTL per $	2.32	Effective rates	2010 = 100
YTL per SDR	3.36	– nominal	...
YTL per €	2.82	– real	...

Trade

Principal exports		Principal imports	
	$bn fob		*$bn cif*
Agricultural products	27.4	Fuels	35.7
Transport equipment	18.2	Chemicals	33.5
Iron & steel	17.5	Mechanical equipment	23.4
Textiles & clothing	16.3	Transport equipment	19.4
Total incl. others	**151.8**	Total incl. others	**251.7**

Main export destinations		Main origins of imports	
	% of total		*% of total*
Germany	8.8	Russia	10.0
Iraq	7.4	Germany	9.8
United Kingdom	5.6	China	9.6
Italy	4.5	United States	5.1
EU28	41.5	EU28	36.7

Balance of payments, reserves and debt, $bn

Visible exports fob	161.8	Change in reserves	11.9
Visible imports fob	-241.7	Level of reserves	
Trade balance	-79.9	end Dec.	131.1
Invisibles inflows	51.7	No. months of import cover	5.6
Invisibles outflows	-37.8	Official gold holdings, m oz	16.7
Net transfers	1.4	Foreign debt	388.2
Current account balance	-64.7	– as % of GDP	47.2
– as % of GDP	-7.9	– as % of total exports	181.1
Capital balance	72.6	Debt service ratio	28.7
Overall balance	10.8	Aid given	3.3
		– as % of GDP	0.4

Health and education

Health spending, % of GDP	5.6	Education spending, % of GDP	...
Doctors per 1,000 pop.	1.7	Enrolment, %: primary	100
Hospital beds per 1,000 pop.	2.5	secondary	86
Improved-water source access,		tertiary	69
% of pop.	99.7		

Society

No. of households, m	20.3	Cost of living, Dec. 2014	
Av. no. per household	3.7	New York = 100	83
Marriages per 1,000 pop.	7.9	Cars per 1,000 pop.	123
Divorces per 1,000 pop.	1.6	Colour TV households, % with:	
Religion, % of pop.		cable	7.0
Muslim	98.0	satellite	51.0
Non-religious	1.2	Telephone lines per 100 pop.	18.1
Christian	0.4	Mobile telephone subscribers	
Other	0.3	per 100 pop.	93.0
Hindu	<0.1	Broadband subs per 100 pop.	11.2
Jewish	<0.1	Internet users, % of pop.	46.3

UKRAINE

Area	603,700 sq km	Capital	Kiev
Arable as % of total land	56.1	Currency	Hryvnya (UAH)

People

Population	45.2m	Life expectancy: men	63.3 yrs
Pop. per sq km	74.9	women	74.8 yrs
Average annual growth		Adult literacy	99.7
in pop. 2015–20	-0.7%	Fertility rate (per woman)	1.5
Pop. under 15	14.5%	Urban population	69.7%
Pop. over 60	21.3%		per 1,000 pop.
No. of men per 100 women	85.7	Crude birth rate	11
Human Development Index	73.4	Crude death rate	17.0

The economy

GDP	UAH1,455bn	GDP per head	$3,900
GDP	$177bn	GDP per head in purchasing	
Av. ann. growth in real		power parity (USA=100)	16.6
GDP 2008–13	-2.1%	Economic freedom index	46.9

Origins of GDP		**Components of GDP**	
	% of total		% of total
Agriculture	10	Private consumption	73
Industry, of which:	27	Public consumption	19
manufacturing	14	Investment	16
Services	63	Exports	47
		Imports	-55

Structure of employment

	% of total		% of labour force
Agriculture	17.2	Unemployed 2013	7.9
Industry	20.7	Av. ann. rate 2000–13	8.3
Services	62.1		

Energy

	m TOE		
Total output	81.8	Net energy imports as %	
Total consumption	126.2	of energy use	32
Consumption per person			
kg oil equivalent	2,767		

Inflation and finance

Consumer price		av. ann. increase 2009–14	
inflation 2014	12.1%	Narrow money (M1)	13.2%
Av. ann. inflation 2009–14	5.8%	Broad money	14.4%
Money market rate, Dec. 2014	24.55%		

Exchange rates

	end 2014		December 2014
UAH per $	15.77	Effective rates	2010 = 100
UAH per SDR	22.85	– nominal	64.20
UAH per €	19.15	– real	72.30

Trade

Principal exports[a]		Principal imports[a]	
	$bn fob		*$bn cif*
Non-precious metals	22.1	Fuels	30.0
Food	12.8	Machinery & equipment	20.0
Machinery & equipment	11.9	Chemicals	8.0
Fuels	10.3	Food	6.3
Total incl. others	**68.5**	**Total incl. others**	**82.6**

Main export destinations		Main origins of imports	
	% of total		*% of total*
Russia	23.8	Russia	27.3
Turkey	6.0	China	9.3
Egypt	4.3	Germany	8.0
China	4.3	Belarus	4.2
EU28	26.5	EU28	35.1

Balance of payments, reserves and debt, $bn

Visible exports fob	59.1	Change in reserves	-4.1
Visible imports fob	-81.2	Level of reserves	
Trade balance	-22.1	end Dec.	20.4
Invisibles inflows	30.4	No. months of import cover	2.3
Invisibles outflows	-26.9	Official gold holdings, m oz	1.4
Net transfers	2.1	Foreign debt	147.7
Current account balance	-16.5	– as % of GDP	81.5
– as % of GDP	-9.3	– as % of total exports	143.5
Capital balance	19.2	Debt service ratio	38.1
Overall balance	2.0		

Health and education

Health spending, % of GDP	7.8	Education spending, % of GDP	6.7
Doctors per 1,000 pop.	3.5	Enrolment, %: primary	105
Hospital beds per 1,000 pop.	9.0	secondary	99
Improved-water source access,		tertiary	79
% of pop.	98		

Society

No. of households, m	17.8	Cost of living, Dec. 2014	
Av. no. per household	2.6	New York = 100	54
Marriages per 1,000 pop.	6.1	Cars per 1,000 pop.	162
Divorces per 1,000 pop.	1.1	Colour TV households, % with:	
Religion, % of pop.		cable	23.2
Christian	83.8	satellite	15.5
Non-religious	14.7	Telephone lines per 100 pop.	26.2
Muslim	1.2	Mobile telephone subscribers	
Jewish	0.1	per 100 pop.	138.1
Other	0.1	Broadband subs per 100 pop.	8.8
Hindu	<0.1	Internet users, % of pop.	41.8

a 2011

UNITED ARAB EMIRATES

Area	83,600 sq km	Capital	Abu Dhabi
Arable as % of total land	0.6	Currency	Dirham (AED)

People

Population	9.3m	Life expectancy: men	76.9 yrs
Pop. per sq km	111.2	women	78.9 yrs
Average annual growth		Adult literacy	...
in pop. 2015-20	2.0%	Fertility rate (per woman)	1.8
Pop. under 15	15.3%	Urban population	85.5%
Pop. over 60	1.0%		per 1,000 pop.
No. of men per 100 women	240.2	Crude birth rate	15
Human Development Index	82.7	Crude death rate	1.1

The economy

GDP	AED1,478bn	GDP per head	$43,050
GDP	$402bn	GDP per head in purchasing	
Av. ann. growth in real		power parity (USA=100)	112.8
GDP 2008–13	2.2%	Economic freedom index	72.4

Origins of GDP		**Components of GDP**	
	% of total		% of total
Agriculture	1	Private consumption	50
Industry, of which:	59	Public consumption	7
manufacturing	9	Investment	23
Services	40	Exports	98
		Imports	-78

Structure of employment

	% of total		% of labour force
Agriculture	...	Unemployed 2013	3.8
Industry	...	Av. ann. rate 2000–13	3.4
Services	...		

Energy

	m TOE		
Total output	213.6	Net energy imports as %	
Total consumption	95.6	of energy use	-188
Consumption per person			
kg oil equivalent	10,383		

Inflation and finance

		av. ann. increase 2009–14	
Consumer price			
inflation 2014	2.3%	Narrow money (M1)	15.1%
Av. ann. inflation 2009–14	1.2%	Broad money	9.3%
Interbank rate, Q4 2014	...		

Exchange rates

	end 2014		December 2014
AED per $	3.67	Effective rates	2010 = 100
AED per SDR	5.32	– nominal	116.20
AED per €	4.46	– real	...

Trade

Principal exports		**Principal imports**	
	$bn fob		*$bn cif*
Re-exports	147.7	Precious stones & metals	62.5
Crude oil	98.4	Machinery & electrical equip.	36.9
Gas	14.7	Vehicles & other transport	
		equipment	27.8
		Base metals & related products	17.9
Total incl. others	**378.6**	Total incl. others	**245.0**

Main export destinations		**Main origins of imports**	
	% of total		*% of total*
Japan	14.5	China	14.3
Iran	11.3	India	13.6
India	10.4	United States	10.5
South Korea	6.2	United Kingdom	5.0

Balance of payments, reserves and debt, $bn

Visible exports fob	378.9	Change in reserves	21.2
Visible imports fob	-241.7	Level of reserves	
Trade balance	137.2	end Dec.	68.2
Invisibles inflows	25.4	No. months of import cover	2.6
Invisibles outflows	-79.0	Official gold holdings, m oz	0.0
Net transfers	-18.9	Foreign debt	168.6
Current account balance	64.7	– as % of GDP	42.0
– as % of GDP	16.1	– as % of total exports	40.4
Capital balance	-44.6	Debt service ratio	5.2
Overall balance	21.1		

Health and education

Health spending, % of GDP	3.2	Education spending, % of GDP	...
Doctors per 1,000 pop.	2.5	Enrolment, %: primary	108
Hospital beds per 1,000 pop.	1.1	secondary	...
Improved-water source access,		tertiary	...
% of pop.	99.6		

Society

No. of households, m	1.7	Cost of living, Dec. 2014	
Av. no. per household	5.0	New York = 100	73
Marriages per 1,000 pop.	...	Cars per 1,000 pop.	226
Divorces per 1,000 pop.	...	Colour TV households, % with:	
Religion, % of pop.		cable	1.0
Muslim	76.9	satellite	98.4
Christian	12.6	Telephone lines per 100 pop.	22.3
Hindu	6.6	Mobile telephone subscribers	
Other	2.8	per 100 pop.	171.9
Non-religious	1.1	Broadband subs per 100 pop.	11.1
Jewish	<0.1	Internet users, % of pop.	88.0

UNITED KINGDOM

Area	242,534 sq km	Capital	London
Arable as % of total land	25.7	Currency	Pound (£)

People

Population	63.1m	Life expectancy: men	79.4 yrs
Pop. per sq km	260.2	women	83.1 yrs
Average annual growth		Adult literacy	...
in pop. 2015-20	0.5%	Fertility rate (per woman)	1.9
Pop. under 15	17.6%	Urban population	82.6%
Pop. over 60	23.2%		per 1,000 pop.
No. of men per 100 women	96.8	Crude birth rate	12
Human Development Index	89.2	Crude death rate	9.3

The economy

GDP	£1,713bn	GDP per head	$41,780
GDP	$2,679bn	GDP per head in purchasing	
Av. ann. growth in real		power parity (USA=100)	72.1
GDP 2008-13	0.3%	Economic freedom index	75.8

Origins of GDP		Components of GDP	
	% of total		% of total
Agriculture	1	Private consumption	65
Industry, of which:	20	Public consumption	20
manufacturing	10	Investment	17
Services	79	Exports	30
		Imports	-32

Structure of employment

	% of total		% of labour force
Agriculture	1.2	Unemployed 2013	7.5
Industry	18.9	Av. ann. rate 2000-13	6.1
Services	78.9		

Energy

	m TOE		
Total output	122.5	Net energy imports as %	
Total consumption	215.7	of energy use	39
Consumption per person			
kg oil equivalent	3,386		

Inflation and finance

		av. ann. increase 2009-14	
Consumer price			
inflation 2014	1.5%	Narrow money (M1)	...
Av. ann. inflation 2009-14	2.9%	Broad money	...
Money market rate, Dec. 2014	0.40%	H'hold saving rate a, 2014	3.9%

Exchange rates

	end 2014		December 2014
£ per $	1.56	Effective rates	2010 = 100
£ per SDR	1.08	– nominal	108.20
£ per €	1.89	– real	115.40

Trade

Principal exports		Principal imports	
	$bn fob		*$bn cif*
Machinery & transport equip.	166.9	Machinery & transport equip.	218.9
Chemicals & related products	76.1	Mineral fuels & lubricants	86.7
Mineral fuels & lubricants	61.7	Chemicals & related products	75.1
Food, drink & tobacco	28.9	Food, drink & tobacco	60.4
Total incl. others	**479.6**	**Total incl. others**	**655.6**

Main export destinations		Main origins of imports	
	% of total		*% of total*
Germany	9.3	Germany	13.2
United States	9.1	China	8.1
Netherlands	7.8	Netherlands	8.1
France	6.6	France	5.7
EU28	43.5	EU28	52.2

Balance of payments, reserves and aid, $bn

Visible exports fob	479.7	Overall balance	7.0
Visible imports fob	-655.9	Change in reserves	-0.8
Trade balance	-176.1	Level of reserves	
Invisibles inflows	578.8	end Dec.	104.4
Invisibles outflows	-480.4	No. months of import cover	1.1
Net transfers	-42.5	Official gold holdings, m oz	10.0
Current account balance	-120.2	Aid given	17.9
– as % of GDP	-4.5	– as % of GDP	0.7
Capital balance	111.7		

Health and education

Health spending, % of GDP	9.1	Education spending, % of GDP	6.0
Doctors per 1,000 pop.	2.8	Enrolment, %: primary	109
Hospital beds per 1,000 pop.	2.9	secondary	95
Improved-water source access,		tertiary	62
% of pop.	100		

Society

No. of households, m	26.8	Cost of living, Dec. 2014	
Av. no. per household	2.4	New York = 100	109
Marriages per 1,000 pop.	4.5	Cars per 1,000 pop.	500
Divorces per 1,000 pop.	2.1	Colour TV households, % with:	
Religion, % of pop.		cable	14.4
Christian	71.1	satellite	41.7
Non-religious	21.3	Telephone lines per 100 pop.	52.9
Muslim	4.4	Mobile telephone subscribers	
Other	1.4	per 100 pop.	124.6
Hindu	1.3	Broadband subs per 100 pop.	35.8
Jewish	0.5	Internet users, % of pop.	89.8

a Gross.

UNITED STATES

Area	9,372,610 sq km	Capital	Washington DC
Arable as % of total land	17.0	Currency	US dollar ($)

People

Population	320.1m	Life expectancy: men	77.3 yrs
Pop. per sq km	34.2	women	81.9 yrs
Average annual growth		Adult literacy	...
in pop. 2015-20	0.8%	Fertility rate (per woman)	1.9
Pop. under 15	19.5%	Urban population	81.6%
Pop. over 60	19.7%		per 1,000 pop.
No. of men per 100 women	96.7	Crude birth rate	13
Human Development Index	91.4	Crude death rate	8.4

The economy

GDP	$16,768bn	GDP per head	$53,040
Av. ann. growth in real		GDP per head in purchasing	
GDP 2008-13	1.2%	power parity (USA=100)	100
		Economic freedom index	76.2

Origins of GDP		**Components of GDP**	
	% of total		% of total
Agriculture	1	Private consumption	68
Industry, of which:	21	Public consumption	15
manufacturing	13	Investment	20
Services	78	Exports	13
		Imports	-17

Structure of employment

	% of total		% of labour force
Agriculture	1.6	Unemployed 2013	7.4
Industry	16.7	Av. ann. rate 2000-13	6.5
Services	81.2		

Energy

	m TOE		
Total output	1,980.3	Net energy imports as %	
Total consumption	2,376.4	of energy use	15
Consumption per person			
kg oil equivalent	7,571		

Inflation and finance

		av. ann. increase 2009-14	
Consumer price inflation 2014	1.6%	Narrow money (M1)	11.4%
Av. ann. inflation 2009-14	2.0%	Broad money	4.8%
Fed funds rate, Dec. 2014	0.12%	H'hold saving rate, 2014	4.1%

Exchange rates

	end 2014		December 2014
$ per SDR	1.45	Effective rates	2010 = 100
$ per €	1.21	– nominal	108.58
		– real	106.72

Trade

Principal exports		Principal imports	
	$bn fob		*$bn fob*
Capital goods, excl. vehicles	534.2	Industrial supplies	681.6
Industrial supplies	509.3	Capital goods, excl. vehicles	591.0
Consumer goods, excl. vehicles	189.1	Consumer goods, excl. vehicles	557.7
Vehicles & products	152.6	Vehicles & products	327.6
Total incl. others	**1,579.6**	**Total incl. others**	**2,344.8**

Main export destinations		Main origins of imports	
	% of total		*% of total*
Canada	19.0	China	20.3
Mexico	14.3	Canada	14.9
China	7.7	Mexico	12.5
Japan	4.1	Japan	6.3
EU28	16.7	EU28	17.0

Balance of payments, reserves and aid, $bn

Visible exports fob	1,593	Overall balance	-3
Visible imports fob	-2,295	Change in reserves	-126
Trade balance	-702	Level of reserves	
Invisibles inflows	1,468	end Dec.	449
Invisibles outflows	-1,043	No. months of import cover	1.6
Net transfers	-124	Official gold holdings, m oz	262
Current account balance	-400	Aid given	30.9
– as % of GDP	-2.4	– as % of GDP	0.2
Capital balance	367		

Health and education

Health spending, % of GDP	17.1	Education spending, % of GDP	5.2
Doctors per 1,000 pop.	2.5	Enrolment, %: primary	98
Hospital beds per 1,000 pop.	2.9	secondary	94
Improved-water source access,		tertiary	94
% of pop.	99.2		

Society

No. of households, m	122.5	Cost of living, Dec. 2014	
Av. no. per household	2.6	New York = 100	100
Marriages per 1,000 pop.	6.8	Cars per 1,000 pop.	394
Divorces per 1,000 pop.	2.8	Colour TV households, % with:	
Religion, % of pop.		cable	56.6
Christian	78.3	satellite	29.5
Non-religious	16.4	Telephone lines per 100 pop.	42.2
Other	2.0	Mobile telephone subscribers	
Jewish	1.8	per 100 pop.	95.5
Muslim	0.9	Broadband subs per 100 pop.	29.3
Hindu	0.6	Internet users, % of pop.[b]	84.2

a Including utilities.
b Includes all hosts ending ".com", ".net" and ".org" which exaggerates the numbers.

VENEZUELA

Area	912,050 sq km	Capital	Caracas
Arable as % of total land	3.1	Currency	Bolivar (Bs)

People

Population	30.4m	Life expectancy: men	72.5 yrs
Pop. per sq km	33.3	women	78.4 yrs
Average annual growth		Adult literacy	...
in pop. 2015-20	1.3%	Fertility rate (per woman)	2.4
Pop. under 15	28.5%	Urban population	89.0%
Pop. over 60	9.4%		per 1,000 pop.
No. of men per 100 women	100.7	Crude birth rate	20
Human Development Index	76.4	Crude death rate	5.5

The economy

GDP	Bs2,651bn	GDP per head	$14,410
GDP	$438bn	GDP per head in purchasing	
Av. ann. growth in real		power parity (USA=100)	34.3
GDP 2008-13	1.2%	Economic freedom index	34.3

Origins of GDP

Components of GDP

	% of total		% of total
Agriculture	4	Private consumption	59
Industry, of which:	35	Public consumption	12
manufacturing	...	Investment	27
Services	62	Exports	26
		Imports	-24

Structure of employment

	% of total		% of labour force
Agriculture	7.7	Unemployed 2013	7.5
Industry	21.2	Av. ann. rate 2000-13	107
Services	70.7		

Energy

	m TOE		
Total output	181.4	Net energy imports as %	
Total consumption	84.1	of energy use	-186
Consumption per person			
kg oil equivalent	2,808		

Inflation and finance

Consumer price		av. ann. increase 2009-14	
inflation 2014	62.2%	Narrow money (M1)	57.4%
Av. ann. inflation 2009-14	34.9%	Broad money	51.7%
Money market rate, Oct. 2014	0.53%		

Exchange rates

	end 2014		December 2014
Bs per $	6.28	Effective rates	2010 = 100
Bs per SDR	9.11	– nominal	45.3
Bs per €	7.62	– real	170.1

Trade

Principal exports		Principal imports	
	$bn fob		$bn cif
Oil	85.6	Intermediate goods	27.9
Non-oil	3.4	Capital goods	12.0
		Consumer goods	9.6
Total incl. others	**89.0**	Total incl. others	**49.4**

Main export destinations		Main origins of imports	
	% of total		% of total
United States	33.2	United States	29.4
India	15.2	China	13.5
China	13.4	Brazil	10.8
Netherlands Antilles	8.0	Colombia	4.7

Balance of payments, reserves and debt, $bn

Visible exports fob	89.0	Change in reserves	-9.2
Visible imports fob	-53.0	Level of reserves	
Trade balance	36.0	end Dec.	20.3
Invisibles inflows	4.2	No. months of import cover	2.8
Invisibles outflows	-33.6	Official gold holdings, m oz	11.8
Net transfers	-1.2	Foreign debt	118.8
Current account balance	5.3	– as % of GDP	33.4
– as % of GDP	1.2	– as % of total exports	127.4
Capital balance	-6.3	Debt service ratio	21.2
Overall balance	-4.3		

Health and education

Health spending, % of GDP	3.4	Education spending, % of GDP	6.9
Doctors per 1,000 pop.	-	Enrolment, %: primary	102
Hospital beds per 1,000 pop.	0.9	secondary	93
Improved-water source access,		tertiary	...
% of pop.	...		

Society

No. of households, m	7.5	Cost of living, Dec. 2014	
Av. no. per household	4.0	New York = 100	45
Marriages per 1,000 pop.	3.5	Cars per 1,000 pop.	134
Divorces per 1,000 pop.	...	Colour TV households, % with:	
Religion, % of pop.		cable	29.3
Christian	89.3	satellite	5.7
Non-religious	10.0	Telephone lines per 100 pop.	25.6
Muslim	0.3	Mobile telephone subscribers	
Other	0.3	per 100 pop.	101.6
Hindu	<0.1	Broadband subs per 100 pop.	7.3
Jewish	<0.1	Internet users, % of pop.	54.9

VIETNAM

Area	331,114 sq km	Capital	Hanoi
Arable as % of total land	20.6	Currency	Dong (D)

People

Population	91.7m	Life expectancy: men	72.2 yrs
Pop. per sq km	276.9	women	80.9 yrs
Average annual growth		Adult literacy	...
in pop. 2015-20	0.8%	Fertility rate (per woman)	2.1
Pop. under 15	22.7%	Urban population	33.6%
Pop. over 60	9.6%		per 1,000 pop.
No. of men per 100 women	97.5	Crude birth rate	17
Human Development Index	63.8	Crude death rate	5.9

The economy

GDP	D3,584trn	GDP per head	$1,910
GDP	$171bn	GDP per head in purchasing	
Av. ann. growth in real		power parity (USA=100)	10.0
GDP 2008-13	5.7%	Economic freedom index	51.7

Origins of GDP		Components of GDP	
	% of total		% of total
Agriculture	18	Private consumption	63
Industry, of which:	38	Public consumption	6
manufacturing	17	Investment	27
Services	43	Exports	84
		Imports	-80

Structure of employment

	% of total		% of labour force
Agriculture	47.4	Unemployed 2013	2.0
Industry	21.1	Av. ann. rate 2000-13	2.3
Services	31.5		

Energy

	m TOE		
Total output	64.4	Net energy imports as %	
Total consumption	58.2	of energy use	-9
Consumption per person			
kg oil equivalent	655		

Inflation and finance

Consumer price		av. ann. increase 2009-14	
inflation 2014	4.1%	Narrow money (M1)	16.2%
Av. ann. inflation 2009-14	9.4%	Broad money	21.3%
Treasury bill rate, Aug. 2014	4.60%		

Exchange rates

	end 2014		December 2014
D per $	21,246.00	Effective rates	2010 = 100
D per SDR	30,781.00	– nominal	...
D per €	25,794.77	– real	...

Trade

Principal exports	$bn fob	Principal imports	$bn cif
Textiles & garments	18.2	Machinery & equipment	18.9
Footwear	8.5	Textiles	8.4
Crude oil	7.3	Petroleum products	6.9
Fisheries products	6.9	Steel	6.7
Total incl. others	**132.7**	Total incl. others	**131.9**

Main export destinations	% of total	Main origins of imports	% of total
United States	18.8	China	28.6
Japan	10.8	South Korea	16.0
China	10.5	Japan	9.0
South Korea	5.2	Thailand	4.9
Germany	3.7	Singapore	4.4

Balance of payments, reserves and debt, $bn

Visible exports fob	132.1	Change in reserves	0.3
Visible imports fob	-123.4	Level of reserves	
Trade balance	8.7	end Dec.	25.9
Invisibles inflows	10.8	No. months of import cover	2.2
Invisibles outflows	-19.5	Official gold holdings, m oz	...
Net transfers	9.5	Foreign debt	65.5
Current account balance	9.5	– as % of GDP	38.4
– as % of GDP	5.5	– as % of total exports	43.2
Capital balance	-8.9	Debt service ratio	3.3
Overall balance	0.6		

Health and education

Health spending, % of GDP	6.0	Education spending, % of GDP	6.3
Doctors per 1,000 pop.	1.2	Enrolment, %: primary	105
Hospital beds per 1,000 pop.	2	secondary	...
Improved-water source access,		tertiary	25
% of pop.	95		

Society

No. of households, m	25.3	Cost of living, Dec. 2014	
Av. no. per household	3.6	New York = 100	76
Marriages per 1,000 pop.	...	Cars per 1,000 pop.	21
Divorces per 1,000 pop.	...	Colour TV households, % with:	
Religion, % of pop.		cable	17.8
Other	45.6	satellite	19.5
Non-religious	29.6	Telephone lines per 100 pop.	10.1
Buddhist	16.4	Mobile telephone subscribers	
Christian	8.2	per 100 pop.	130.9
Muslim	0.2	Broadband subs per 100 pop.	5.6
Jewish	<0.1	Internet users, % of pop.	43.9

ZIMBABWE

Area	390,759 sq km	Capital	Harare
Arable as % of total land	10.3	Currency	Zimbabwe dollar (Z$)

People

Population	14.1m	Life expectancy: men	61.3 yrs
Pop. per sq km	36.1	women	63.6 yrs
Average annual growth		Adult literacy	83.6
in pop. 2015-20	2.3%	Fertility rate (per woman)	3.8
Pop. under 15	39.5%	Urban population	32.4%
Pop. over 60	5.7%		per 1,000 pop.
No. of men per 100 women	97.1	Crude birth rate	33
Human Development Index	49.2	Crude death rate	8.1

The economy

GDP	$13.5bn	GDP per head	$950
Av. ann. growth in real		GDP per head in purchasing	
GDP 2008-13	9.1%	power parity (USA=100)	3.5
		Economic freedom index	37.6

Origins of GDP		**Components of GDP**	
	% of total		% of total
Agriculture	12	Private consumption	94
Industry, of which:	31	Public consumption	20
manufacturing	13	Investment	13
Services	57	Exports	29
		Imports	-57

Structure of employment

	% of total		% of labour force
Agriculture	...	Unemployed 2013	5.4
Industry	...	Av. ann. rate 2000-13	5.1
Services	...		

Energy

	m TOE		
Total output	3.3	Net energy imports as %	
Total consumption	4.3	of energy use	8
Consumption per person			
kg oil equivalent	316		

Inflation and finance

			av. ann. increase 2009-14
Consumer price			
inflation 2014	-0.2%	Narrow money (M1)	...
Av. ann. inflation 2009-14	2.3%	Broad money	...
Treasury bill rate, Aug. 2014	...		

Exchange rates

	end 2014		December 2014
Z$ per $	...	Effective rates	2010 = 100
Z$ per SDR	...	– nominal	...
Z$ per €	...	– real	...

Trade

Principal exports		**Principal imports**	
	$bn fob		*$bn cif*
Platinum	0.9	Machinery & transportation	
Gold	0.7	equipment	0.5
Tobacco	0.4	Fuels & energy	0.4
Ferro-alloys	0.3	Manufactures	0.3
		Chemicals	0.2
Total incl. others	**3.1**	Total incl. others	**4.8**

Main export destinations		**Main origins of imports**	
	% of total		*% of total*
China	19.9	South Africa	50.9
South Africa	11.2	Zambia	9.3
Congo-Kinshasa	10.2	China	8.5
Botswana	9.1	India	3.6
Zambia	3.4	Botswana	3.2

Balance of payments, reserves and debt, $bn

Visible exports fob	3.1	Change in reserves	-0.1
Visible imports fob	-4.6	Level of reserves	
Trade balance	-1.4	end Dec.	0.5
Invisibles inflows	0.2	No. months of import cover	1.1
Invisibles outflows	-0.6	Official gold holdings, m oz	0.0
Net transfers	1.2	Foreign debt	8.2
Current account balance	0.6	– as % of GDP	20.8
– as % of GDP	4.3	– as % of total exports	225.9
Capital balance	1.7	Debt service ratio	79.8
Overall balance	3.4		

Health and education

Health spending, % of GDP	...	Education spending, % of GDP	...
Doctors per 1,000 pop.	0.1	Enrolment, %: primary	109
Hospital beds per 1,000 pop.	1.7	secondary	47
Improved-water source access,		tertiary	6
% of pop.	79.9		

Society

No. of households, m	3.1	Cost of living, Dec. 2014	
Av. no. per household	4.5	New York = 100	...
Marriages per 1,000 pop.	...	Cars per 1,000 pop.	...
Divorces per 1,000 pop.	...	Colour TV households, % with:	
Religion, % of pop.		cable	...
Christian	87.0	satellite	...
Non-religious	7.9	Telephone lines per 100 pop.	2.2
Other	4.2	Mobile telephone subscribers	
Muslim	0.9	per 100 pop.	96.4
Hindu	<0.1	Broadband subs per 100 pop.	0.7
Jewish	<0.1	Internet users, % of pop.	18.5

EURO AREA[a]

Area	2,578,704 sq km	Capital	–
Arable as % of total land	24.5	Currency	Euro (€)

People

Population	333.9m	Life expectancy: men	79.0 yrs
Pop. per sq km	129.4	women	84.7 yrs
Average annual growth		Adult literacy	98.8
in pop. 2010–15	0.1%	Fertility rate (per woman)	1.5
Pop. under 15	15.2%	Urban population	76.0%
Pop. over 60	25.1%		per 1,000 pop.
No. of men per 100 women	96.0	Crude birth rate	10.0
Human Development Index	88.3	Crude death rate	10.1

The economy

GDP	€9,896bn	GDP per head	$39,120
GDP	$13,194bn	GDP per head in purchasing	
Av. ann. growth in real		power parity (USA=100)	71.3
GDP 2008–13	-0.5%	Economic freedom index	67.3

Origins of GDP

Components of GDP

	% of total		% of total
Agriculture	2	Private consumption	56
Industry, of which:	25	Public consumption	21
manufacturing	16	Investment	19
Services	74	Exports	43
		Imports	-39

Structure of employment

	% of total		% of labour force
Agriculture	3.6	Unemployed 2013	11.9
Industry	25	Av. ann. rate 2000–13	9.2
Services	71.3		

Energy

	m TOE		
Total output	457.3	Net energy imports as %	
Total consumption	1,278.7	of energy use	60
Consumption per person			
kg oil equivalent	3,838		

Inflation and finance

Consumer price		av. ann. increase 2009–14	
inflation 2014	0.4%	Narrow money (M1)	5.6%
Av. ann. inflation 2009–14	1.7%	Broad money	2.0%
Interbank rate, Dec. 2014	0.08%	H'hold saving rate, 2014	7.9%

Exchange rates

	end 2014		December 2014
€ per $	0.82	Effective rates	2010 = 100
€ per SDR	1.19	– nominal	96.01
		– real	96.65

Trade[b]

Principal exports

	$bn fob
Machinery & transport equip.	941.1
Other manufactured goods	508.3
Chemicals & related products	363.0
Mineral fuels & lubricants	162.7
Food, drink & tobacco	138.7
Total incl. others	**2,306.4**

Principal imports

	$bn cif
Mineral fuels & lubricants	664.6
Machinery & transport equip.	577.0
Other manufactured goods	507.2
Chemicals & related products	209.7
Food, drink & tobacco	124.3
Total incl. others	**2,237.7**

Main export destinations

	% of total
United States	16.7
Switzerland	9.7
China	8.5
Russia	6.9
Turkey	4.5
Japan	3.1

Main origins of imports

	% of total
China	16.6
Russia	12.3
United States	11.6
Switzerland	5.6
Norway	5.4
Japan	3.4

Balance of payments, reserves and aid, $bn

Visible exports fob	2,569	Overall balance	-10
Visible imports fob	-2,346	Change in reserves	-161
Trade balance	223	Level of reserves	
Invisibles inflows	1,605	end Dec.	748
Invisibles outflows	-1,363	No. months of import cover	2.4
Net transfers	-160.2	Official gold holdings, m oz	347
Current account balance	305	Aid given	42.7
– as % of GDP	2.3	– as % of GDP	0.4
Capital balance	-317		

Health and education

Health spending, % of GDP	10.6	Education spending, % of GDP	5.5
Doctors per 1,000 pop.	3.9	Enrolment, %: primary	103
Hospital beds per 1,000 pop.	5.6	secondary	108
Improved-water source access,		tertiary	68
% of pop.	99.9		

Society

No. of households, m	146.7	Colour TV households, % with:	
Av. no. per household	2.8	cable	41.0
Marriages per 1,000 pop.	4.0	satellite	25.4
Divorces per 1,000 pop.	1.9	Telephone lines per 100 pop.	27.9
Cost of living, Dec. 2014		Mobile telephone subscribers	
New York = 100	...	per 100 pop.	113.2
Cars per 1,000 pop.	516	Broadband subs per 100 pop.	27.3
		Internet users, % of pop.	390.7

a Data generally refer to the 17 EU members that had adopted the euro as at December 31 2013: Austria, Belgium, Cyprus, Estonia, Finland, France, Germany, Greece, Ireland, Italy, Luxembourg, Malta, Netherlands, Portugal, Slovakia, Slovenia and Spain.

b EU28, excluding intra-trade.

WORLD

Area	148,698,382 sq km	Capital	...
Arable as % of total land	10.8	Currency	...

People

Population	7,162.0m	Life expectancy: men	68.8 yrs
Pop. per sq km	48.2	women	73.3 yrs
Average annual growth		Adult literacy	84.3
in pop. 2015–20	1.0%	Fertility rate (per woman)	2.5
Pop. under 15	26.2%	Urban population	54.0%
Pop. over 60	11.7%		per 1,000 pop.
No. of men per 100 women	101.6	Crude birth rate	25
Human Development Index	70.2	Crude death rate	8.1

The economy

GDP	$75.6trn	GDP per head	$10,610
Av. ann. growth in real		GDP per head in purchasing	
GDP 2008–13	3.3%	power parity (USA=100)	27.2
		Economic freedom index	57.8

Origins of GDP		**Components of GDP**	
	% of total		% of total
Agriculture	3	Private consumption	60
Industry, of which:	27	Public consumption	18
manufacturing	16	Investment	22
Services	70	Exports	30
		Imports	-30

Structure of employment[a]

	% of total		% of labour force
Agriculture	30.5	Unemployed 2013	6.0
Industry	24.2	Av. ann. rate 2000–13	6.2
Services	45.1		

Energy

	m TOE		
Total output	13,431.7	Net energy imports as %	
Total consumption	13,101.9	of energy use	-3
Consumption per person			
kg oil equivalent	1,858		

Inflation and finance

Consumer price		*av. ann. increase 2009–14*	
inflation 2014	3.5%	Narrow money (M1)[a]	8.5
Av. ann. inflation 2009–14	4.1%	Broad money[a]	4.9
LIBOR $ rate, 3-month, Dec. 2014	0.24%		

Trade

World exports

	$bn fob		$bn fob
Manufactures	12,694	Ores & minerals	758
Fuels	2,842	Agricultural raw materials	379
Food	1,705	Total incl. others	**18,947**

Main export destinations		Main origins of imports	
	% of total		% of total
United States	12.5	China	12.1
China	10.4	United States	8.7
Germany	6.3	Germany	7.5
Japan	4.5	Japan	3.9
France	3.6	Netherlands	3.6
United Kingdom	3.3	France	3.1

Balance of payments[b], reserves and aid, $bn

Visible exports fob	18,158	Overall balance	0
Visible imports fob	-17,713	Change in reserves	260
Trade balance	445	Level of reserves	
Invisibles inflows	8,038	end Dec.	13,361
Invisibles outflows	-7,954	No. months of import cover	6.2
Net transfers	-60	Official gold holdings, m oz	1,024
Current account balance	469	Aid given	...
– as % of GDP	0.6	– as % of GDP	...
Capital balance	-253		

Health and education

Health spending, % of GDP	10	Education spending, % of GDP	4.8
Doctors per 1,000 pop.	1.5	Enrolment, %: primary	108
Hospital beds per 1,000 pop.	...	secondary	73
Improved-water source access,		tertiary	32
% of pop.	89.3		

Society

No. of households, m	1,831.5	Cost of living, Dec. 2014	
Av. no. per household	3.7	New York = 100	...
Marriages per 1,000 pop.	...	Cars per 1,000 pop.	126
Divorces per 1,000 pop.	...	Colour TV households, % with:	
Religion, % of pop.		cable	...
Christian	31.5	satellite	...
Muslim	23.2	Telephone lines per 100 pop.	20
Non-religious	16.3	Mobile telephone subscribers	
Hindu	15.0	per 100 pop.	101
Other	13.8	Broadband subs per 100 pop.	19.8
Jewish	0.2	Internet users, % of pop.	132.9

a OECD countries.   b 2012

Glossary

Balance of payments The record of a country's transactions with the rest of the world. The **current account** of the balance of payments consists of: visible trade (goods); "invisible" trade (services and income); private transfer payments (eg, remittances from those working abroad); official transfers (eg, payments to international organisations, famine relief). Visible imports and exports are normally compiled on rather different definitions to those used in the trade statistics (shown in principal imports and exports) and therefore the statistics do not match. The **capital account** consists of long- and short-term transactions relating to a country's assets and liabilities (eg, loans and borrowings). The **current and capital accounts**, plus an errors and omissions item, make up the **overall balance. Changes in reserves** include gold at market prices and are shown without the practice often followed in balance of payments presentations of reversing the sign.

Big Mac index A light-hearted way of looking at exchange rates. If the dollar price of a burger at McDonald's in any country is higher than the price in the United States, converting at market exchange rates, then that country's currency could be thought to be over-valued against the dollar and vice versa.

Body-mass index A measure for assessing obesity – weight in kilograms divided by height in metres squared. An index of 30 or more is regarded as an indicator of obesity; 25 to 29.9 as over-weight. Guidelines vary for men and for women and may be adjusted for age.

CFA Communauté Financière Africaine. Its members, most of the francophone African nations, share a common currency, the CFA franc, pegged to the euro.

Cif/fob Measures of the value of merchandise trade. Imports include the cost of "carriage, insurance and freight" (cif) from the exporting country to the importing. The value of exports does not include these elements and is recorded "free on board" (fob). Balance of payments statistics are generally adjusted so that both exports and imports are shown fob; the cif elements are included in invisibles.

CIS is the Commonwealth of Independent States, including Georgia, Turkmenistan and Ukraine.

Crude birth rate The number of live births in a year per 1,000 population. The crude rate will automatically be relatively high if a large proportion of the population is of childbearing age.

Crude death rate The number of deaths in a year per 1,000 population. Also affected by the population's age structure.

Debt, foreign Financial obligations owed by a country to the rest of the world and repayable in foreign currency. The **debt service ratio** is debt service (principal repayments plus interest payments) expressed as a percentage of the country's earnings from exports of goods and services.

Debt, household All liabilities that require payment of interest or principal in the future.

Economic Freedom Index The ranking includes data on labour and business freedom as well as trade policy, taxation, monetary policy, the banking system, foreign-investment rules, property rights, government spending, regulation policy, the level of corruption and the extent of wage and price controls.

Effective exchange rate The nominal index measures a currency's depreciation (figures below 100) or appreciation (figures over 100) from a base date against a trade-weighted basket of the currencies of the country's main trading partners. The real effective exchange rate reflects adjustments for relative movements in prices or costs.

EU European Union. Members are: Austria, Belgium, Bulgaria, Croatia, Cyprus, Czech Republic, Denmark, Estonia, Finland, France, Germany, Greece, Hungary, Ireland, Italy, Latvia,

Lithuania, Luxembourg, Malta, Netherlands, Poland, Portugal, Romania, Slovakia, Slovenia, Spain, Sweden and the United Kingdom.

Euro area The 19 euro area members of the EU are Austria, Belgium, Cyprus, Estonia, Finland, France, Germany, Greece, Ireland, Italy, Latvia, Luxembourg, Malta, Netherlands, Portugal, Slovakia, Slovenia and Spain. Lithuania joined on January 1 2015. Their common currency is the euro.

Fertility rate The average number of children born to a woman who completes her childbearing years.

G7 Group of seven countries: United States, Japan, Germany, United Kingdom, France, Italy and Canada.

GDP Gross domestic product. The sum of all output produced by economic activity within a country. GNP (gross national product) and GNI (gross national income) include net income from abroad, eg, rent, profits.

Household saving rate Household savings as % of disposable household income.

Import cover The number of months of imports covered by reserves, ie, reserves ÷ $\frac{1}{12}$ annual imports (visibles and invisibles).

Inflation The annual rate at which prices are increasing. The most common measure and the one shown here is the increase in the consumer price index.

Life expectancy The average length of time a baby born today can expect to live.

Literacy is defined by UNESCO as the ability to read and write a simple sentence, but definitions can vary from country to country.

Median age Divides the age distribution into two halves. Half of the population is above and half below the median age.

Money supply A measure of the "money" available to buy goods and services.

Various definitions exist. The measures shown here are based on definitions used by the IMF and may differ from measures used nationally. Narrow money (M1) consists of cash in circulation and demand deposits (bank deposits that can be withdrawn on demand). "Quasi-money" (time, savings and foreign currency deposits) is added to this to create broad money.

OECD Organisation for Economic Co-operation and Development. The "rich countries" club was established in 1961 to promote economic growth and the expansion of world trade. It is based in Paris and now has 34 members.

Official reserves The stock of gold and foreign currency held by a country to finance any calls that may be made for the settlement of foreign debt.

Opec Organisation of Petroleum Exporting Countries. Set up in 1960 and based in Vienna, Opec is mainly concerned with oil pricing and production issues. Members are: Algeria, Angola, Ecuador, Iran, Iraq, Kuwait, Libya, Nigeria, Qatar, Saudi Arabia, United Arab Emirates and Venezuela.

PPP Purchasing power parity. PPP statistics adjust for cost of living differences by replacing normal exchange rates with rates designed to equalise the prices of a standard "basket"of goods and services. These are used to obtain PPP estimates of GDP per head. PPP estimates are shown on an index, taking the United States as 100.

Real terms Figures adjusted to exclude the effect of inflation.

SDR Special drawing right. The reserve currency, introduced by the IMF in 1970, was intended to replace gold and national currencies in settling international transactions. The IMF uses SDRs for book-keeping purposes and issues them to member countries. Their value is based on a basket of the US dollar (with a weight of 41.9%), the euro (37.4%), the Japanese yen (9.4%) and the pound sterling (11.3%).

List of countries

	Population	GDP	GDP per head	Area	Median age
	m, 2013	$bn, 2013	$PPP, 2013	'000 sq km	yrs, 2013
Afghanistan	30.6	20.3	1,950	652	16.5
Albania	3.2	12.9	9,930	29	32.9
Algeria	39.2	210.2	13,320	2,382	26.9
Andorra	0.085	3.3	37,200[ab]	5	41.8
Angola	21.5	124.2	7,740	1,247	16.3
Argentina	41.4	609.9	22,400	2,780	31.1
Armenia	3.0	10.4	7,780	30	32.7
Australia	23.3	1,560.4	43,200	7,741	37.2
Austria	8.5	428.3	45,080	84	42.7
Azerbaijan	9.4	73.6	17,140	87	29.7
Bahamas	0.4	8.4	23,260	14	31.8
Bahrain	1.3	32.9	43,850	0.8	30.1
Bangladesh	156.6	150.0	2,950	144	25.1
Barbados	0.3	4.2[a]	15,570[a]	0.4	36.9
Belarus	9.4	71.7	17,620	208	39.3
Belgium	11.1	524.8	41,570	31	41.6
Benin	10.3	8.3	1,790	115	18.4
Bermuda	0.069	5.5[a]	53,060[a]	0.1	42.6
Bolivia	10.7	30.6	6,130	1,099	22.4
Bosnia & Herz.	3.8	17.9	9,540	51	39.5
Botswana	2.0	14.8	15,750	582	22.5
Brazil	200.4	2,245.7	15,040	8,515	30.3
Brunei	0.4	16.1	71,780	6	30.5
Bulgaria	7.2	54.5	15,730	111	43.0
Burkina Faso	16.9	12.9	1,680	274	17.1
Burundi	10.2	2.7	770	28	17.6
Cambodia	15.1	15.2	3,040	181	24.4
Cameroon	22.3	29.6	2,830	475	18.3
Canada	35.2	1,826.8	42,750	9,985	40.1
Central African Rep.	4.6	1.5	600	623	19.7
Chad	12.8	13.5	2,090	1,284	15.8
Channel Islands	0.162	9.2[b]	56,610[b]	0.2	42.0
Chile	17.6	277.2	21,940	756	33.1
China	1,385.6	9,240.3	11,910	9,600	35.4
Colombia	48.3	378.4	12,420	1,142	27.7
Congo-Brazzaville	4.4	14.1	5,870	342	18.8
Congo-Kinshasa	67.5	32.7	810	2,345	17.4
Costa Rica	4.9	49.6	13,880	51	29.7
Croatia	4.3	57.9	21,350	322	42.6
Cuba	11.3	68.2[a]	18,800[a]	57	40.1
Cyprus	1.1	21.9	28,220	110	35.2
Czech Republic	10.7	208.8	29,020	9	40.3
Denmark	5.6	335.9	43,780	79	41.1
Dominican Rep.	10.4	61.2	12,190	43	25.8
Ecuador	15.7	94.5	10,890	49	26.1
Egypt	82.1	272.0	11,090	256	25.2
El Salvador	6.3	24.3	7,760	1,001	24.1

	Population	GDP	GDP per head	Area	Median age
	m, 2013	$bn, 2013	$PPP, 2013	'000 sq km	yrs, 2013
Equatorial Guinea	0.8	15.6	33,770	21	20.6
Eritrea	6.3	3.4	1,200	28	18.4
Estonia	1.3	24.9	25,820	118	40.9
Ethiopia	94.1	47.5	1,380	45	18.2
Fiji	0.9	3.9	7,750	1,104	27.1
Finland	5.4	267.3	39,740	18	42.3
France	64.3	2,806.4[c]	37,530	338	40.6
French Guiana	0.2	5.0[a]	18,390[a]	549	24.9
French Polynesia	0.3	6.4	26,100[ab]	90	30.9
Gabon	1.7	19.3	19,260	4	20.7
Gambia, The	1.8	0.9	1,660	268	17.0
Georgia	4.3	16.1	7,160	11	37.6
Germany	82.7	3,730.3	43,880	70	45.5
Ghana	25.9	48.1	3,990	357	20.6
Greece	11.1	242.2	25,670	239	42.8
Guadeloupe	0.5	12.2[a]	26,750[a]	132	37.7
Guam	0.2	4.6[ab]	28,700[a]	2	29.8
Guatemala	15.5	53.8	7,300	0.5	19.4
Guinea	11.7	6.1	1,250	109	18.6
Guinea-Bissau	1.7	1.0	1,410	246	19.1
Haiti	10.3	8.5	1,700	36	22.2
Honduras	8.1	18.6	4,590	28	21.9
Hong Kong	7.2	274.0	53,220	112	42.4
Hungary	10.0	133.4	23,330	1	40.6
Iceland	0.3	15.3	41,860	93	35.5
India	1,252.1	1,875.1	5,420	103	26.4
Indonesia	249.9	868.4	9,560	3,287	27.8
Iran	77.4	368.9	15,590	1,905	28.5
Iraq	33.8	229.3	14,950	1,745	19.7
Ireland	4.6	232.1	45,680	435	35.3
Israel	7.7	290.6	32,490	70	30.1
Italy	61.0	2,149.5	35,280	22	44.3
Ivory Coast	20.3	31.1	3,210	301	19.0
Jamaica	2.8	14.4	8,890	11	27.7
Japan	127.1	4,919.6	36,220	378	45.9
Jordan	7.3	33.7	11,780	89	23.4
Kazakhstan	16.4	231.9	23,210	2,725	29.4
Kenya	44.4	55.2	2,790	580	18.8
Kosovo	1.8	7.1	8,880	11	27.4
Kuwait	3.4	175.8	83,840[a]	18	29.2
Kyrgyzstan	5.5	7.2	3,210	200	24.6
Laos	6.8	11.2	4,820	237	21.4
Latvia	2.1	31.0	22,570	64	41.5
Lebanon	4.8	44.4	17,170	10	29.8
Lesotho	2.1	2.3	2,580	30	20.7
Liberia	4.3	2.0	880	111	18.5
Libya	6.2	74.2	21,050	1,760	26.6

	Population	GDP	GDP per head	Area '000 sq	Median age
	m, 2013	$bn, 2013	$PPP, 2013	km	yrs, 2013
Liechtenstein	0.037	5.7	89,400[ab]	0.2	42.1
Lithuania	3.0	45.9	25,450	65	39.3
Luxembourg	0.5	60.1	91,050	3	39.0
Macau	0.6	51.8	142,600	0.03	37.4
Macedonia	2.1	10.2	11,610	26	37.1
Madagascar	22.9	10.6	1,410	587	18.4
Malawi	16.4	3.7	780	118	17.2
Malaysia	29.7	313.2	23,340	331	27.4
Mali	15.3	10.9	1,640	1,240	16.3
Malta	0.4	9.6	29,130	0.3	40.9
Martinique	0.4	11.8[a]	26,750[a]	1	41.7
Mauritania	3.9	4.2	3,040	1,031	19.8
Mauritius	1.2	11.9	17,710	2	34.6
Mexico	122.3	1,260.9	16,370	1,964	27.0
Moldova	3.5	8.0	4,670	34	35.8
Monaco	0.031	6.1[a]	78,700	0.002	50.5
Mongolia	2.8	11.5	9,430	1,564	26.8
Montenegro	0.6	4.4	14,130	14	37.1
Morocco	33.0	103.8	7,200	447	27.0
Mozambique	25.8	15.6	1,110	799	17.3
Myanmar	53.3	63.0	4,350	677	29.0
Namibia	2.3	13.1	9,580	824	21.2
Nepal	27.8	19.3	2,240	147	22.4
Netherlands	16.8	853.5	46,160	42	41.8
New Caledonia	0.3	9.7	38,800[ab]	19	32.8
New Zealand	4.5	185.8	34,730	268	37.0
Nicaragua	6.1	11.3	4,640	130	23.1
Niger	17.8	7.4	920	1,267	15.0
Nigeria	173.6	521.8	5,600	924	17.8
North Korea	24.9	15.5	1,800[b]	121	33.6
Norway	5.0	512.6	64,410	324	39.0
Oman	3.6	79.7	45,330[a]	310	26.3
Pakistan	182.1	232.3	4,600	796	22.5
Panama	3.9	42.7	19,420	75	27.9
Papua New Guinea	7.3	15.4	2,640	463	20.9
Paraguay	6.8	29.0	8,090	407	23.9
Peru	30.4	202.4	11,770	1,285	26.5
Philippines	98.4	272.1	6,540	300	23.0
Poland	38.2	525.9	23,690	313	38.8
Portugal	10.6	227.3	27,800	92	42.2
Puerto Rico	3.7	103.1	34,750	9	35.7
Qatar	2.2	203.2	136,730	12	31.7
Réunion	0.9	22.4[a]	23,960a	3	30.7
Romania	21.7	189.6	18,970	238	39.4
Russia	142.8	2,096.8	25,250	17,098	38.3
Rwanda	11.8	7.5	1,470	26	18.2
Saudi Arabia	28.8	748.5	53,640	2,150	27.5

	Population	GDP	GDP per head	Area	Median age
	m, 2013	$bn, 2013	$PPP, 2013	'000 sq km	yrs, 2013
Senegal	14.1	14.8	2,240	197	18.1
Serbia	7.2	45.5	13,020	88	38.7
Sierra Leone	6.1	4.1	1,540	72	19.1
Singapore	5.4	297.9	78,760	0.7	38.1
Slovakia	5.5	97.7	26,500	49	38.2
Slovenia	2.1	48.0	28,860	20	42.4
Somalia	10.5	1.4	600[ab]	638	16.3
South Africa	52.8	366.1	12,870	1,219	26.0
South Korea	49.3	1,304.6	33,060	100	39.4
South Sudan	11.3	11.8	2,030	644	18.6
Spain	46.9	1,393.0	33,090	506	41.4
Sri Lanka	21.3	67.2	9,740	66	31.4
Sudan	38.0	66.6	3,370	1,879	19.2
Suriname	0.5	5.3	16,070	164	28.5
Swaziland	1.2	3.8	6,690	17	20.1
Sweden	9.6	579.7	44,660	450	41.0
Switzerland	8.1	685.4	56,950	41	42.0
Syria	21.9	35.2	5,100[ab]	185	22.4
Taiwan	23.3	511.3	43,680	36	38.7
Tajikistan	8.2	8.5	2,510	143	21.7
Tanzania	49.3	43.7	2,440	947	17.5
Thailand	67.0	387.3	14,390	513	36.9
Timor-Leste	1.1	1.3[a]	2,080[a]	15	16.6
Togo	6.8	4.3	1,390	57	18.9
Trinidad & Tobago	1.3	24.6	30,450	5	33.3
Tunisia	11.0	47.0	11,120	164	30.3
Turkey	74.9	822.1	18,780	784	29.4
Turkmenistan	5.2	41.9	14,000	488	25.6
Uganda	37.6	24.7	1,670	242	15.8
Ukraine	45.2	177.4	8,790	604	39.7
United Arab Emirates	9.3	402.3	59,850[a]	84	30.0
United Kingdom	63.1	2,678.5	38,260	244	40.2
United States	320.1	16,768.1	53,040	9,832	37.4
Uruguay	3.4	55.7	19,590	176	34.4
Uzbekistan	28.9	56.8	5,170	447	25.3
Venezuela	30.4	438.3	18,200	912	27.0
Vietnam	91.7	171.4	5,290	331	29.8
Virgin Islands (US)	0.1	1.6[ab]	14,500[ab]	0.4	40.2
West Bank & Gaza	4.3	11.3[a]	4,920[a]	6	19.1
Yemen	24.4	36.0	3,960	528	19.1
Zambia	14.5	26.8	3,930	753	16.6
Zimbabwe	14.1	13.5	1,830	391	19.5
Euro area (17)	333.9	13,194.0	37,800	2,629	42.8
World	7,162.0	75,621.9	14,400	136,162	29.2

a Latest available year.   b Estimate.
c Including French Guiana, Guadeloupe, Martinique and Réunion.

Sources

Academy of Motion Pictures
AFM Research
Airports Council International, *Worldwide Airport Traffic Report*
Avascent Analytics

Bloomberg
BP, *Statistical Review of World Energy*

CAF, *The World Giving Index*
CBRE, *Global Prime Office Occupancy Costs*
Central banks
Central Intelligence Agency, *The World Factbook*
Clarkson Research, *World Fleet Register*
Company reports
The Conference Board
Council of Tall Buildings and Urban Habitat

The Economist, www.economist.com
Economist Intelligence Unit, *Cost of Living Survey; Country Forecasts; Country Reports*
Encyclopaedia Britannica
ERC Group
Euromonitor International
Eurostat, *Statistics in Focus*

FIFA
Finance ministries
Food and Agriculture Organisation

Global Democracy Ranking
Global Entrepreneurship Monitor

H2 Gambling Capital
The Heritage Foundation, *Index of Economic Freedom*

IFPI
IMD, *World Competitiveness Yearbook*

IMF, *International Financial Statistics; World Economic Outlook*
International Agency for Research on Cancer
International Centre for Prison Studies
International Civil Aviation Organisation
International Cocoa Organisation, *Quarterly Bulletin of Cocoa Statistics*
International Coffee Organisation
International Cotton Advisory Committee, *March Bulletin*
International Cricket Council
International Diabetes Federation, *Diabetes Atlas*
International Grains Council
International Institute for Strategic Studies, *Military Balance*
International Labour Organisation
International Organisation of Motor Vehicle Manufacturers
International Publishers Association
International Rubber Study Group, *Rubber Statistical Bulletin*
International Sugar Organisation, *Statistical Bulletin*
International Telecommunication Union, *ITU Indicators*
International Tennis Federation
International Union of Railways
Inter-Parliamentary Union

Johnson Matthey

McDonald's

National statistics offices
Nobel Foundation

OECD, *Development Assistance Committee Report; Economic Outlook; Government at a Glance; OECD.Stat; Revenue Statistics*

Olympic.org

Pew Research Centre, *The Global Religious Landscape*

Population Reference Bureau

Reporters Without Borders, *Press Freedom Index*

Rugby World Cup

Shanghai Ranking Consultancy

The Social Progress Imperative, *Social Progress Index*

Sovereign Wealth Fund Institute

Stockholm International Peace Research Institute

Taiwan Statistical Data Book

The Times, *Atlas of the World*

UN, *Demographic Yearbook; National Accounts; State of World Population Report; World Population Database; World Population Prospects; World Urbanisation Prospects*

UNCTAD, *Review of Maritime Transport; World Investment Report*

UNCTAD/WTO International Trade Centre

UN Development Programme, *Human Development Report*

UNESCO Institute for Statistics

UN High Commissioner for Refugees

UN Office on Drugs and Crime

US Census Bureau

US Department of Agriculture

US Energy Information Administration

US Federal Aviation Administration

Visionofhumanity.org

WHO, *Global Immunisation Data; World Health Statistics*

World Bank, *Doing Business; Global Development Finance; Migration and Remittances Data; World Development Indicators; World Development Report*

World Bureau of Metal Statistics, *World Metal Statistics*

World Economic Forum, *Global Competitiveness Report*

World Federation of Exchanges

World Shipping Council

World Tourism Organisation, *Yearbook of Tourism Statistics*

World Trade Organisation, *Annual Report*

Yale University